THE
ILLUSTRATED
ENCYCLOPEDIA
OF
DREAMS

HAMLYN

This edition published in 1989 by
the Hamlyn Publishing Group Limited
a division of the Octopus Publishing Group,
Michelin House,
81 Fulham Road,
London SW3 6RB

A-Z text and some illustrations (see p. 192) taken from the work:
Conoscerti, Enciclopedia dei Test
© 1986 Gruppo Editoriale Fabbri SpA
Milan

© Translation, all other text and design: Octopus Books Limited 1988

ISBN 0 600 56705 2

Produced by Mandarin Offset.
Printed and bound in Hong Kong

INTRODUCTION

From time to time we all experience vivid dreams which are difficult to explain. The impression most of us are left with when we wake up after such a dream is one of confused, muddled images which have no logical form. It is often as though we have been watching or taking part in a strange fantasy which seems to have nothing to do with our everyday lives. In fact, dreams probably reflect more about ourselves than we realize. Our dream world, however nonsensical, disturbing or beautiful, is in many ways more real than what we call 'reality'. In most cases dreams reflect our deepest desires, fears and frustrations – what we could term our 'inner' or 'private' face, which only emerges through our subconscious when we are asleep.

Our 'outer' or 'public' face, however, is different. Most of us habitually hide behind a barrier or system of convention imposed by society. We usually try to be like everyone else because we are happier being one of a crowd. To some extent our behaviour is 'coded' – that is, we behave according to our situation and who we are with. For example, we might hide certain personality traits that we think could be unacceptable to one person, while later, when talking to someone else, we may allow these traits to show but will repress another aspect of ourselves. We all use different types of self-censorship when we are mixing with others and establishing relationships, although we may not always be aware that we are adjusting our behaviour to fit in with others. Adapting our public face to suit various situations tends to become second nature. The question then arises as to which face – the private or the public – gives a true picture of what we are really like. It can be argued that it is the private and not the public face that provides an accurate indication of our true self. This is because the private self is not bound by the rigid constraints which we constantly put on ourselves while we are awake.

A master key to dreams

This book will help to find the key to your private self, by making sense of the puzzling images and strange symbolism that dreams are made of. Once we understand more about our private thoughts

and fears, and when our true strengths and weaknesses have been revealed in our dreams, we can use this knowledge to our advantage. It would be comforting to believe that we alone hold the key to the private or inner self, but this is not necessarily the case. Although dreams are personal, all of us dream about ideas and symbols which can be easily interpreted. So the secrets that our dreams hold can be revealed by someone who has no personal knowledge of us but who is versed in dream symbols and interpretation.

Using the *Encyclopedia*

The Illustrated Encyclopedia of Dreams incorporates the wisdom of some of history's most notable interpreters of dreams, from the Greek Artemidorus through to Freud, Jung and their successors. The interpretations provided in the main part of the book – an extensive A-Z with explanations of the most common images and symbols encountered in dreams – are based on knowledge gathered by experts in the subject. When there is more than one interpretation put forward for a specific image, you should select the most appropriate one. Obviously, the greater one's self-knowledge, the more accurate the selection of an interpretation will be. Furthermore, each specific interpretation should be modified and adjusted in the light of particular circumstances affecting your life at the time a dream comes to you. If you dream that you are lost in a maze, for example, and yet your work is going well, you should look to another domain of your life to understand the uncertainty and indecision the dream suggests is nagging at you.

The basic tools of interpretation provided by the A-Z should also be used in conjunction with the knowledge acquired from 'Sleep – The Pathway to Your Dreams'. This section answers questions about the complex relationship between sleep and dreaming, explains the process of sleep and describes why both sleep and dreaming are vital to our physical and mental wellbeing. With practice, the information in this book should enable you to understand dimensions of yourself that have, until now, been no more than strange, disordered images within your dream world.

SLEEP

THE PATHWAY TO YOUR DREAMS

Man has always slept and his sleep has always seemed mysterious; often it was believed to be magical. The dreams that come unbidden when we are sunk in slumber seem not of our doing: they concern people and creatures we have never seen, they bring loved ones back to life, they play fast and loose with geography and chronology. In many cultures dream interpretation was a highly-prized skill and dreams were often felt to prophesy future disasters or triumphs.

Today the study of dreaming and sleep is no less fascinating than the pronouncements of the High Priests of yesterday, although modern researchers rely more on the measurement of the brain's electrical responses than on esoteric books of omens. Yet the mechanics of sleep and of dreaming remain elusive. Much is known now, but more remains in the realms of theory.

The circadian rhythm

Every creature on Earth reacts instinctively to the alternating phases of day and night, light and dark. For some animals, such as the bat, night time means activity, while daytime means inactivity and sleep. Mammals tend to be light-lovers and sleep at night, although extreme fatigue and danger may cause the pattern to alter occasionally.

Research has shown, however, that newly-born infants have to acquire the 24-hour rhythm. In their first days outside the womb babies seem to respond to an inborn hourly cycle, which extends gradually to multiples of one hour – any new parent knows what little respect a baby has for the hours of darkness! As the child becomes accustomed to the habits of its family it will generally oblige them by sleeping when they do and waking at daybreak. A mixture of social conditioning and adjustment to the 24-hour hour cycle regulates the growing child's patterns of sleep and wakefulness.

Once acquired, the daily or 'circadian' rhythm remains with us to our dying day. As with all learned functions its operation lies in the cerebral cortex, the 'grey matter', of the brain. Dogs also obey the circadian rhythm but if their cerebral cortex is removed (as happened in a controversial experiment in Chicago in the 1950s) they sleep most of the time, waking irregularly, and they no longer dream.

Our biological clock depends on more than the functioning of the cerebral cortex, however. The part of the brain known as the hypothalamus regulates the body temperature, which regularly falls from the 'normal' 37.0°C to as low as 35.5°C in the early hours of the morning. (Sweating attacks during the night are usually associated with illness or severe sleep disturbances.) At noon the temperature may rise to over 37.0°C; this is the time when most people achieve optimum efficiency, physically and mentally. Roughly two hours later a sharp change in the biological clock will mark the onset of the 'post-lunch dip', whether or not one has actually eaten lunch.

The hypothalamus also regulates the flow of chemicals in the blood and urine. Normal sleepers often find they can drink a fair amount of fluid before retiring and sleep through to dawn without visiting the bathroom. This is because the production of urine dramatically decreases at the onset of sleep. Poor sleepers or those with organic problems tend to wake often to relieve themselves. 'Do you have to get up during the night?' is a standard medical enquiry in ascertaining the state of a patient's general health.

The body can gradually adjust to a reversal of its learned cycle over a period of time. Shift workers, for example, changing from a day to a night shift or vice versa have been found to need a week or so before they can regain their normal performance level. Repeatedly scrambling the body's biological rhythms is harmful; pilots and air stewardesses, for example, are frighteningly at risk from this phenomenon. Consider, too, the implications of international businessmen or jet-setting politicians taking major decisions while suffering from the effects of a long flight.

There is something paradoxical about sleep. Although when we are asleep we are apparently deaf and blind to the outside world, sleep is an *activity*. We are seemingly unconscious, yet at one level – the level of dreams – another kind of consciousness operates vividly. In some cases, as in nightmares, our dreaming consciousness evokes such an extreme response that it propels us into normal consciousness – and we wake screaming.

We seem to be doing nothing as we snore gently, yet we are being 'repaired'. Soon after falling asleep, body cells begin to divide faster than during wakefulness. Great surges of the 'growth hormone' are released into the bloodstream when we are sleeping most deeply, repairing and renewing our bodies while our brainwaves can be seen to be slow and long. Minor ailments such as colds are often completely better after a 'good night's sleep' – due to increased production of the growth hormone, made more urgent by the presence of infection. Insomniacs or light sleepers do not receive their full share of this invaluable hor-

mone and are often more prone to accident and illness – they are the ones that can't shake off colds and sore throats – than deeper sleepers.

Darting eyeballs
When we fall asleep we initiate a complex series of changes in consciousness that succeed each other throughout the night. There is no one uniform state that we call 'sleep'. The deepest sleep comes almost immediately after we first fall asleep, then a short period of lighter sleep follows in which our eyeballs dart about beneath closed eyelids, as if we're watching some secret activity. This phase of Rapid Eye Movement (REM) sleep is associated with dreaming. (During REM phases in dogs this is often accompanied by growling and tail twitching, as if they are catching rabbits in their dreams.) We have an average of five peaks of REM sleep during an eight-hour period, generally wakening just after the last one. People wakened during REM sleep tend to remember their dreams, however briefly, although the shrill clamour of an alarm clock, with its associations of work and duty, may drive all memory of our dreams away instantly.

Many people claim they never dream. Put these same people in a dream research laboratory, wire them up to an electroencephalogram (EEG) machine (which measures electrical activity within the brain), and wait for the REM phases to begin. If woken in the middle of one such phase our 'non-dreamer' will tell of vivid and bizarre dreams. Everyone dreams, every night.

EEG machines have established that there is a universal pattern of sleep that we all more or less conform to. As we become drowsy our brainwaves become longer and slower, finally becoming the 'delta' waves of the deepest sleep. During this time our body undergoes a rapid shutting down of its systems; digestive processes and the production of urine diminishes rapidly. The heart slows down, under closed eyelids the pupils contract, and our bodies

require less air to breathe.

As we enter unconsciousness we experience two forms of sleep – orthodox and paradoxical. There are four separate phases of brainwave activity in orthodox sleep. The first is accompanied by a slower pulse and is a light sleep during which the brainwaves slow down. At this stage a small noise or the light from a street lamp may wake you.

Phases two and three take us into a far deeper state of relaxation and an even slower rate of breathing. In phase four we are truly in a 'deep, dreamless sleep', while the EEG records very long, slow delta waves – proof positive that there is no mental activity in any accepted sense taking place.

For approximately 90 minutes every night we enter paradoxical sleep, with rapid eye movements, increased heart beat and blood pressure and fast, erratic brainwaves indicating a sudden agitation of mental activity. We are dreaming. Certain physical processes may mimic wakefulness, such as the production of adrenalin (the fight-or-flight hormone) during dreams of danger or horror, but in fact during this phase the muscles are at their weakest, almost as if we were paralyzed. Particularly horrific dreams may be accompanied by a feeling of helplessness, of being rooted to the spot – a direct reflection of our physical state on our sleeping minds.

The physiological dream
An interesting aspect of this relationship between the mind and body during sleep is the so-called 'physiological dream', where either physical activity or outside influences are dramatized in our dreams. A ringing telephone may become dream alarm bells, or a full bladder turn into a dream of drowning! A classic dream in this category was that of the psychologist L. F. A. Maury whose dream featured the French revolutionary Robespierre: during the night an ornamental bedrail became dislodged and fell across his neck – he dreamed it was

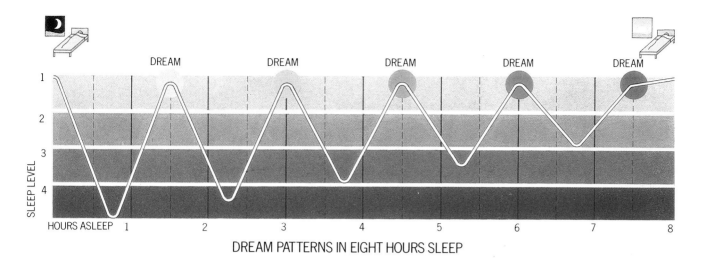

DREAM PATTERNS IN EIGHT HOURS SLEEP

A chart showing the dreaming patterns of a sleeping person during an eight hour night. Each night everyone experiences five phases of dreaming which coincide with light periods of sleep. Timed, these phases amount to a total of ninety minutes a night.

the guillotine, but woke at its touch, as if his brain censored the experience of death.

There is growing evidence that people who are particularly active during the day, especially if their experiences have been dangerous or traumatic, require more paradoxical sleep than those who are less emotionally or physically stretched. 'Nervous exhaustion' calls for the restoration of harmony, the soothing power that sleeping and dreaming brings. Enforced sleep deprivation has appalling results: nightfliers in the RAF during the Second World War were under particular strain due to the terrors of flying over enemy country in the dark, often at a moment's notice – a pattern that was repeated without respite for weeks at a time. Sleep was necessarily inadequate in both quantity and quality; interrupted dreams soon become inextricably interwoven with a distressing reality. Many airmen cracked under the strain. With sleep their situation would have been traumatic enough, but without it, normal functioning

was impossible and life became – literally – a nightmare.

Studies of sleep deprivation reveal a tendency for forbidden dreams to intrude into reality in the form of hallucinations or paranoid delusions. After about 100 hours of continuous wakefulness all perceptions, physical and mental, become distorted. The pattern of a carpet turns into a seething mass of writhing snakes, the innocent comments of a passer-by are interpreted as sinister threats and we become wary of eating or drinking in case of poison or contamination. We hear voices talking about us, as in Evelyn Waugh's *The Ordeal of Gilbert Pinfold*, which was based on the author's own experience of hallucinations during a period of great strain. Research shows that there is no greater strain than sleep deprivation.

Drunk without drink
There is a marked similarity between a very sleepy person and someone in the later stages of drunkenness. Both mumble incoherently, stumble and bump into furniture. They exhibit curious mood changes and their judgment is seriously impaired. Putting a cup on a table becomes a complicated task – they often miss by inches – and more seriously, their driving ability is very poor, although they may believe otherwise.

Long-distance bus or lorry drivers have discovered the detrimental

effects of sleep deprivation to their cost. An estimated two-thirds of all long-distance drivers' near-misses or accidents are due to falling asleep at the wheel. A wise driver snatches some sleep at regular intervals during a long haul: one driver took a short nap in a lay-by even though he was only fifteen minutes from home. Mix tiredness with alcohol and, of course, you double the risk of killing and being killed.

Performance of routine tasks, on the other hand, is impaired less than one might imagine during extended periods of sleeplessness. If a task is wholly predictable, a worker can continue doing it well into a third day without sleep. But alter the rhythm of the task, or give the subject an exercise that requires instant reaction and they soon prove themselves to be hopeless at it. Ask a normally rested subject to write down a complicated list of words and he will get it ninety per cent right at the beginning, dropping to seventy per cent or less as the task continues, due to eyestrain and boredom. But ask a sleep-deprived person to write down even familiar words and errors creep in almost immediately; 'West Bromwich' might become 'wild bromide' and eventually – as in the very drunk – the writing degenerates into a meaningless scrawl.

There have been newspaper reports about the dangers of doctors working long hours without sleep.

One joked: 'My writing's bad enough normally, but after an 80-hour shift what it says is anybody's guess!' A love letter written in such a state might be amusing; a prescription is considerably less so. Sleepy people confuse names and figures; there were several reported cases of exhausted doctors telling nurses to administer the wrong drugs in the wrong dosage.

The twilight zone

This confusion is also exhibited during the period of drowsiness immediately before sleep. This 'hypnagogic' state – a kind of twilight zone of normal consciousness – is often taken to be reality. We may hear voices calling our name or see frightening figures lurking in the shadows; we may believe we have had visions, been 'called' by God, or seen a ghost. We have lost control of reality, due to the drop in 'cortical vigilance' – the brain's cortex is the guardian of our waking state.

During the hypnagogic phase we may suddenly 'come to' with a jerk, strange thoughts and phrases echoing inside our heads. Many people actually coin new words or make nonsensical comments when this happens. In 1960 the *New Statesman* held a competition for hypnagogic creativity. The most paradoxically coherent bit of nonsense came from a Mr Singleton of London, who wrote:

'Only God and Henry Ford
Have no umbilical cord.'

One woman, convinced she wrote brilliant poetry while sinking into slumber, managed to wake up and record the immortal line: 'Milton, Oh Milton, my feet are so cold . . .'

It was believed for a few years during the 1960s that one could actually learn while asleep. Enterprising electronics companies patented learning devices, basically

An electroencephalogram (EEG machine) reveals the full extent of the often hectic mental activity taking place behind the external tranquillity of the dreaming sleeper.

personal stereos, on which one could play tapes of facts and figures to one's sleeping self for as long as the tape lasted. Some machines automatically rewound themselves repeatedly until they were switched off in the morning. Ingenious though these were, they possessed one major drawback – they did not work. Further research showed that thinking and grasping facts requires consciousness – cortical vigilance.

Some people hypnagogically visit other times and places, but curiously few report being 'present' at historic events. Experiences are more likely to include watching an unknown peasant from some South American country tinkering with a car, or listening to two middle-aged women chatting on a bus in surreal and possibly obscene language.

As sleep itself draws nearer one may participate in the dramas being enacted on one's inner screen. Nonsense words and phrases, unusual or bizarre scenes and physical sensations come together. One dream researcher reported watching a visionary typist at work while a voice could be heard saying: 'Scramblaceous words several points in or over.' At the word 'over' the typewriter carriage flew across, knocking over a cup of coffee and the dreamer awoke with a violent bodily jerk.

Sensations of falling often precede an abrupt jerking into wakefulness. (Freud believed that in women it indicated a desire to become a 'fallen woman'; his explanation for male dreamers was a little more complicated.) Sometimes people experience strange surges of almost mystical feeling, or hear an explosion at the point when they are jerked awake. Alpha rhythms (signifying the electrical activity of the brain in drowsiness) are absent for the few seconds before the awakening and the brainwaves are particularly slight and slow.

Voices of the night

Coming to full wakefulness in the morning involves a similar state to night-time hypnagogia, this time

called 'hypnopompia'. Hypnopompic experiences again involve bedroom figures or strange voices talking close to one's ear. Sometimes these voices seem to be extending the content of the last dream of the night; sometimes they come out of the blue and are carried through into wakefulness, perceived as a real voice.

Between the curious half-dreaming phases of hypnagogia and hypnopompia there are roughly one and a half hours of 'pure' dreaming per eight-hour night. The nature and content of dreams can vary enormously from the almost mechanical replaying of the day's events, to precognitive or prophetic dreams of great vividness. Often people who claim they never dream confuse memories of their more prosaic dreams with ordinary thinking: to them a dream must have some fantastical quality to mark it out clearly from common events and everyday consciousness.

The mother in the teapot

Laboratory dreamers wakened from REM sleep tend to report lengthy narrative dreams, although all descriptions of dreams suffer from our innate desire to impose order and cogency on what is essentially chaotic and incoherent. A dreamer may tell of a car chase, of feeling trapped and frightened in a runaway car, of being saved by the appearance of his mother by the roadside and of his getting out of the car to go and take tea with her on the lawn. What he may really have dreamt was that he was taking tea with his mother in a car, which turned into a teatable which chased him – then without warning he was standing quite calmly by the side of the road again, waving to his mother in a giant teapot. Without realizing it, the dreamer had 'sorted' the dream material out into a more acceptable form for his wakeful scientific listeners.

Hard-headed rationalists often assert that our dreams are similar to the 'dreaming' of a computer, where random phrases and figures appear on the screen while programmes are being adjusted. At the other extreme are the parapsychologists who urge dreamers to keep dream diaries in order to discover precognitive dreams, or who believe it is possible for two dreamers to engage in a 'dream dialogue'. Today most psychologists and psychoanalysts find themselves roughly halfway between such positions – acknowledging the chemical and physiological components of dreaming, but also recognizing the creative potential and symbolism of our dreams.

Dreams are undeniably useful, whether they are remembered upon waking or not. They seem to act out our fears and anxieties, and somehow help to solve our problems while we sleep. One writer went to bed searching in his mind for a specific word which steadfastly eluded him. He dreamt he was wandering in the crypt of a church muttering 'I've forgotten, I've forgotten.' Some dream analysts might say that he had obviously gone down into the depths of his mind (the crypt) taking his problem with him. No doubt – as is the way with problems left to the subconscious in sleep – he would wake up with the word on his lips. In fact he did so, not mysteriously, but as a direct result of his dream. The word had been *cryptmnesia* – the forgetting of facts once learnt! The crypt in the writer's dream here had been both symbolical and literal.

In the long term, keeping a dream diary can help those who have a deep-rooted problem or who can't make up their minds which path to take. Often people literally don't know their own minds, being too sophisticated or repressed to trust their instincts. Dreams certainly reveal the inner self. If one is lucky enough to wake up with a dream still fresh in the mind it is useful to jot down the general outline immediately, and any images or phrases that are associated with it.

One woman was anxious about her future: she had the choice of remaining in a stressful but well-paid job, or becoming a freelance writer, with good prospects of writing a book. Security appealed to her personality but she also felt that her creativity was being stifled in her job. After a series of dreams in which she was trying to catch a train but could not remember her destination, and attempting to fly but remaining firmly on the ground, she had a very short, simple dream: she was in a 'tall, new, very impersonal office block and was being edged towards the window by persons unknown. . . . I found myself hanging on to a filing cabinet with a book in my hand and, to my disbelief, the filing cabinet, the book and I were being hurled out into thin air. So this is it, I thought, I'm falling to my death. But I didn't feel frightened; the fall was ridiculously slow and I almost felt an imposter as I gently bumped to the ground holding the book. The filing cabinet had disappeared on the way down. People came running. I told them, I should be suffering from shock, shouldn't I? But I could hardly stop myself from dancing with joy.'

She left her job and enjoyed herself enormously writing a first book, despite the warnings of more cautious friends. She never did 'suffer from shock'.

Dreams and sex

Sigmund Freud's sex-obsessed dream analysis is often seen as something of a joke these days, but his emphasis on sexual repression may well have been appropriate to his own time and place. Sex is a powerful driving force and must therefore regularly appear, like other strong urges such as hunger or ambition, in our dreams. Researcher Dr Calvin Hall made a list of no less than 102 commonly-agreed dream symbols for penis, such as pistol, pen or truncheon, and 55 symbols for sexual intercourse such as 'to plough' and 'to ride'. He was aware that many people would accuse psychoanalysts of being a bunch of dirty old men – but when he went to the *Dictionary of Slang and Unconventional English* he found over 200 expressions for penis and 212 for the sexual act – including 'to plough' and 'to ride' . . .

Judging by the coarse and obscene language that even the most respectable spinsters use when waking from a general anaesthetic it would seem that we all have 'dirty' minds. In dreams ideas become symbols, and naturally many of these have a sexual meaning. Yet dreams, as Carl Jung asserted, are much more than symbolical sex shows. He acknowledged other desires in man, including the desire to worship, and personal ambition. He reaffirmed the ancient idea of *archetypes*, symbols that we all have in common, which mean that, to a large extent, a stranger can unlock the secret of our dreams.

For Freud a dream of drowning in the wide ocean would have an obviously sexual connotation, while for Jung it was more profound. To him the sea was the archetypical symbol of the unconscious, which we all share. Sinking down into it might mean becoming aware of our most profound levels of being.

As the twentieth century progressed, psychoanalysts noticed an interesting phenomenon. Patients tended to report typically Freudian dreams to Freudian psychoanalysts, and Jungian ones to Jungian analysts. It was as if their subconscious minds set out to please the doctors.

In the 1970s Dr Ann Faraday cautioned against a too-stringent adherence to psychoanalytical schools of thought. She told of an incident involving one of her own dreams, which had to be recalled for her student dream class. She recalled dreaming that her legs were covered in thick, black hair and of a feeling of disgust. Her tutor, a staunch Freudian, happily began to interpret the dream as her horror at discovering the masculine elements in her sexuality. She stopped him: she had just remembered she had to dash to keep an appointment to have her legs waxed!

To the extent that we create our own dreams, they are intensely

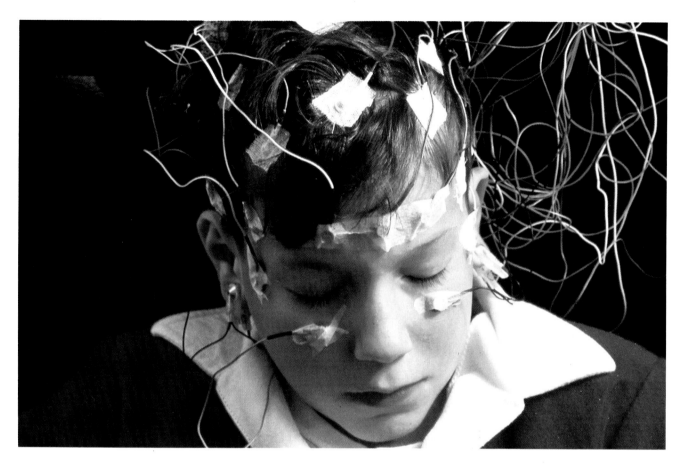

personal. People often say: 'I had the most astonishing dream last night – I've no idea where it came from.' Yet the subconscious, the left-brain function, is continuously creative, like the animation and script departments of Walt Disney Inc. operating simultaneously. Even the most down-to-earth people have glorious, exciting and fantastic dreams, once their everyday, repressive personality is asleep.

Dreams in the genes

There does seem to be a very large reservoir of common symbolism, a universal dream code, 'programmed' into each one of us. Research has shown that almost totally uneducated people dream in the symbolism of ancient myths, sometimes even dreaming the myths themselves.

Because all humans share a common heritage and use the same everyday objects it makes sense to acknowledge that some dreams are open to universal interpretation. More controversially, some theorists assert that we all share a genetic

pool of dream symbolism: stories and myths handed down from generation to generation, like the Cinderella theme, are encoded in our psyches at birth, it is said. Much research remains to be done in this area, however.

Sometimes horrific memories of real life recur in vivid dreams. A bus driver who had once, through no fault of his own, run over and killed a little child, regularly dreams he's bearing down on her again and cries out, slamming his foot down on the imaginary brake so hard that he once broke the bedrail. Soldiers relive battles, yelling commands, ducking imaginary shells and waking in terror, dripping sweat. To them the 'jerk', common in first falling asleep, might be accompanied by the sound of a bomb exploding.

Frequently ex-servicemen dream of attacking an enemy – one American woke to find his hands around his wife's neck. He had strangled her, believing she was a Japanese soldier. When the circumstances of the incident became known he was

The electroencephalogram (EEG machine) is used specifically to monitor brain activity and dreaming patterns.

acquitted of murder, as was an Englishman in the 1980s who, driven from the same sleep-motive, also killed his wife. Yet he had never seen combat and had never been a Japanese prisoner-of-war. His nightmare was pure fiction, but had the same tragic result.

Depression and insomnia

It has been found that depressed people have a high content of masochistic imagery in their dreams. 'I dreamt I waited all night for you to ring and you didn't,' said one patient, adding gratuitously, 'It was a very boring, depressing dream.' Many clinically depressed people retreat into bed and appear to sleep the clock round. This is the opposite pattern of behaviour to that of the classic insomniac: a highly-anxious, conscientious type who is beset with problems that loom especially large at night. Insomniacs suffer from more than mere lack of sleep and consequent fatigue – they suffer from fear.

A vicious circle is soon formed: anxiety causes adrenalin to flow as in any threatening situation, real or imagined, and the adrenalin heightens the cortical vigilance that keeps sleep at bay. In effect the insomniac is poisoned by his own adrenalin, and can do nothing except toss and turn and worry more.

Old people sleep less – and complain of it more – than the young or middle-aged, and women suffer from insomnia more than men. Insomnia cannot last forever: human beings must sleep or they literally go mad. Many insomniacs actually manage about three hours' sleep a night, punctuated with bad dreams and great restlessness, and wakefulness during REM peaks. Often continual waking during dreams means the bedroom itself becomes a threatening place, reinforcing the dread of the night-time vigil while – so it seems – the rest of the world sleeps happily.

To some extent insomnia can be self-inflicted: late-night cups of coffee, for example, can reduce a night's sleep by a full two hours. Recent research has also shown that food allergies, which may or may not be known to the sleeper, can disrupt the night's sleep or inhibit the onset of sleep. Interestingly, at least one old wives' tale has been validated by sleep research: a hot malted drink last thing at night does indeed promote better sleep. It appears to be the malt, rather than the milk, that has a soporific effect.

One of the more frustrating aspects of insomnia is the tendency to spend the night fretting, then to drift off to sleep at around seven in the morning – just when the alarm clock reminds you of a full day's work ahead. Left to themselves, insomniacs would manage to sleep their full quota, but during the day, which is obviously perceived (subconsciously) as a less threatening time. Unfortunately most people have to earn a living and it is not practicable to sleep during the

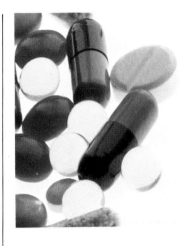

Tranquillizers and sleeping pills make you dream less vividly but sleep for longer. Withdrawal from them can cause nightmares.

hours of daylight. This, rather than the lack of sleep at night, is the major motivation behind taking tranquillizers to promote 'normal' patterns of sleep.

Drugged sleep

Millions of regularly repeated prescriptions for such drugs as Nitrazepam (Mogodon) are handed out every year to otherwise healthy people. They are also prescribed as daytime drugs for some highly anxious patients, but those who work tend to take them just at night. Although they are considerably less dangerous than the old favourites, barbituates (such as Nembutal, which killed Marilyn Monroe), these mild tranquillizers are now being recognized as addictive and ultimately unhelpful. They tend to suppress normal restlessness during sleep, decrease the vivid dreams of paradoxical sleep and increase the duration of sleep. They also decrease the amount of stress hormone in the bloodstream, found in large quantities in poor sleepers. Over weeks of pill-taking the chemistry of the brain adjusts to these new situations, accepting them as 'normal'. If the sleeper is deprived of his tranquillizer, even for one night in some cases, he will react with high anxiety (with accompanying high levels of stress hormone in his blood), less sleep and more night-

mares. For many it is easier to remain hooked. As one G.P. said to an addict: 'If I were on tranquillizers and working, goodness knows how I'd come off them.' It takes approximately six full weeks for the addict to become used to living without the drug, with nights so full of terror that some doctors believe it is harder to come off tranquillizers than heroin.

Insomnia can be helped by hypnotherapy. With this treatment, a post-hypnotic suggestion that you *will* sleep reduces anxiety and prevents the release of the stress hormone into the bloodstream – and in ways not entirely understood, often ensures a more normal balance between paradoxical and orthodox sleep. Acupuncture has also helped insomniacs, although the mechanisms involved are not known.

Alcohol may make us drowsy (at any time of the day) but the initial sleepiness induced by late-night toddies rapidly becomes shallow sleep and restlessness. Even after a drunken stupor the sleeper finds himself a victim of 'rebound anxiety' in the form of palpitations, and 'the shakes' of delirium tremens in the morning.

Clearly paradoxical sleep is what we all need and crave; it provides us with the basis for normal mental functioning. It is much less intense in retarded children, and senility is also accompanied by less REM sleep. Dreaming periods are essential to the growth and development of normal brains, but for many, dreaming is a magical world – inexplicable in terms of brain chemistry or cortical functioning.

Sleep is essential. All beings must sleep, even if only in 'microsleeps' of a few split seconds a day. Birds sleep wtih their heads tucked under their wings and dolphins sleep with first one eye open and then the other. But living things need more than rest – they need to dream to be healthy and happy. To understand ourselves we must understand our dreams. This book will help you to unravel the profound wisdom of your sleeping self.

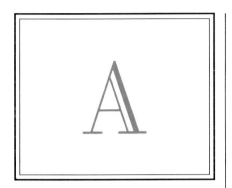

ABANDONMENT

Dreaming about abandoning someone is an unfavourable sign: it means the loss of a friendship or a loved one whom you relied upon. Dreaming about being abandoned yourself means problems on the horizon.

ABASEMENT

Dreaming about being in a state of degradation indicates that you are about to enter a period of financial problems; but if you find you are smiling or happy in the dream, it suggests that these problems will be of short duration, and that you will overcome them.

ABBEY   This signifies liberation from anxiety or unexpected good fortune.

ABBEY

This dream symbolizes being freed from anxieties, and you may look forward to a period of general tranquillity and calm. A dream about a ruined abbey indicates unexpected good fortune (possibly financial).

ABORIGINE

Any dream about a tribesman such as an aborigine augurs well for the future: it signifies new experiences and increased energy.

ABORTION

This is almost always an unfavourable sign. If a man dreams about abortion, it indicates that his partner is likely to have problems; if a woman has this dream, it means illness or some form of unhappiness is on the way.

ABYSS

Seeing an abyss or crevasse or, worse still, falling into one, is a sign of great danger which even your friends are unlikely to be able to help you out of. Take particular care in your life and keep your eyes open.

ACCOUNTANT

Dreaming about being an accountant suggests a strong adaptability and practicality on the part of the dreamer; if you speak to one, it suggests intrigues among those around you; and if you dream about paying one, you are likely to be facing a major decision. If the accountant is honest, a very important piece of business is about to be concluded; if, on the other hand, he or she is dishonest, you must avoid complications at all costs. Having your accounts checked by an accountant suggests you are making wrong moves in your working life.

ACCUMULATION

Dreams about accumulating money, pure and simple, are a sign of greed. If you dream about heaping up goods or grain, this means wealth and success in business. Conversely, if you dream about accumulating food and provisions it suggests you have a sense of insecurity.

ACNE

If you find you have spots on your face in a dream, this indicates an imminent betrayal, but if it is someone else who is suffering from acne, it symbolizes protection and security.

ACORN

This is a dream which indicates good luck coming the way of the dreamer. It guarantees success in business or at work and happiness in love, as well as good health and happiness in life in general. If a pregnant woman dreams about acorns there is a strong chance she will have healthy twins.

ACQUITTAL

Dreaming about being acquitted or found innocent in a trial is a sign of good fortune: it shows you are about to enter a period of stability where you will be safe from attack.

ADDER

Like all biting or stinging animals, the adder is a symbol of evil. Dreaming about one symbolizes suffering in love: your partner will prove unfaithful and deceitful and may bring you into discredit with their wayward behaviour.

ADDRESS

If you give your address to someone else in your dream, it shows you have a highly original imagination. If you change addresses, you need to change some of your attitudes because they are making life difficult for other people. If this address is at or near a hotel, you need to overcome a certain amount of natural laziness in a new project or piece of work. If this address is a friend's, you are likely to be very shy with new colleagues or acquaintances.

ADMIRATION

This is a good subject to dream about. If you are admiring someone else, this is a sign that your partner is genuinely in love with you; if the dream is about someone admiring you, you have many friends that respect you a great deal.

ADULTERY

Any dream about committing adultery shows problems in your love life; you are likely to be undergoing traumas and may be frequently at your wits' end. If you resist the temptation, however, it is a sign of a peaceful and contented existence guided by common sense and strong principles.

ADVERSARY

An adversary or competitor signifies imminent danger: you need to get your affairs in order before you start getting into difficulties.

ADVERTISEMENT

Seeing a TV advertisement or hearing one on the radio does not augur well, as it shows nervousness and worry overcoming your normal ability to reason, to the point where your judgment will be affected and you will start making silly mistakes. If you see an advertisement hoarding in your dream, there are unexpected changes on the way.

ADVICE

Dreaming about giving advice is a sign that you want to be respected and appreciated by other people,

ADULTERY   Giving way to temptation will cause trouble.

but also indicates a need to act quickly. If the dream is about someone else giving you advice this suggests problems, probably of a fairly temporary nature.

AEROPLANE

Any dream about an aircraft or a trip in one is a sign that good fortune is on the way. If you dream about seeing or being in a plane, you are about to receive some good news: if the plane crashes, on the other hand, this suggests a major failure, possibly in business.

AFFLICTION

Any affliction, or illness, in a dream heralds a change in your domestic situation such as moving house. As far as love is concerned, being afflicted or ill in a dream means you need to take great care in choosing the partner who is right for you.

AIR

If you dream about clear, clean air, this is a favourable sign; there is the chance to recoup some money you have spent or lost and also the chance of a pleasant journey to be made.

ALARM CLOCK

An alarm clock can take a number of different forms in a dream. If it is

AEROPLANE   An image denoting that either good fortune or good news is on the way.

gold, you need to be rather more prudent than you are at the moment; if it is silver, you have high aspirations and ideals. If it is simply a metal one, you are rather short on will-power, and if it is a small travelling alarm you need more balance and discipline in your life. If you buy an alarm clock in your dream, you are about to discover a secret, while if you hear one going off, a project you are involved in, at work or outside, will come to a successful conclusion.

ALLIGATOR

An alligator or crocodile in a dream is a warning that you need to watch out for a powerful enemy who may be creeping up on you behind your back.

ALMONDS

There are a number of different interpretations which can be placed on a dream about almonds. Eating them symbolizes problems at work and obstacles to love, as well as unsatisfied desires in general. Seeing someone else eating them indicates calm in your life and success in projects you are involved in. A sweet almond is a symbol of temptations which are attractive but potentially dangerous, while if the almond is bitter you are worried

about a weighty obligation which threatens to tie you down. If they are roasted or cooked in some way, this suggests you have unusually strong powers of observation.

ALTAR

Dreaming about being in front of an altar, or receiving communion, are both signs of an inner peace and harmony in your life at the moment and in the future.

AMPUTATION

This is a dream which indicates risks or danger. You may be about to lose something dear to you: a friend may be departing from your life, or a task you are enjoying may be taken away from you.

ANCHOR

There are a number of interpretations which can be given to the symbol of an anchor. The anchor may be heavy and difficult to lift, in which case you will attain prosperity and peace despite problems you may be having at the moment. If you can see the anchor on the sea bed, it is a sign of good fortune, but if it cannot be seen because the water is not clear, your desires are not likely to be fulfilled. If a girl dreams about an anchor, someone in her future family will choose a life at sea.

ANGEL

The appearance of an angel is an extremely favourable sign in a dream, as it indicates a major increase in other people's respect for you. If there are many angels and you are in their midst, you can look forward to a happy life with many friends you can trust and rely upon.

ANNOUNCEMENT

If the announcement is of a birth, you can expect a long wait which eventually will end in a major success. If it is death that is being announced, however, there are a great many physical and psychological weak spots in your life; you need to listen to people who are giving you advice because they

ALMONDS   A dream about these nuts can symbolize dangerous temptations.

respect you and because it will help you overcome major problems. If the announcement is of a marriage, you should no longer hesitate about discussing a problem that is worrying you with your partner; once you have confided in your partner you will find that he or she is the perfect person to help you find a lasting solution to it.

ANSWER

The meaning of an answer in a dream depends very much on what spirit it is given in. If it is polite and open, there is a visit from someone who lives a long way away in the offing, but if it is given reluctantly or evasively, people who are envious of you and your successes are gossiping about you behind your back. If you dream about replying to a letter from a friend, your relationship with your partner is a very profound and understanding one. If the answer you receive is a short one, this indicates pleasure and enthusiasm, leading to unexpected success.

ANTS

The ant is a well-known symbol of hard-working industriousness, and – by extension – being well-off financially. If you dream of winged ants, however, this shows carelessness in work. Dreaming about a long line of ants walking across the ground is very much a symbol of good luck.

ANXIETY

Despite what one might think, being anxious in a dream is actually a sign that your frequent disquiet and worry is unjustified and something you expect to fail will in fact succeed.

APPLES

Dreaming about apples is a sign of a long and happy life, with success in business and good fortune in love. If the apples are bitter, though, there may be disappointment on the way. Ripeness is a sign of a mature sensible attitude to life, while cooked apples signify a pleasant encounter or discussion with someone. A dream about eating apples contains a warning that if you want to complete a major project at work, you need to be a little less proud and try to work out a compromise with your colleagues.

APPOINTMENT

If you dream about asking for an appointment with someone, a rather uncertain situation is indicated, with much indecision and doubt assailing your already rather fragile personality, and the result could be a crisis which will be very difficult to get over.

APRICOTS

If you dream about apricots (either picking or eating them), this is a sign that fate is on your side and that health and wealth will be yours. You are also very likely to marry during your life.

APRON

A clean, white, newly-washed apron is a sign of happiness, but if it is dirty or black, it signifies impending danger. Putting on an apron suggests a visit from relatives. If you dream about washing an apron, this indicates that there is a new love on the way.

ARGUMENT

An argument in a dream suggests one in real life: disputes, business problems and a possible break with a loved one.

ARMY

This is a dream which indicates danger, anxiety and fear, all the more so if the army is actually fighting. An army in retreat is a symbol of failure, but an army marching indicates success in life.

ARRANGING

Arranging books on a shelf is a symbol of beginning again on a project which you thought had been abandoned for good. Arranging objects in a drawer shows a life which is full of problems and worries. Arranging a meal-table is a sign of good health and physical strength; you are being decisive and confident in your actions and they deserve praise from your employer. Arranging a tea or coffee service suggests a need to be less over-enthusiastic about something in your life. If it is a meeting that is being arranged, this dream means you need to call in others to help you with a problem.

ARREST

This is a classic example of a dream which means its opposite: freedom of action and behaviour.

ARROW

This is not a favourable thing to dream about. Shooting an arrow is a sign of insecurity, and hitting someone shows you are taking a serious risk somewhere in your life. If you

ASSASSINATION   As might be expected, such a dream does not augur well: turbulent times lie ahead.

are hit by an arrow it means misfortune of some kind. A poisoned arrow means major worries and unhappiness.

ARTICHOKE

A dream involving artichokes suggests dangers and anxieties, but they can be overcome much more easily than might appear. Eating artichokes is a sign of having painful decisions to make, while cooking them suggests strange and mysterious encounters.

ASHTRAY

A great deal depends on what the ashtray is made of: if it is a glass one, it suggests a feeling of disquiet with some aspect of your partner's

ARTICHOKE   This signifies danger and strange meetings.

behaviour; if it is an onyx one, you are being unjustifiably shy about something; and if it is a metal one, there is a chance of disputes and disagreements with your superiors. If the ashtray is clean, you need to make a decision soon or there is the risk that you will make a mistake. If it is dirty, your fortunes have taken a turn for the worse.

ASSASSINATION

Any dream about an assassination or murder is a bad sign, whether it is you or someone else carrying it out. It suggests possible misadventures in almost any sphere of your life: the loss of some money, a fire, a violent argument, misunderstandings with your loved ones. At all events, a rather black period is on the way, and it is better to sit tight and see what happens.

ASYLUM

This is a fairly common subject to dream about: it is neither the bringer of good nor bad tidings, but simply a warning. If you are in a psychiatric hospital of some kind in the dream, there is something causing you bewilderment or incomprehension in your life, and you need to do something about it pretty quickly or it will cause you problems. If you dream about visiting one, it suggests differences between you and your superiors or your parents. Leaving one is a symbol of regret for something that has happened in the past, but there is no need to be afraid as better times are coming.

ATHLETE

An athlete or sportsman in a dream is not a sign of good luck: you could be entering quite a difficult phase of your life in many respects. You may experience a break with someone you love and with whom you have been building up a relationship for some time. In work you are likely to make a series of mistakes which will lose you the respect of one of your superiors; and ill health is also indicated. If you dream about being an athlete yourself, you will experience a disappointment in love.

AUDIENCE

Having an audience watching you do something suggests a certain amount of insecurity in your life – you need others to approve of what you are doing. If you are asking for an audience, say with royalty or the Pope, there is a chance that you may be getting yourself into difficulties which you may find rather difficult to overcome.

AVALANCHE

An avalanche signifies a high degree of impressionability and nervousness in the dreamer. If you are buried in the avalanche, you will be overwhelmed with sadness, and if the avalanche buries a house or hut or similar building, there will be discontent among your family.

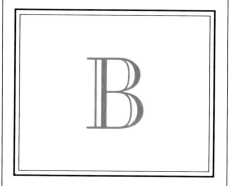

BABY

This is a very auspicious dream to have, as it symbolizes happiness and success in everything you do. But if a girl dreams about babies, it is possible that someone is trying to seduce her.

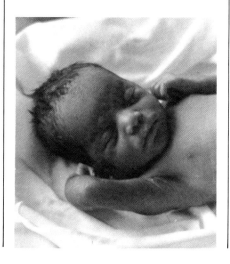

In most cases, a dream about a newborn baby is not a healthy sign: it suggests a strong, almost childlike dependence on your part or that of someone close to you. It also indicates that you are exhausted because of the repeated failure of something you are involved in at work, leading to a general feeling of hopelessness. If the baby is crying, it means you can take courage because you will be helped by advice given by someone very close to you.

BACK

A man's back is a sign of short-lived traumas, while a woman's indicates emotional instability. A donkey's back means a change of direction in your career. If you find yourself scratching your back in your dream, you can expect irritation caused by the people you work with.

BADGER

The badger is an animal which brings good luck, and in dreams it symbolizes prosperity due to your business acumen; sometimes it also indicates long journeys to unfamiliar places.

BAKER

A baker in a dream is a good omen. If he is kneading dough, there is an important piece of news on the way, while if you see him putting bread into the oven, you can expect a pleasant surprise. But if he is taking something out of the oven, something unpredictable and possibly unpleasant is about to happen.

BALCONY

A balcony represents the idea of openness and receptiveness to others' ideas. A balcony draped with cloth, flags or the like is a symbol of a peaceful future. If there is a birdcage on it, you can expect minor disappointments, but if it is covered in flowers a pleasant surprise is on its way.

BABY   This dream is one that bodes well for adults of both sexes – but girls should be wary of male acquaintances!

BALDNESS

Dreaming about baldness is a sign of impending loss, though not necessarily of hair! A man dreaming about baldness may be going through a period of physical weakness or illness, while a woman may experience emotional complications which could lead to a break with someone or something.

BALL

The ball is one of the symbols most frequently seen in dreams. The meaning depends on the type of ball: if it is any colour other than white, it symbolizes dangerous illusions; a tennis ball means guaranteed success; while a football suggests that projects which have been abandoned need to be taken up again. A snooker or billiard ball shows you have obstacles to surmount. If you buy a ball in a dream, you are generous and kind-hearted, and if you give it to someone as a present you are being loving and faithful towards your partner. If you see one rolling along, there are a number of contradictory impulses in your personality.

BALLOON

A balloon in a dream is unlikely to herald much in the way of good fortune. You are going through a period of nervousness and agitation, and risk compromising a business relationship; if you calm down and accept the help of someone who loves you, things will settle down. If you see a balloon floating off into the sky, you will be involved in projects which take a long time to come to fruition, while if you see one landing your business affairs will undergo a certain amount of change and alteration. Getting into the basket of a hot-air balloon signifies pleasant encounters to come.

BANDIT

Bandits and other criminal types are a sign of the unexpected: for example, if you dream of people robbing a bank there will be an unexpected visit from a friend. If a woman dreams about being attacked by bandits, it means that she is surrounded by admiration from the opposite sex. The image of a bandit brandishing a knife is a sign of imminent danger.

BANKRUPTCY

This is a warning signal to the dreamer. Dreaming about being bankrupt suggests that you need to be extremely cautious in business matters: it is better to follow the advice of others at the moment.

BANNER

A banner is not a sign of particularly good luck. If it has writing on it, there are minor financial problems

Where do the images in dreams come from?

How do the events and images of dreams actually come into being? According to the Canadian expert, Wilder Penfield, it is the memory which serves as a huge storage area for images and sounds which form the raw material for dreams. By stimulating the memory area of the brain using a tiny charge from an electrode, Penfield managed to make a person hum a tune, even though they were asleep and dreaming at the time. This was clearly a tune being stored in the subject's memory, and when Penfield briefly switched off the charge and then switched it back on again, the person started the tune again from the beginning instead of carrying on where they had left off. Other experiments have shown that events which happened many years ago, and of which a person has no conscious memory, can nevertheless be remembered in dreams. This is because when the conscious part of the brain is no longer active, images and memories locked away in the subconscious are released.

Even before sleep begins, images are forming which can be recalled if the person wakens.

in the air, while if it is coloured or decorative, you need to provide an explanation for actions which others might see as a little odd. Seizing a banner in battle is a sign that you are about to undergo a short-term change of direction, though your finances will not suffer as a result. Losing one in battle means a period of painful dilemmas either now or in the near future.

BANQUET

This is one of the many symbols which means the opposite of what one might expect. Being present at a banquet indicates problems such as illness, a feud, having a rival in love, or depression.

BAPTISM

Many dreams which involve going into a church are an ill omen, but attending a baptism is quite the opposite: it is a symbol of new life and happiness, though also a caution against complacency when one is happy.

BARBER

Dreaming about going to a barber's or having one's hair cut means an impending loss of money.

BARLEY

Dreaming about barley shows progress in one's career, while watching it being ground indicates an organized mind and a high degree of foresight. If you buy barley in your dream, you are person who makes decisions quickly, and they are usually the right decisions. Selling barley suggests a meeting where tempers could be roused.

BARN

Going into a barn or hay-loft in a dream indicates good luck and success with tasks you are currently involved in. If the barn falls down or catches fire there may be trouble in the air in your daily life.

BASIN

A basin of water symbolizes the successful pursuit of happiness. Trying to drink from one means

there may be a romantic affair in the near future, but be careful because the first person you meet is not necessarily Mr or Miss Right.

BASKET

A basket is a message of caution: just as small objects can easily slip through the bottom of your basket, so money can easily slip through your fingers if you are not careful. If your dream involves making or buying a basket, you need to make positive moves to clear up possible problems within your family.

BAT

A bat flying around in daylight is a symbol of reassurance and calm, but if it is at night, there is a problem just around the corner – possibly financial worries or family conflicts. A bat which brushes against you as it flies past is a reminder that ill fortune often brushes past and is soon forgotten.

BATH

The precise meaning of the dream depends on what the water in the bath looks like. If it is clear and

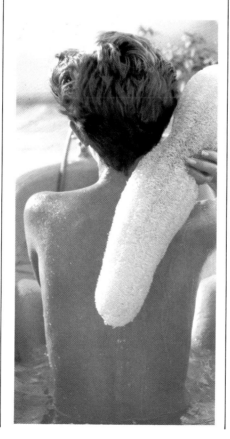

BATHING   Be cautious if you dream about bathing and are contemplating major changes, because the water may be deeper than it looks!

mirror-like, it is a sign of success in business and in love, but if it is dark and dirty, you are entering a troubled period in your life.

BATHING

Actually getting into a bath or a pool of water of any kind, as opposed to looking at it, shows that you are a person who likes to get involved in situations rather than observing them from afar; the water, though, may be much deeper than it looks, so you should take care and look before you leap.

BATHROBE

Getting into a bathrobe or dressing-gown suggests jobs that need your family's help to carry them out, while giving one to somebody as a present suggests you may be being presumptuous.

BATTLE

What this dream means depends on the result of the battle. If you win, success is on the way, but if you lose things will not go so well.

BEACH   You are in a secure and contented frame of mind.

BAZAAR

Going into an Eastern Bazaar or buying things in one shows that you probably make decisions without proper reflection. But if the bazaar is full of toys or trinkets, it signifies that there is the chance of a pleasant encounter very soon.

BEACH

An empty beach indicates a favourable opportunity which should be grasped as soon as possible. If there are people bathing on it, you have a great sense of security and confidence with yourself at the moment and an innate trust in the future. If you dream about sunbathing on a beach, business relationships will improve.

BEANS

Dried beans are a bad sign because they suggest worsening health. But if they are fresh ones, they may indicate favourable business deals. Eating beans signifies arguments and disagreements, while planting them shows that although obstacles may seem insurmountable, they are not.

BEAR

Dreaming about a bear is a reminder of major problems and the possible presence of an adversary or rival in your life. But killing a bear is a symbol of overcoming one's difficulties and defeating the adversary.

BEARD

Here the meaning of the dream depends on the colour and type of beard involved. Dreaming about having a short beard indicates a victory which is short-lived, while if it is long, this is a sign of good fortune in one's financial affairs. A large, shaggy beard is a symbol of abandoned hopes, a white one of conscientiousness in one's work. A false beard indicates problems with one's health.

BEAUTY

Dreaming about being beautiful in fact indicates quite the contrary: it reveals a fear of losing one's attractiveness because of illness or advancing age. Dreaming about a person one knows and finding them beautiful in the dream indicates that they may be in some kind of peril, while an unknown beauty is a sign that our own ideal partner exists and we are likely to meet them soon.

BED

Dreaming about being in bed can either indicate a period of illness on the way, or it may be that a new relationship is about to begin in your life. Making a bed is a sign of change or a major move. An iron bed is a sign of hopelessness and unhappiness, and a brass one a symbol of the betrayal of trust.

BEER   A thirst-quenching brew for the thirst-making episode ahead of you. Drink it – but avoid speculation.

BEDBUG

Being bitten by a bedbug or flea in a dream is a good sign: you are about to receive a proposal or suggestion which will be to your advantage. Dreaming about killing them is a less favourable sign, and seeing a bed full of them indicates possible health problems.

BEE

Bees are a symbol of hard work and success. They also symbolize prudence because they always stay close to the hive if there is a storm in prospect. They are an indication of success in business and happiness in love. If you are stung by a bee in your dream, this indicates a minor difference of opinion with someone.

BEER

A glass of beer with a fine head to it is a symbol of animated discussions in the near future. If you are drinking the beer in the dream, there may be a loss of money in the offing, but if others are drinking it, this loss will be a minor one. But either way, you should steer clear of any kind of speculation.

BEETLE

Seeing a flying beetle in a dream is an indication of good fortune in everything you do (love, work, finances) and with everyone you meet, from shop assistants to lovers. A beetle beating against some kind of obstacle and falling to the ground is a sign that projects you are involved in will not be completed until much later than you expected.

BEGGAR

Despite what it might seem to imply, seeing a beggar in a dream shows that a period of happiness and lack of worry is just around the corner. Most importantly, financial matters are likely to go well, while in love you will meet the person you were looking for and they will give you happiness. But if you dream about seeing a beggar, you are the object of hostility though this will not cause you any harm.

BELL

Hearing a bell ringing in the distance is a sign of good news. A bell being struck with a hammer indicates problems and worries, while a bell tolling for the dead is a sign that someone who is highly placed is looking after your interests. For lovers, the sound of a bell suggests that there will be a wedding.

BELT

The meaning of the dream depends on what the belt is made of. If it is of poor-quality material, or looks old, there is better luck in prospect than you have been having up to now, while a new leather belt signifies a relaxation in relationships where there has been tension recently. A belt made of silk or similar fabric shows that some of your desires are not capable of being fulfilled.

BERRY

The type of berry is important here, though any dream which involves eating berries indicates health problems. Blackberries are a sign of illness or injury, while finding juniper berries represents an improvement in one's health. Strawberries or raspberries symbolize a secret love. Picking any kind of berry in a dream is a sign of an impending improvement in one's finances.

BETRAYAL

Betraying a husband in a dream indicates fears and suspicions which are unfounded, while a wife betrayed shows that violent pent-up emotions need releasing. If it is a lover being betrayed, you are being diplomatic and at the same time managing to seize opportunities being presented to you; if it is a friend, there are problems to be sorted out. If you dream about betraying the whereabouts of a thing, as opposed to a person, take care who you choose as friends.

BIBLE

Reading a Bible or giving one as a gift indicates sensitivity and discretion. If you dream about swearing an

oath on the Bible, you need to push very hard to assert yourself over a particular issue, but you will triumph in the end. Seeing a Bible open on a lectern is a sign of a mind which is full of inner turmoil.

BICYCLE

Any dream which involves riding a bicycle shows there is an important decision that needs to be taken: if you give it a good deal of careful thought, you will eventually make the right decision.

BIRD OF PREY

Any bird of prey, such as an eagle or kestrel, is an ill omen, symbolizing a decline in one's physical strength. If you dream of the bird hunting by day, a gain you make will be quickly squandered, and if it is a nocturnal bird, such as an owl, there are sacrifices and privations to be undergone.

BIRTH

Dreaming about a birth is generally a good omen, as bringing a son or daughter into the world indicates both a firm, decisive personality and financial and physical well-being. If the birth is a difficult one, there are major problems to be overcome and decisions to be made, though these will be resolved in

BIRTHDAY   A good omen, signifying health and happiness.

your favour because you have a practical, rational mind. If the birth is an easy one, this reveals that you have considerable resistance to pain and suffering.

BIRTHDAY

Any birthday – your own or someone else's – is a good omen in a dream, signifying good health and a peaceful, tranquil existence.

BISCUIT

Eating biscuits is a favourable omen; a prize or distinction which is well-deserved will be received. But giving biscuits reveals ill intentions on the part of the giver.

BISHOP

A bishop seen in a church is a sign of new developments in an old situation. If he is standing at the altar, the outlook for the future is highly optimistic, and if he is in a procession calm and serenity is indicated. If the bishop is giving communion, there will be a happy event within your family.

BITING

This dream often indicates a highly-strung personality, possibly frustrated in its ideals, with a tendency to regard the future with considerable trepidation. Biting into a piece of bread, on the other hand, shows some kind of threat to those nearest and dearest to you. Biting into fruit is a sign of tact and diplomacy. Biting someone else shows that arguments and lies may disturb your relationship with your partner despite both of you declaring your love.

BITTERSWEET

The idea of bitter-sweetness in a dream is a favourable sign, and eating anything which is bitter-sweet shows that you have an incisive mind which should have no trouble tackling the occasional difficulties you encounter.

BLACKMAIL

A man being blackmailed in a dream shows a need to be understood and loved, while if a woman is being blackmailed a lack of financial stability is indicated. A friend being blackmailed shows a lack of self-confidence and optimism. If you dream about blackmailing someone who is dependent on you, you are being excessively vain and overambitious at the moment, while if a superior is being blackmailed you see yourself as being threatened by someone else at work.

BLINDING

This dream can have various meanings, depending on who or what is blinded. If it is a person, there is a family conflict on the way, while a bird being blinded is a sign of impending bad news. If someone else blinds you, it suggests you have fears which are unfounded.

BLINDNESS

Going blind yourself shows that a lover may be in some kind of danger from someone else and suggests that there may be disappointment in love on the way. Dreaming about a blind person asking for money is a warning to be cautious in something you are involved in, and a blind person with a guide dog is a bringer of interesting news.

BLISTER

A blister on your hand is a sign of irritability and lack of self-confidence in actions you have recently carried out. If the blister is on your foot, you are displaying weakness and being indecisive in your work environment and putting yourself at risk as a result. If you dream about pricking a blister, you will overcome obstacles at work.

BLOOD

Human blood is a symbol of success in one's endeavours, while animal blood means that you need some of your responsibilities taken off your shoulders if you are to function efficiently. Dried blood is a symbol of a fairly major problem at work. Any dream in which you see blood suggests that you should keep contacts with a new acquaintance to the minimum for the time being.

BLOW

Being dealt a blow of some kind actually suggests a stroke of good fortune, though hitting someone else is not a good sign. Being hit with a stick is an indication of good health, while a blow from a club of some kind suggests respect from others. If you receive a blow from a gun, your projects at work are likely to be highly successful.

BOAT

If you dream about steering a boat through calm waters, your life will be calm and unruffled, but if the water is stormy, you can expect your life to be the same. A sinking boat suggests a hidden peril on the way.

BOMB

Contrary to appearances, a bomb is not a bad sign if it appears in a dream. A bomb exploding indicates heated but friendly discussions with other people, while a hand grenade is a sign of an impending gift.

BONES

Human bones show that a person who is dear to you is going to be away for a short period of time, while animal bones are a sign that

BOAT   Life should be correspondingly tranquil if you dream of steering a boat through calm waters.

you may be about to lose or spend money and be caused a certain amount of worry as a result. If you find a bone in your dream, you can expect painful differences between yourself and the rest of your family; if you pick it up, you will be dissatisfied with work you have done recently and are about to enter a period of apathy and listlessness which worries you. Any very large bone in a dream symbolizes problems in one's relations with the opposite sex.

BONFIRE

This is a symbol which indicates a number of things: nostalgia, regret for mistakes you may have made, and also rebellion against the present state of affairs you find yourself in. Whether it is leaves, paper or wood which are being burned, the meaning is always the same.

BOOK

Buying a book, being given one or reading one are all hopeful omens, but lending or borrowing a book foreshadows a disappointment in love. A finely bound book stands for inner happiness, but if it is torn or falling apart it is a sign of disquiet and anxiety. A textbook reflects passing whims and fancies, while a prayerbook indicates an undeveloped interest in all things mystical and spiritual.

BOOTS

A pair of men's boots seen in a dream indicates that we should follow advice being given to us by others because it is practical and sensible, while women's boots betoken new relationships at work. Buying boots denotes a long period of cheerful good humour ahead.

BOREDOM

Getting bored at some kind of festival or banquet is a sign that you lack imagination. If your dream is full of a general feeling of boredom this is because you are dissatisfied at the moment.

BOSS

The appearance of your boss in a dream implies that you are feeling insecure and mentally fragile. If the boss displays pleasant, likeable behaviour it is because you are being over-sensitive and feel let down by something a friend has done to you, but if he or she is being unreasonable it portends a very difficult and stormy period in your career and you need to be calm and decisive.

BOTTLE

The precise significance of the dream depends on what the bottle contains. If it is full, it inevitably

BOTTLE   An empty wine bottle denotes a period of uncertainty ahead.

foretells prosperity; should it be full or wine or some kind of alcoholic drink, then extremely good health is on the way, and if it is empty, there is a period of uncertainty coming. A bottle being dropped or spilt can mean that you are about to experience family problems.

BOTTLING

Putting any liquid into a bottle is generally a slightly ominous sign: if it is wine that the bottle is being filled with, the dream symbolizes fear of what the future holds in store, while milk being put into a bottle indicates betrayal by a friend. Bottling vinegar suggests a major upset in one's love life.

BOUQUET

Being given a bouquet of flowers by someone of the opposite sex in a dream augurs particularly well, suggesting that someone is in love with you even though you may not be aware of it. Dreaming about holding a bouquet of flowers means that you are afraid of becoming unwanted and discarded, just as the flowers will be when they die.

BOX

A cardboard box is a harbinger of speculation and money being put at risk, while one made of wood also foretells uncertainty in business matters. A silver box shows an activity you are involved in coming to an end, and a gold one new friendships on the way. If the box is empty, you are suffering from a feeling that life is empty and meaningless.

BOXER

A boxer in the ring signifies that you are having difficulty in choosing from a variety of options open to you, while if he is on the ropes you have been brought down to earth after a period in which you were suffering from illusions. If the boxer wins the match, you can expect exciting new events to occur soon, but if he is knocked out you may lose something which is precious to you. A black boxer symbolizes

BOXER   This dream subject can mean that you are in for a buffeting.

wasted energies, while a white one shows up conflicts and friction with relations and friends.

BOY

Dreaming about a schoolboy indicates breadth of vision and generosity. A boy in church, possibly an altar boy, means you are being too impulsive and flighty. If you see boys eating in a dream, your feelings towards your partner are genuine, but if the boys are arguing or fighting, you lack understanding and affection for your partner.

BRA

Putting on a bra in a dream suggests you are extremely adaptable, while buying one is a sign of a well-considered decision. If the bra is a new one, you will have a pleasant meeting with a person close to you, while if it is old, you have a number of ideas which others may consider strange but which have a spark of genius about them. A small bra suggests that you are aggressive and ill-tempered, while a large one means that your obstinacy will cause you to make serious errors of judgment at work. A white bra is a symbol of contentment.

BRACELET

This is a dream which brings good luck. Dreaming about having a bracelet on your arm is a sign of happiness in love, while if someone else puts a bracelet on your arm, you will fall in love and marry soon – if you have not done so already. If you dream about finding a bracelet, you can expect an encounter which will cause a great deal of confusion in the short term.

BRAIN

Dreaming about eating brains is a sign of great mental agility leading to financial or other benefits. An animal or human brain seen in a dream is a premonition that caution is needed in everything you are doing at the moment.

BRAKING

Braking in a vehicle, or reining in a horse, both mean involvement in work which takes a considerable toll on your resources. But it is also a sign of satisfaction obtained from hard work.

BRACELET   A twin-headed symbol: love and happiness, or confusion?

BRASS

Tarnished brass shows a strong, decisive personality; worked into an object, it shows satisfaction in the field of love; and melted brass indicates a conflict with people around you. If you see a brass shield, the professional ambition you are displaying at the moment will be amply rewarded in due course; if you see tools and instruments máde of brass, you are going through a phase where you have great physical and emotional strength. Brass candlesticks connote pleasant emotional experiences, particularly if a birthday or some other festival is at hand.

BRAWL

A brawl or riot in a dream prefigures doubts and worries, while taking part in one betrays secret pain or troubles in you or someone close to you. Causing a riot shows you are suffering from a shortage of affection and want to be the centre of others' attention. If the brawl involves only women, you will be let down by someone you thought was a friend. If it involves motorists, you need to moderate some of your opinions.

BREAKFAST   A hearty breakfast is symbolic of starting each day well.

BREAD

Seeing bread in your dreams indicates a gamble coming to a successful conclusion, while eating it is a sign of physical health and fitness. Making bread means a message or a piece of news from someone a long way away may be coming to you; putting it into the oven means a problem which has troubled you for a long time being resolved at last; and taking it out of the oven means stability and constancy in your relations with others. White bread shows that you may be oversensitive and in a rather fragile condition psychologically but brown suggests you will receive help and support from friends in your time of need. Buying bread in a dream tells you that you should be profiting from a potentially advantageous situation, and selling it suggests involvement with a large company or organization in the not-too-distant future. Any dream involving a bread roll is likely to mean that a period of calm and confidence is coming to an end.

BREAKFAST

Starting a new day with a large, healthy meal is a good habit: in a

dream it suggests promise for future projects and tasks, and success for any initiatives you may take.

BREAKING

Breaking plates in a dream is a token of great material well-being, and breaking cups or glasses indicates generosity and enthusiasm. Breaking any other household object shows a private life which is difficult and full of frustrations and disappointments, mainly due to the fact that a close relationship with someone else is being harmed by major upheavals.

BREAST

Dreaming about a woman's breast is a sign of an unexpected item of income or piece of good fortune. If the breast is covered, you are likely to undergo an experience which will have a formative effect on the rest of your life, while if the breast is not covered, some kind of minor pain or illness is indicated in the near future.

BREATHING

Having trouble breathing, or being out of breath for some reason, signifies that you will experience remorse and guilt for something you did some time ago. If, however, you are breathing slowly and calmly in your dream it is because in real life you are going through a period of confidence in yourself and your future. This new-found confidence will allow you to attain new heights of achievement in anything you choose to do in connection with your professional life.

BRIAR

A briar pipe is a sign of material and physical well-being, while seeing a table or other furniture made of this rare wood foreshadows disagreements with relatives caused by something you have done which might be regarded as extravagant; if you try to be a little less self-willed, and emphasize the realistic, practical side of your personality, you will obtain more understanding from others. Getting caught up in a briar bush suggests you are involved in something you regret.

BRICKLAYER

Building a house or a wall, or getting bricklayers to do it for you, is a very positive subject for a dream; in your present state of mind, you are well-placed to take on

Why do we not always remember our dreams?

Freud said that the interpretation of dreams was the main route to an understanding of the human mind as a whole. The trouble with interpreting dreams is that very often we cannot remember the contents of our dreams after we wake up. Either we forget them totally, or we remember only brief instants which we cannot express in words or organize in rational terms. So why do we forget?

Dreams are an expression of desires we cannot admit to others, or often even to ourselves, because they are socially unacceptable. Dreaming them is the only way we have of expressing them. All of us think we have a fairly clear-cut idea of what we are and what we want, and the fact is that we would find it very hard to accept some of the messages given to us in dreams if we were given them point-blank. So we use a kind of censorship on our dreams, and can only remember and interpret them selectively.

The content of a dream is therefore heavily loaded with emotion which distorts our memory of what happened in it. The material from our memory which makes up the dream is reprocessed to a different set of rules to those which govern our conscious existence, and this makes them difficult to remember.

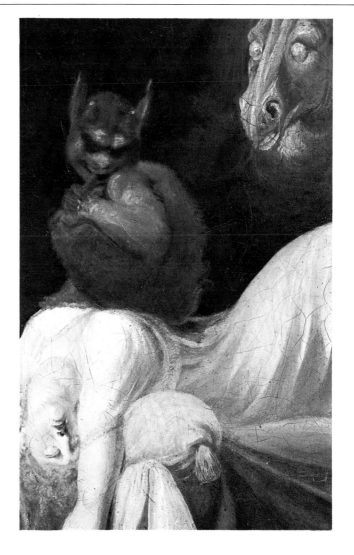

new initiatives and tasks because your powers of imagination and industriousness are at their height. Watching bricklayers working in a dream reflects your own physical health and strength, but if they are taking a tea-break, you need to put more energy than you are at the moment in your work, because things are threatening to stagnate.

BRIDE

A bride at the altar presages good news in almost everything you do; but if she is on her own, without a bridegroom, your health is at slight risk. If you find yourself standing beside the bride at the altar, a desire you have been nurturing for a long time will soon come to fruition.

BRIDGE

A wooden bridge is a hint that you may be rather lacking in will-power, but if it is made of concrete or stone, you have great ambitions for the future which are likely to be realized. A railway bridge is a sign of good health and luck in any risky enterprise, while a road bridge suggests that you are being far too ambitious and may be experiencing painful disagreements in relationships with your partner. A bridge being built is a sign of a fertile

BROTH   A negative symbol that signifies disappointment or fatigue.

imagination, and a covered bridge indicates an imminent emotional encounter which will be surprisingly pleasant. A curved bridge is often a sign that financial problems are on the way.

BROOM

A broom with a modern rectangular-type head is a prediction of new emotional experiences, while a traditional witches' broom or besom suggests money wasted or lost because of thoughtlessness on your part. A broom with a wooden handle indicates a sudden change in the

BRIDE   A bride in company is a good omen; alone, a bad one.

near future which will complicate everyday affairs for you.

BROTH

A broth or thick soup denotes a number of slightly negative feelings, such as disappointment, fatigue at work and overall lack of energy.

BROTHER

Dreaming about an older brother denotes an act of courage, or a courageous personality, while the appearance of a younger brother in a dream portends a family argument. A brother you like, or one who behaves kindly towards you in the dream, actually suggests a break with a friend, but if the brother behaves badly or is seen in an unfavourable light in the dream, good luck is indicated.

BRUISE

Dreaming about having bruises on your body because of being hit or having some kind of accident suggests ill health in real life. It means that you should definitely avoid any kind of energetic activity or over-exertion for the time being, as it could precipitate this ill health.

BRUSH

A soft brush indicates the beginning of a period of great creativity and imagination, while a hard one is a sign of open-heartedness and generosity. A hairbrush shows that you need to make some fairly major sacrifices if you want to go on with a relationship with someone you care about, while a paintbrush shows that you have a great deal of *joie de vivre* and considerable optimism at the moment. Using any kind of brush may indicate your having to argue to get your ideas across, and washing one means there are difficulties in your life.

BUBBLE

Soap bubbles floating through the air are a symbol of a carefree, happy existence, but if they burst, your present cheerful state of mind may dissipate likewise and give way to disappointments.

need to calm down and look at your problems rationally if you are going to solve them and take advantage of the potential solutions being offered to you by other people. If you dream about buying buttercups, you are about to embark on a particularly favourable period in your life from the emotional point of view.

BUTTERFLY

A brightly-coloured butterfly on the wing points to some particularly stimulating times ahead, but if it is trapped inside a room or a box it indicates minor difficulties which can easily be surmounted. A butterfly or moth flying round a light

BUTTER   Well-being and comfort are signified by a dream of butter.

indicates a short-lived victory, while finding a dead butterfly is a sign of danger.

BUTTON

Dreaming about losing a button often means that you are going through an anxious period to the detriment of your health. Sewing a button back on after it has come off indicates that you are involved in a futile hunt for an unattainable ideal. Undoing buttons often has an erotic significance, but it may also mean that you are acting in a detached and possibly callous way in your relationships with the opposite sex.

BURNING

Any kind of fire burning in a dream has a positive significance, though the exact meaning depends on what substance or object is burning. Burning wood indicates liveliness of mind and inventiveness, as does smoking tobacco; while burning incense or perfume of any kind stands for sympathy or warmth coming from a source you had not expected. Burning oil or petrol is sounding a note of caution to the dreamer, but a house burning signifies that relief is on the way from problems or illnesses that have been distressing you.

BUSH

A bush is a symbol of change and innovation. Dreaming about fighting one's way through a clump of bushes or a hedge signifies that any changes taking place in your life at the moment will be for the best in the long term, although you may not regard them as such at this particular point in your life.

BRIDGE   A road bridge symbolizes over-ambition or personal problems.

BUTCHER

Meeting a butcher in a dream does not necessarily bode ill: it indicates the chance of your meeting someone dear whom you have not seen for a long time, or the renewal of an acquaintance which may be very important to you in later life.

BUTTER

This is a very pleasant portent, signifying material comfort and welcome guests in your household. For lovers, butter denotes an impending marriage, and arguments or disputes you are involved in at the moment will eventually be sorted out to everyone's satisfaction, not least your own.

BUTTERCUPS

Dreaming about buttercups indicates that you are in a delicate state emotionally and financially and you

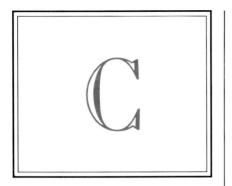

CABBAGE

This is a highly favourable portent when seen in a dream. Planting cabbage seeds is a sign of money on the way, and harvesting cabbages signifies great inner strengths which will see you through a difficult situation. Cutting up a cabbage suggests a family misunderstanding will soon be resolved.

CABIN

The precise meaning of a cabin in a dream depends on what it is being used for. If the cabin has people living in it, a surprise at work is indicated. If the cabin is a beach-hut or one used for changing, it is a premonition of petty behaviour, while a cabin on a ship shows that you are viewing a situation from a distorted perspective.

CABBAGE   This is a very favourable portent both financially and morally.

CAGE

A birdcage is a symbol of a happy marriage, but an empty cage with an open door is a sign of betrayal. A dream which involves either buying or making a cage indicates the end of what has been in many ways an unpleasant period in your life, while dreaming about being put in one is a sign of disagreements on the horizon.

CALCULATION

Doing any kind of sum or calculation in a dream – whether you get it right or wrong– reflects the fact that you are using a great deal of positive energy at the moment and there may be good news on the way.

CALENDAR

This is an auspicious sign in a dream. Writing in an appointment on a calendar shows a meeting with a happy outcome if you are in love – one which may end in marriage.

CALF

Dreaming about a calf or calves is a precursor to happiness and a care-free existence, particularly if there is a partner involved.

CALM

Calm after a storm or other major event in a dream shows an end to worries and a period of peace and quiet after rows and disagreements.

But if the dream involves a calm sea, it is a warning that you may be at risk from some kind of snare or ambush lying beneath the surface of an apparently innocent situation. Dreaming about someone who is calm in the face of a stressful situation indicates that you are an unflappable, reflective type of person.

CALUMNY

A calumny or slander suggests its opposite: if someone speaks ill of you in your dream it is because you are highly respected and admired by people you meet in your everyday life. If you slander someone else, it actually means they are receiving a

CANDLE   A burning candle indicates an unexpected letter or event.

great deal of intellectual stimulation and attention from you, and they may mean more to you than you are prepared to admit.

CAMEL

A camel or dromedary is a noble, long-suffering animal, and its appearance in a dream shows the need to bear a heavy burden – illness or misfortune – until it is overcome, which may be later rather than sooner.

CAMELLIA

Being given camellias (especially white ones) indicates intense but

short-lived joy. Giving them to someone else shows that there is a humorous, even facetious side to your nature. A dead or dying camellia tells you that you have temptations to overcome.

CAMPING

Going camping, or coming across a camping ground in a dream is a sign of new developments in general, and more specifically financial improvements and new friendships. A caravan site is a sign both of success and of new respect from your family.

CANARY

This is an auspicious bird to dream about: its yellow colour signifies freedom, success, money and new developments in your life, while for lovers it indicates a happy and long-lasting union.

CANDLE

A burning candle is a hopeful sign, indicating unexpected events: a letter, perhaps, or a visit from someone. Lighting a candle symbolizes trust and faithfulness, and extinguishing one a loss, perhaps in business, love or sport. Buying candles shows a desire to break out of routines and celebrate or spend some time enjoying something you do not often do.

CANDLESTICK

The appearance of a candlestick in a dream indicates a period of uncertainty, doubt and indecision, especially if it is made of a precious material of some kind. But if the candlestick contains lighted candles, the difficult period will be short-lived.

CANNON

Dreaming about a cannon is a sure sign that you have too many worries and may be contemplating risky projects. If a man dreams about a cannon going off, it means he has risks to overcome in his professional and public life. For a woman, it simply means a meeting with someone in the armed forces or in uniform.

CAR   Driving a car in a dream signifies control over your destiny.

CAR

A car has a variety of meanings depending on exactly how it appears in the dream. Dreaming about buying a car suggests you are about to acquire an unfavourable reputation for something, while selling one indicates that you owe someone some money which needs to be paid back. Driving a car symbolizes being in control of your own destiny.

CARDINAL

Dreaming about seeing a cardinal or kissing his ring is a sign of good fortune. A cardinal giving a blessing, saying prayers or walking in a procession foretells new experiences, important proposals being made and advances in one's career.

CARDS

Playing cards are not harbingers of good fortune in a dream; instead they suggest minor irritations and differences with others. Playing a game of cards yourself, or watching someone else playing, is a sign of innovation and change as well as of possible arguments with friends.

CARESS

Caressing a child is a sign that doubts need to be cleared up as soon as possible, while caressing a husband or wife or other loved one suggests an important piece of business which is gradually slipping away from you. Caressing an object reflects delays and holdups which could jeopardize your plans.

CARNIVAL

This is not a positive dream, as it suggests melancholy, suffering and disorder, while a masked carnival or ball indicates duplicity and dishonesty. Dreaming about taking part in a carnival procession points to an obstacle to be overcome.

CARPENTRY

Any craftsman at work is a bringer of good fortune to the dreamer, and a carpenter is no exception to this, suggesting as it does a task being brought to a successful conclusion. A carpenter joining pieces of wood together symbolizes success, and banging nails into wood is an indication of unexpected and pleasant occurrences. However, a carpenter making a coffin suggests disappointments to come.

CARPET

A frequently encountered image in dreams, the carpet is a sign of projects currently being undertaken coming to a successful conclusion, even if they seem complex at the moment. Beating a carpet heralds the arrival of potentially important news, while walking on one is a portent of a period which is uncomplicated and serene.

CARRIAGE

A horse-drawn carriage indicates an enigma that needs to be clarified, while a railway carriage shows a desire to be given more freedom. Seeing a carriage with no-one inside it means that you will soon be involved in a power-struggle with someone you do not like very much.

CARROT

This is a vegetable which brings a dreamer good fortune, and a bunch of carrots indicates the birth of a baby.

CARRYING

Carrying news heralds the fact that a problem which has been troubling you for a long time is about to be solved, while carrying gifts is a warning to you to take care in business matters. Carrying a letter is a symbol of secrets which need to be kept. Carrying a heavy bag in a dream represents a burden you are bearing for someone else's sake. Carrying another person on your shoulders shows that you have a strong personality which others feel they can rely on.

CART

Pushing or pulling a cart suggests some kind of loss or deprivation. But if you see someone else with a cart, or if it is standing on its own, an improvement in your financial situation may be on its way.

CARTRIDGE

Dreaming about a cartridge is a sign of hard-won conquest, either in business or in love. An unused cartridge means a short-lived infatuation, while a used cartridge, perhaps lying on the ground, shows that a weighty problem has been solved.

CASTLE

Usually this means arguments with others caused by your shortcomings, but a castle can also have other meanings. An ancient castle, possibly a medieval one, indicates that long-term investments need to be reviewed, while a castle being demolished or burnt down is a foreboding of danger. A castle under siege shows that you are involved in a quest for freedom.

CAT

The well-known black cat crossing one's path also brings good luck if seen in a dream. Generally speaking, though, cats are not a good omen, suggesting unfaithfulness in love and complications in one's working life. Killing a cat means you are causing your enemies discomfort.

CATACOMB

Dreaming about going into a catacomb indicates an adaptable personality with a strong capability for self-sacrifice. Coming out of a catacomb means changes in your work environment, and getting lost in one means there is a chance that you will meet people you have not seen for a long time.

CAULDRON

A cauldron of food indicates ambitions and desires being fulfilled, while one full of water shows transitory worries. A cauldron being used by witches is a symbol of disturbed relationships within your family. A cauldron bubbling on a fire means you will receive the fruits of a highly advantageous business transaction, while a tureen on a table suggests your imagination and creativity will be rewarded. Overturning a cauldron suggests you may be putting your health at risk.

CASTLE Dreaming of an ancient castle suggests long-term investments.

CAVE

A damp, dark cave underground is a danger signal, but one situated on a hill or mountain can mean new possibilities and opportunities are in the offing. A cave which is full of animals is a sign of insecurity.

CEILING

A white ceiling is a sign of romantic ardour, while a coloured one shows that you are full of ideas at the moment and particularly creative in your work. An ornate, decorated ceiling shows a finely developed critical sense and great powers of reason. Seeing a ceiling crumbling or falling down means you are about to suffer financial loss.

CELEBRATION

A birthday celebration signifies the beginning of an untroubled period in your life, while celebrating a festival such as Christmas shows you have a complex personality. Dreams which involve celebrating an unexpected event indicate that a period of stability and good health is beginning.

CELLAR

The appearance of a cellar in a dream can tend to reflect a state of depression, though the precise

meaning varies depending on the contents of the cellar. If it is full of wood or coal, the indications are that although you feel downhearted now, this gloom will be short-lived; if there are bottles of wine in it, there is a period of depression to come fairly soon. An empty cellar is a much more cheerful sign, though: it signifies a refreshed, relaxed frame of mind and receptivity to new ideas.

CEMENT

This is usually an encouraging subject for a dream. Bags of cement symbolize wealth; wet cement indicates long-lasting affection and hardened concrete represents success and stability in your business affairs.

CEILING   A highly ornamented ceiling is a symbol of your good sense.

What do violent dreams mean?

Violence is one of the more common subjects in dreams. Often such dreams create a feeling of worry or guilt when we wake up from them, because they show forbidden situations which the conscious mind rejects.

Although society instils the fear of punishment in us for violent actions, it cannot stop us having the thoughts in the first place, so we experience them in dreams instead.

"I saw it as though in slow motion. The car driven by my wife went straight into the wall of our house. I ran over and saw her lying there limply, like a rag doll. She looked as though she was dead, but I didn't care." The narrator of this dream had no children, but very much wanted them, and he felt he was fast approaching an age where it would be too late. He believed that if only he could regain his freedom, and get out of his unhappy marriage, all this would be put right. So while his life consisted of periods of profound depression, with occasional thoughts of suicide, his dream revealed the desires he felt deep down, but could never express. There was no reason why he should feel any guilt about the dream: the main thing was to confront his problems and try to find an acceptable solution to them.

CEMETERY

Contrary to what one might expect, dreaming about a cemetery holds out great hope for the future: it indicates the fulfilment of many of your desires. Going to a cemetery with someone else is a sign of true friendship, while putting flowers on a grave denotes a sensitive but also somewhat indecisive personality.

CEREMONY

A ceremony to celebrate something indicates a positive outlook, while a religious ceremony is an indicator of a wish coming true. A ceremony involving important dignitaries, or perhaps royalty, indicates an ability to react rapidly to a new situation; and a military ceremony or parade means new-found pleasures within your family.

CERTIFICATE

Asking for a certificate generally means you mistrust someone or something in your life at the moment, but certain types of certificate have other meanings. A birth certificate is a symbol of new life and increased creative powers; a medical certificate reflects long-term good health, but a death certificate foreshadows a major family upset.

CHAIN

A chain of flowers means that all your worries are about to be solved in a very short space of time, while a metal chain joining things together suggests the chance of major success after lengthy strivings.

CHAINING UP

Dreams about chaining other people up denote victory over one's foes, but being chained up yourself suggests other people are making life unduly difficult for you without your realizing it.

CHAIR

An armchair indicates important negotiations are under way, while a beach chair or deckchair shows dishonesty and lies have been found out. A stool indicates a new relationship with someone of the oppo-

CHEESE   In the main signifies greatly improved fortunes.

site sex, not necessarily romantic, but which will be long-lasting and give you a great deal of satisfaction. The act of sitting down on a chair in a dream means you are starting to face up to difficulties which will prove easier than you thought to sort out. Sitting in a chair and reading indicates a feeling of contentment with the way life is going at the moment, but getting up out of a chair means you need to overcome a certain amount of natural laziness. Sleeping in a chair means you are both optimistic and patient in your outlook.

CHAMPAGNE

Toasting someone with Champagne in a dream is an indicator of enthusiasm and optimism, but getting drunk on it suggests that the euphoria you may feel at the moment is unlikely to last very long. Dreaming about other people drinking Champagne suggests that you are feeling bitter and disappointed about being left out of something.

CHAMPION

If you dream about being a champion of justice trying to right wrongs that have been committed, you are in need of understanding and help from other people. If you are cham-

pioning the honour of a woman, you may have an insecure and unpredictable personality. Being the champion in a sporting context suggests that your current enthusiasm may not last very long.

CHANGING ONE'S MIND

Changing your mind about your father in a dream heralds a major victory or success, while if your mother is involved, you will soon receive news from a long way away. If you change your mind about someone you disliked – someone who now turns out to be a friend – there are misunderstandings in your life which need to be cleared up as soon as possible. Changing your mind on impulse means that you will be justly rewarded for displaying honesty and uprightness, but if you take a long time to change your opinions in the dream, it is because you are irritated by your failure to complete something at work. Buying an item and then deciding you do not like it after all means that the naïve, childish and impressionable side of your character has recently got the better of you.

CHAPEL

Dreaming about a chapel suggests you have psychological problems at the moment, while the appearance of a chapel of rest in your dreams symbolizes *amour propre*: a knowledge of your own virtues.

CHEATING

Cheating someone else, or pretending to have feelings that you do not in fact have, is a bad sign in a dream: it suggests you are worried about a project you have a particular interest in and it is more than likely you will not achieve what you hope. If you cheat in a game of cards or sporting activity, it means you are not being consistent in your actions and risk losing the trust or affection of your partner.

CHEESE

Eating cheese in a dream is a symbol of improving physical and psychological health. Buying

CHOCOLATE   With nuts, suggests general dissatisfaction and boredom.

cheese denotes aspirations and ambitions coming to fruition. Grating it indicates minor setbacks. To lovers, though, cheese is a symbol of unfaithfulness.

CHERRIES

Dreaming about a cherry tree indicates the approach of a rather strained period as far as both love and work are concerned. Eating cherries represents good health, while picking them signifies boredom and dissatisfaction with one's lot in life.

CHESS

The game of chess occurs often in dreams and has a precisely defined meaning. When the dreamer finds him or herself playing chess, highly developed critical faculties and a decisive, astute personality are indicated. Losing at chess means you have been setting your sights too high, while winning reflects success in your personal life. A chess piece on its own suggests a certain amount of unhappiness which can be lessened by thinking very carefully about the way others see you.

CHESTNUT

The chestnut is a bearer of good fortune. Dreams about picking or buying them suggest financial advantage, good news and freedom to pursue long-cherished plans. Eating roasted chestnuts foretells the success that you will experience in every field of activity you are involved in.

CHICKEN

Like many birds, the chicken symbolizes gains and profits, both spiritual and material; all the more so if the chicken is laying an egg in the dream. Even a dead chicken suggests justifiable confidence in the future. A newly hatched chick is a sign of your own or someone else's displeasure at something you have done.

CHIMNEY

A factory chimney indicates unexpected income, while a chimney on top of a house (particularly if it is smoking) is a sign of short-term instability. A funnel on a ship is a symbol of new horizons and opportunities presenting themselves to you.

CHOCOLATE

Dreaming about chocolate reflects your current state of well-being and ease, while eating it means there may be an unexpected loss of money or a major item of expense. Chocolate with nuts in it suggests dissatisfaction and boredom, while filled chocolate of any kind symbolizes fleeting pleasures.

CHOIR

Although a choir might logically suggest people working together to achieve harmony, in fact it normally means the opposite in dreams: you can expect disagreement and lack of tolerance from people. But a choir singing outdoors has a more favourable significance, suggesting a delightful surprise in store.

CHRISTMAS   This reflects a time of happiness with friends and loved ones.

CHRISTMAS

Dreaming that it is Christmas is almost always a harbinger of good fortune, suggesting a favourable time for friendships, especially new ones, and a happy and fulfilling relationship with the person you love. Your health will be at its best. If you dream about Christmas Eve, though, this indicates a period of waiting, being kept in suspense, though eventually an unexpected and advantageous piece of news will arrive and make you believe the waiting was worthwhile.

CHRISTMAS CAKE   Making one suggests the completion of a project.

CHRISTMAS CAKE

The process of making a Christmas cake is a fairly complicated one, and when it happens in a dream it indicates a task which has taken you a long time to complete will finally bear fruit. Dreaming about cutting a Christmas cake means you are being too cautious in your relations with a new acquaintance, while if you are eating a slice of cake, you will soon be given a favourable opportunity of some sort. Buying a Christmas cake indicates a minor failure, and giving one to someone else suggests a precarious financial situation.

CHURCH

Seeing the outside of a church in a dream denotes good fortune, but going into one suggests you are being plagued with anxieties. Praying in a church is a sign of pleasure and comfort, while going into church dressed in mourning indicates a marriage in the near future.

CIGARETTE

Loose cigarettes are a token of disillusion and disappointment, while cigarettes in a packet indicate important negotiations or business dealings are under way. Dreaming about lighting up a cigarette means you have new ideas and projects in mind for your future career; smoking a cigarette right down to the end

is a sign that you need to postpone an important appointment until you are better prepared for it.

CINEMA

A cinema is a symbol of light-heartedness and superficiality. Dreaming about going to the cinema is a warning not to trust appearances, particularly in the case of a beautiful woman or handsome man. If the cinema is empty, slanderous gossip is circulating about you.

CIRCUS   The present state of affairs may only be short-lived.

CIRCLE

Dreaming about drawing a circle indicates that there are many opportunities in your life which you have still to take advantage of. The circle itself is a symbol of perfection, and any dream involving something circular, such as a wheel or a barrel, has favourable implications.

CIRCUS

Although it might seem strange at first, a dream about a circus emphasizes the fact that things are temporary and short-lived, that happiness may be replaced by sadness, that

projects and ideals may not come to fruition, and that friendships may place you at risk.

CITY

Dreaming about a big city shows you have ambitious ideals, and if you find yourself living in a big city in the dream, these ideals will shortly be realized.

CLAY

Wet clay is a malleable substance with many uses, and its appearance in a dream suggests that although you are being flexible in your behaviour there may be someone who is harming your interests without your realizing the fact. Shaping clay with your hands indicates you have ideas which are precise and clearly-defined.

CLEANING

Dreaming about cleaning vegetables suggests petty arguments within your family. Cleaning or washing clothes means excessive extravagance, while cleaning or polishing shoes means an aggressive exchange with a friend. Cleaning a house is a sign of joy and happiness, and cleaning a bath suggests your ideas are particularly well-thought-out and lucid at the moment. Cleaning a kitchen means that you are going through an optimistic phase and can expect good health; while cleaning or dusting furniture means you have inner vitality and great strength of will: both will stand you in good stead. Sweeping a path means you can expect to meet with obstacles which are fairly difficult, but not impossible, to overcome.

CLIMBING

Climbing a mountain in a dream suggests that you have worries and preoccupations which seem to be insurmountable, but it is more than likely that you are exaggerating their importance. If you try to reassert the calm, clear-headed side of your nature, you will see everything starting to turn out for the good. Climbing a ladder indicates that you are ascending the ladder of

business success, and is thus a favourable sign – so long as you do not set your sights unrealistically high. Seeing a climbing plant such as ivy or runner beans in your dream suggests long-lasting, faithful friendships: do not let yourself be discouraged by any minor hiccups in these relationships.

CLOAK

Any cloak or cape, no matter what colour it is or what it is made of, suggests a period of uncertainty and indecision ahead before you can start functioning normally again.

CLOCK

A clock or watch is a favourable omen in a dream. If it is made of gold, it signifies major successes and satisfaction, while if the clock or watch is a silver one there is a new emotional relationship in store. A man's watch is a sign of small successes in everyday life, and a

CLIMBING   Mountain-climbing means exaggerated worries.

woman's one indicates a desire to get ahead in the world of work. A grandfather clock is a sign that you should place more trust and reliance on others when they offer you support. Buying a clock or watch suggests you are suspicious about something – with good reason as it happens. Wearing a watch means you need to keep an eye on expenditure or it could get out of hand, while losing a watch means you should not give in to any temptations because they could later make life very difficult for you.

CLOISTER

A cloister is a symbol of peace and tranquillity and is an entirely good omen, except if you cannot find your way out of it, in which case you may be feeling trapped by circumstances which are out of your control.

CLOTH

A woollen cloth indicates new relationships, while a linen one signifies financial gains. A white cloth means you have a lot of negative thoughts about someone which are unjustified, and a black cloth indicates differences of opinion between you and members of your family. A large cloth means your health is likely to be extremely good in the near future; if the cloth is coloured, you should not place too much trust in someone recently encountered and already important in your life. If it is striped, you need to face up to a fairly major problem in your work before it gets out of hand. A shroud covering a dead body reflects a lack of stability and coherence in your emotional relations with others.

CLOTHES

Putting on or buying clothes in a dream symbolizes that you are making progress in a difficult situation. This can vary from minor progress to brilliant success, depending on how bright the clothes are. Dirty clothes are an indication of happiness.

CLOUDS

If the sun is covered by clouds in your dream, you have a strong sense of duty and a careful, practical mind. If it is the moon that disappears behind the clouds, you are a patient and persevering person and these features of your personality will help you overcome the

problems you are having at work at the moment. Any deterioration in the weather in your dreams reflects a change for the worse in your emotional stability: you are probably being unduly irritable and gloomy in your outlook. But white clouds which do not look as though they are bringing bad weather are an indication of advancement and improvement in your working life.

CLOUDS   When the clouds obsure the sun, the dreamer is practical.

CLOWN   If you are among clowns it indicates superficial relations.

CLOVER

Fresh clover suggests that advice you are being offered at work should be followed unswervingly, while if the clover is dried there is a period of fatigue and physical weakness ahead which may worry you somewhat. Picking clover is a sign of easy financial gain – especially, of course, four-leafed clover.

CLOWN

Seeing a clown performing in your dream shows astuteness and shrewdness which are not always directed to the proper ends. If you yourself are dressed up as a clown,

you are likely to be faced with a very worrying problem and need to give careful thought to any decision you make because any mistakes at this stage could lose you a lot of money. If you dream about being one of a group of clowns, you are seeing things rather too superficially and need to be less frivolous in your relations with those around you.

COACHMAN

A person driving a coach or carriage is a sign of well-being. Dressed in livery, a coachman heralds particularly pleasant news. If the coach is empty, though, it is a sign that you are not taking life seriously enough at the moment and this could cause you problems.

COAL

Dreaming about a coal-heap or a slag-heap is an ill omen, but coal burning merrily in a grate is an indicator of financial or other gain. Wet coal which will not burn is a sign that you are experiencing a particularly important event in your life and are worried about its consequences.

COBWEB

A spider's web with a spider in it is a sign that you are at risk from someone close to you who is cynically using you, but if there is no spider in the web, then happy events and days of tranquillity are in prospect. If you dream about a spider spinning a web you may be being criticized and slandered by people who dislike you, but if the dream involves walking into a spider's web current financial projects will turn out successfully.

COCKROACH

This is an unpleasant omen in a dream: it reflects problems in your work, loss of energy and possibly money too. Killing a cockroach is a sign of difficulties to be overcome.

COFFEE

Coffee is a pleasant sign in a dream: it denotes a healthy financial position and a state of happiness and

COBWEB   A spider in its web warns that someone close is exploiting you.

harmony with one's loved one. Dreaming about drinking bitter coffee shows a cheerful and friendly personality, while sipping sweet coffee indicates a sympathetic and co-operative nature.

COFFIN

This is usually a negative subject to dream about, though if it is you laid out in a coffin it simply signifies sudden change in your life.

COIN

Dreaming about having coins in your pocket signifies good fortune, though not necessarily financial. You are likely to be making rapid progress in your job because of your extrovert, imaginative personality, but you have to be careful not to exaggerate things or get them out of proportion. Giving coins to a beggar means you can expect a prosperous period financially, while someone else giving you a coin or coins means you are about to experience a loss which will make you excessively cautious and pessimistic.

COLD

Cold of any kind is unlikely to be a good sign in a dream. Being cold yourself is a sign of disloyalty to others, while trying to keep out of the cold means things are not going your way. If your hands are cold your financial situation is insecure, while if it is your legs that are feeling the cold it is because you are depressed and anxious.

COLLAPSE

If you or someone else collapses in a dream, much depends on the reason for the collapse. If it was due to sorrow or pain, this actually means an end to your sorrows and the beginning of a period of happiness; likewise if the collapse was because of some kind of illness it suggests a period of better health is on the way. If someone else collapses through fatigue, your own problems are likely to be solved very soon. If a building collapses, on the other hand, faith which you had placed in a person or thing has proved to be unjustified.

COLLECTING MONEY

Collecting entrance fees for some kind of performance or show means that your promises are not being kept. Collecting a debt means you are running unacceptable risks in your professional life, while collecting for charity suggests that you have a desperate need for affection and for the understanding of others.

COLONEL

The appearance of a colonel in a dream can have a number of meanings. A colonel on a horse, or at the head of a group of soldiers, indicates a business trip being made in the near future, while one in old-fashioned uniform suggests financial improvements. A colonel who has been killed or wounded, or stripped of his rank, is a sign of worries and intrigues.

COLUMN

A dream involving a broken or fallen column is a sign of hopes being shattered. A fine intact classical column means changes for the better are on the way. A marble column is a sign of financial stability, but if the column is made of plaster or some other easily breakable material, your dream indicates that you are deluding yourself where romance is concerned.

COMB

Dreaming of a comb which has all its teeth shows difficult business matters must be resolved, while one which has some of its teeth missing shows that some points need clearing up in a complex situation. A metal comb suggests success in the sporting or gambling fields, while a plastic comb means that you are being vain and over-confident and this could be counter-productive. Finding a comb suggests problems on the emotional front, and losing one, strained friendships. Buying a comb indicates an unexpected change of address.

COMBAT

Dreaming about taking part in armed or unarmed combat suggests that you are an enterprising person who enjoys taking risks. Watching a combat means you are indifferent to events and people around you. The idea of combat in general suggests the presence of enemies and rivals, while emerging victorious from combat reflects success in love.

COMBING

Combing a child's hair shows good relationships with your family and the person you love. Combing a woman's hair is a sign of fears about a project at work you have a particular interest in. Combing straight hair suggests that your friendships are solid, secure ones, but combing curly hair indicates that you are emotional and impressionable. Combing your own hair shows generosity and a reflective nature, but if you have trouble doing so because your hair is too tangled, this can indicate friction or disagreements at work.

COMET

A comet has long been regarded as a harbinger of some major world event. This event need not necessarily be a favourable one – it could be a natural disaster such as an earthquake. Dreaming of the passage of a comet across the sky can also indicate major upsets on a personal level, so you'd be best advised not to take any undue risks.

COMMITTEE

Sitting on a committee suggests the possibility of a happy event as well as the development of your own spirit of adventure. A noisy, argumentative committee meeting can suggest the danger of doing something in excess, but a quiet, orderly meeting suggests a relaxed period in your own life.

COMMUNION

A dream in which you make your first communion heralds especially good news, while an ordinary communion service is an indicator of good fortune, talents being used to the full, and events which help you gain recognition for those talents. A girl dreaming about a communion service is likely to have, or to meet, a partner who is affectionate.

COMPASS

A compass appearing in a dream foreshadows major debts, important decisions at work, and disharmony.

COMPETITION

Dreaming about taking part in a competition, whether on the sporting field or elsewhere, indicates putting a disproportionate amount of effort into obtaining a result which does not justify the work involved; it also suggests a need to make use of all the reserves of tact and diplomacy you have at your disposal.

COMPLAINT

Making any kind of complaint in a dream augurs ill for the future: because of ups and downs you are experiencing in your fortunes at the moment, you may be distracted from grasping favourable opportunities held out to you. Complaining to any kind of company or government official means you are obsessed by the feeling that no-one understands you, while complaining to someone about the way they are behaving means you are anxious and worried for no particular reason.

COMPLIMENTS

Contrary to what one might expect, giving or being paid compliments does not bode well in a dream. Complimenting someone else actually suggests the idea of falsehood and using flattery to deceive, while being complimented yourself reflects internal jealousy and discord.

CONCERN

This concern may be directed towards your mother, and if so it betrays a certain amount of nervousness and irritability which you need to keep under a tight rein. If it is your mother you are concerned about, you are hard-working and very scrupulous in your dealings with others. Concern about a son or daughter means that there are agreements to be reached within a project which has important financial implications. If you are worried about someone's health, there will be tensions within your family, while if you are afraid about the future, you have shyness to overcome.

CONCERT

Going to a concert symbolizes an independent, entrepreneurial personality. Taking part in one shows that you are stubborn and obstinate, either in your current business relationships or generally as a person. Conducting a band or orchestra in concert suggests you will be in the public eye in some way, but that your 'fame' will be short-lived.

CONFESSION

Going to confession, or seeing a confessional with or without a priest in it, is a sign of loss and deprivation, though it also reflects intelligence and lofty ideals. Making a confession to a friend or colleague simply shows a feeling of guilt about something you have recently done.

CONFETTI

Despite its happy connotations in real life, confetti in a dream suggests that you are behaving irrationally and irritably.

CONFIDING

Confiding in someone in a dream means you need to relax and slow down the pace of your life for a while. This is particularly true if it is a man you are confiding in: you may be at considerable risk if you do not start taking things easy.

I dream in colour: do you do the same?

Many of us are able to remember the colours of things in our dreams. In fact there is no doubt that colours have a quite precisely defined significance in dreams. Strong, bright colours tend to reflect sexual impulses; dark colours signify worries and fears; and pale colours show a feeling of relaxed contentment, provided of course that the dreams they appear in are pleasant ones.

Recent studies of dreaming have brought out two interesting facts. The first is that dreaming in colour has become more frequent and widespread since the advent of colour cinematography, and in all likelihood (though there are few statistics to support this assumption) still more so since colour television became common. The second is that some drugs, in particular tranquillizers and sleeping tablets, make it more likely that a person will dream in colour. A doctor dealing with elderly patients has noted that "nothing on earth" would induce him to deprive the more lonely and unhappy of his patients of one particular tablet. This "helps them to dream in colour, and has a noticeable effect on their general morale". He added: "For these poor old people, dreaming is like going to the cinema. And dreaming in colour is the only amusement they can allow themselves."

Often in dreams, colours do not correspond to what we would expect to find in reality. This

Whether or not we dream in colour is still a matter of debate. One thing is certain: different colours correspond to different states of mind.

is because, as we have seen, they express states of mind, and it has been shown that particular colours reflect different moods. Many experts believe that all our dreaming is done in colour, but we often forget this because when we try to remember and decipher our dreams, what we recall is their content, and not the form they took.

CONFIRMATION

Going to a confirmation service, whether it is you or someone else that is being confirmed, means that in every part of your life at the moment there is balance and harmony and an awareness of your responsibilities.

CONGRATULATIONS

These are a favourable portent. Being congratulated in a dream, or congratulating someone else, either for an achievement, or for some happy event such as a birth or a marriage, is a sign of happiness in your own daily life, loves and work.

CONSPIRACY

Taking part in a conspiracy in a dream shows that you are labouring under a major misapprehension or illusion. Discovering a conspiracy among others shows a piece of business being compromised to the point where it is no longer feasible.

CONVALESCENCE

Dreaming that you are recovering from a major illness has favourable implications entirely unconnected with your health: it signifies a major success is imminent in your work.

CONVENT

Seeing a convent in a dream is a sign of change and new developments. Dreaming about going into one or living in it suggests you have an openness, generosity and friendliness which makes you popular with others; and any dream involving a convent has generally favourable connotations.

COOKING

The precise implications of a dream which involves cooking depends on what is being cooked, but generally it means that a piece of work that would cause worry were it not finished in time, is in fact coming to a successful conclusion.

COPPER

A dream in which a copper object appears indicates ungrounded fears and worries. Beate copper shows that you are experiencing a period of discomfort or a minor crisis. If the copper is engraved with some sort of design, the dream suggests you have particularly refined tastes, while if it is inlaid with silver, it shows that appearances can be deceptive. An old-fashioned copper pot indicates someone else may be willing to help you to get a project finished. A copper coin being given to you signifies a doubt you have had for a long time finally being resolved, while copper wire signifies an uncertain situation.

COPYING

Dreaming about copying a letter is a sign of nervousness and anxiety; while copying a document indicates a strong, tenacious personality. Copying someone's signature shows you are involved in a difficult struggle with people who are much stronger than yourself, and unless you put your reason and practicality to work you could end up being humiliated. Copying someone else's behaviour in a dream, or following their instructions, suggests you have an unpredictable and extravagant personality and you should be careful to keep things in perspective.

CORAL

Acquiring something made of coral in a dream is a sign of strength of personality and perseverance, but if you sell it or give it away, it denotes weakness. A coral reef is a danger sign for anyone who is in love.

CORN

Dreaming about fields of corn, or about eating it, symbolizes financial and material well-being. Sowing corn is a sign that you are likely to become increasingly busy in your work, and harvesting corn is an indication of good health.

CORPSE

This is a symbol of separation, parting, a break in a relationship or unfaithfulness in love. Dreaming about burying a corpse is a sign of good fortune at work. A dead body in a coffin is a sign of a bond being

COSTUME   Children in costume signify the fertility of your imagination.

broken, while if you see one in a mortuary it indicates financial losses. The body of a woman reflects your being severely let down by a friend, while the body of a man means that you need to face up to those things in your life which are going wrong at the moment.

CORRIDOR

Corridors appear frequently in dreams. If the corridor is a narrow one, there are possible losses of some kind in store for you, while a wide one reflects your considerable ambition. A dark corridor is a sign of worries looming on the horizon, and a brightly-lit one shows misunderstandings being cleared up.

COSTUME

Wearing a bathing costume in a dream is a sign of great physical sensitivity to your surroundings and environment. Putting on a historical costume indicates the arrival of favourable news, while a regional or national costume reveals your highly-developed powers of imagination.

COTTON WOOL

The appearance of a pad of cotton wool in a dream is a sign of a difficult and problematic situation, while if it is bloodstained it indicates that you may soon receive important news on the work front. If the cotton wool is packaged, you have a secret which needs to remain that way whatever happens. If it is loose, you may be about to lose something you were particularly fond of. If you use cotton wool to keep yourself clean in the dream, you are experiencing a lack of energy and will-power at the moment which creates setbacks at work. If you use cotton wool to polish something, a dangerous situation may be in the offing.

COUGHING

Having a cough in a dream is an ominous sign; you will soon find yourself at the centre of a very complex and delicate situation which you may not be able to get out of. If you have a serious fit of coughing in the dream, it is because there are many problems to be dealt with at work.

COUNTRY

Dreaming about having a house in the country indicates the beginning of a period free from financial worries. Being surrounded by green countryside indicates satisfaction and the comforts of a good life, but if the landscape is a barren one, without trees or flowers, it indicates the beginning of a period of your life which is grey and unexciting. A foreign country in a dream shows you have a high degree of awareness of things which do not relate directly to your everyday life. Coming back to your home country after being abroad means that you should think carefully about any decision you are about to make, as it could otherwise cost you a great deal of money.

COURT

A magistrates' court in a dream indicates initiative and enterprise, while a criminal court suggests that a decision of consequence needs to be taken very soon. A court martial shows that you are concerned about someone whose merits are unrecognized by others. Being a witness in court means you are about to overcome a difficult obstacle, but being taken to court yourself can often be a premonition of something unpleasant.

COURTYARD

A dream in which a courtyard features is an optimistic one, in-

COUNTRY   When you dream of being in the country, you are happy and content.

dicating hopes being fulfilled, while if there are children or animals in the courtyard it suggests that you have managed to skirt dangers that were placed in your path.

CRADLE

A cradle with a baby in it is an obvious sign of hope for the future, and indicates success in projects undertaken. A doll's cradle symbolizes unrealizable aims, and an empty cradle means health problems.

CRAMP

A cramp is a painful but short-lived affliction, and this is exactly what it suggests in a dream. Cramp in your hands and feet indicates very short-lived worries, while stomach cramp is a sign of immoderate ambition and unrealistic ideas.

CRATER

Climbing into or out of a crater suggests that you are getting involved in activities which could place you at severe risk; falling into a crater means you should stay away from people who could be leading you astray. An active crater with smoke or flames coming out of it reflects a pressing need for money, but if the crater is that of an extinct volcano a piece of business will soon be successfully concluded.

CRAYFISH

Crayfish in a dream are not a good sign: they indicate poor judgment, and when dead, or cooked, a disappointment in emotional affairs.

CREAM

Although cream itself is generally sweet, in dreams its significance is a bitter one. Dreaming about whipping or beating cream means ill-humour and irritability, and eating

CREAM   You may have made a bad buy if you eat cream in a dream.

it denotes an acquisition or purchase which should not have been made. Coffee with cream in it symbolizes secret pleasures. A medicinal cream or ointment, though, holds out the promise of objectives being realized and major financial gains being made.

CRICKET (the game)

Cricket is a game with complex rules, and seeing or taking part in a cricket match in your dream suggests you feel yourself bound by rules imposed on you by other people, but now is an opportunity to escape some of them. A cricket ball is a symbol of impatience which needs to be kept under control, and a cricket bat indicates petty jealousies and rivalries.

CRICKET (the insect)

The cricket, like Dickens' magical Cricket on the Hearth, is a sign of good luck. A cricket which comes into the house in your dream suggests that money will be coming into the house as well. But trying to catch the cricket in a dream is likely to bring ill luck.

CRIME

Any type of crime occurring in a dream is a sign of difficulties to come. A crime committed as a matter of honour or conscience is a sign that you have major worries, while a political crime suggests there are matters in your life which need clarification. Committing any type of crime yourself indicates that you are about to incur the displeasure of friends or colleagues.

CRIMINAL

A criminal confessing his or her crimes in a dream shows a personal success being delayed or held back, while the appearance of a suspected criminal symbolizes a lack of stability in your personal relationships. A murderer, strangely enough, suggests unexpected help from someone you had underestimated. Generally speaking, the activities of a criminal in a dream suggest change for the worse.

CROSSING   If you cross a fence in a dream it indicates wasted energy.

CROSS

A cross is an auspicious symbol to dream about, signifying comfort and security. The meaning of the cross can also vary depending on what it is made of. A wooden cross indicates a surprise, while a gold one indicates favourable comments being made about you at work.

CROSSING

Here the meaning of the dream depends on what it is that is being crossed. Crossing a boundary, such as a fence or a frontier between countries, is a sign of energies not being put to good use, while crossing a river or other natural barrier is a symbol of dangers put behind you. However there may be unexpected new developments at work, and you need to keep cool and avoid making mistakes because at the moment these would be more harmful to you than usual.

CROSSROADS

Being at a crossroads symbolizes a decision that has to be taken. If you dream about taking one of the roads available to you, much of course depends on whether this proves to be be the right road in the dream — in which case a correct decision is

CROWN   Dreaming of a royal crown suggests improvements in social life.

indicated – or the wrong one, in which case you need to review the situation and avoid getting into even more trouble.

CROW

The crow, with its black body and wings, is not a good dream omen: it is a harbinger of disappointment, financial worries and health problems. Hearing its cawing in your sleep is a symbol of unpleasant occurrences to come.

CROWD

Any crowd of people in a dream means an improvement in your fortunes. A crowd celebrating means business affairs turning out advantageously, and a crowd which is demonstrating or protesting is a warning to you to be cautious.

CROWN

Dreaming about a royal crown is a sign of social advancement, but if you dream about donning it yourself you may be rather uncommunicative and untrustworthy at the moment. A golden crown symbolizes responsibilities involving trust; and a crown of flowers, delicate health.

CRUMBS

Dreaming about breadcrumbs is a healthy sign. If the crumbs are being eaten by birds, it is a clear sign that good news or gifts are on the way.

CRY

Crying with sadness actually indicates your overcoming an obstacle, while crying with happiness indicates disputes and arguments. A woman crying is an indication that you need to take more care in things you are involved in, while a baby crying suggests there may be improvements in your domestic situation in the near future.

CRYSTAL

Crystal is a delicate, fragile material, and dreaming of crystal suggests your emotions may be in a delicate condition. A broken crystal is a sign of disagreements, discord and recriminations in your relations with others. If the crystal item is dirty, people may be taking offence at your actions without your realizing it, but if it is clean your course of action is the right one.

CUCKOO

Dreaming about seeing or hearing a cuckoo implies problems between lovers – such as arguments or even a split – while the cuckoo can also presage jealousy and lack of understanding in a marriage.

CUCUMBER   Like any vegetable in a dream, cucumbers signify good health.

CUCUMBER

The appearance of this vegetable, or indeed any other vegetable, in a dream usually indicates that you are in good health and have an iron constitution.

CUP

A china cup in a dream reflects an appointment not being kept, while one made of glass suggests interesting proposals being made to you at work. A plastic cup concerns your general financial interests. If the cup is full, you are in the middle of a very favourable and cheerful period of your life, but if it is empty, you can expect difficult discussions with members of your family. If the cup is overflowing it signifies that you are ruled by your heart.

CUP   A full teacup shows you are enjoying a contented phase of life.

CURLING UP

Curling up on the ground is not a very auspicious thing to do in a dream, as it suggests you are being exhibitionistic and extravagant, and creating many illusions for yourself; you need to keep your feet firmly on the ground or you will put your career at risk. If you curl up in a sitting position, you have extraordinary reserves of energy which are helping you overcome fatigue and pain; while if you curl up in a comfortable armchair, you are shutting off your thoughts to avoid facing a problem of your own making.

CURTAIN

A white curtain in a dream indicates a burdensome responsibility; a coloured one, a modest standard of living. A thin or flimsy curtain indicates a calm, serene temperament. If you raise or open the curtain during your dream, you can regard a work project as having been successfully completed.

CUSHION

This is one of those dream symbols which indicates its opposite: the bigger, softer and more comfortable the cushion, the more thorny are the problems you have to resolve.

CUT

Cutting yourself by mistake in a dream bodes ill for the future, suggesting imminent problems, bad decisions or sad news. Someone

else being cut or wounded indicates advancement in your career. Anything else which is intentionally cut, such as food, or wood, suggests that you should sever a relationship with someone who is bringing you nothing but unhappiness.

CYCLIST

Dreaming about a cyclist toiling up a hill, flying down it, or heading for the finishing post in a race indicates progress, triumphs over adversaries and problems, and favourable

CYPRESS TREE   This may be an unwelcome sign, predicting that money and health problems lie ahead.

changes. The only cycle dream which does not augur well for the future is that in which a cyclist falls off his bicycle – but he can always get back on and carry on riding!

CYPRESS TREE

The cypress of our dreams is a sad tree, indicating problems and difficulties, either financial or in health.

DAHLIA

The dahlia is an auspicious flower to dream about: it suggests prestige and lofty ambitions being fulfilled. Picking dahlias indicates an unexpected journey to be made, while a lover giving his partner a dahlia suggests that misunderstandings may arise between them.

DANCING

Dreaming about dancing is, in general, a good sign. If it is you dancing, there are gains and benefits on the way, while being at a ball indicates that a friend will enjoy a piece of good fortune. Dancing in a public place indicates a meeting which may change your life. It is only dancing on your own that brings sadness in real life: you have hopes which will never be realized.

DANGER

If you feel you are in some kind of danger in your dream, without knowing exactly what it is, this shows you have a careful and prudent personality which will help you make major gains in a short space of time. If you come face-to-face with danger, you will go through a phase of being lazy and apathetic towards everything and you will not find it easy to free yourself from this state of mind. Even once you achieve this, you may find yourself having difficulties with your partner.

DARKNESS

If you find yourself in darkness in your dream – for example in a cave or a tunnel – there may be a major emotional upset on the way in which your inner strength and outward decision-making ability will be tested to the full. But if you manage to escape from the darkness back into the sunlight, this promises success in your work and happiness in love. Fear of the dark in a dream suggests that you have very major obstacles to overcome in your life. A dark or shadowy person or thing you cannot quite identify indicates a subconscious fear that needs to be brought out into the open and rationalized. Someone being kept in the dark, figuratively or literally, means that relationships with your loved one, or someone close to you, may be difficult.

DATE (appointment)

A date with someone of the opposite sex whom you find attractive suggests you are probably feeling unwanted or unattractive yourself; but if there are no romantic overtones, and the date is merely an appointment, it suggests there may be an important meeting in real life very soon.

DATE (fruit)

The date, and the date palm, are both signs of good luck, suggesting an adventurous existence and a possible long journey. Dreaming about eating dates means an interesting proposal coming out of your working life.

DAUGHTER

Dreaming of a daughter is a sign of important news to come. A daughter who is ill or injured is a sign of your own worries, while if your daughter is pregnant, you may need help to deal with a difficult problem. A disobedient daughter is a symbol of uncertainty for the future.

DEAFNESS

Being deaf in a dream is not a particularly good sign. There is news on the way which you will not like and which may leave you

DAHLIA   This flower suggests your ambitions are being achieved.

depressed. A dream about trying to make yourself understood to a deaf person means you are deluding yourself in matters of love.

DEATH

Death occurs quite often in dreams, and is rarely an ill omen: it simply shows that you are in a nervous or agitated state and being excessively pessimistic. Dreaming about your own death is a sign both of good health and improvements on the business or financial front, while it can also indicate meeting a person you have been attracted to for a long time on a more intimate footing than hitherto. Dreaming of being about to die indicates that your health may be at risk in a small way.

DEBT

Owing someone money, or being owed money, is a sign of a certain amount of nervous tension on your part. Repaying a debt indicates confidence in your financial situation.

DECEPTION

Deceiving someone else, or being deceived yourself, indicates ill-humour, anxiety, worry and loneliness. It also indicates complications or losses in your business life.

DEER

Dreaming about deer points to pleasant events on the way, but hunting deer is a symbol of postponing these events through your own actions. A deer being hunted can also symbolize a prison, either real or metaphorical.

DELAY

Being delayed and hence late for an appointment in a dream in fact means you have considerable skills of enterprise and initiative. A delay in payment suggests hidden dissatisfaction and worry which appears to have no particular cause. A delayed departure, perhaps of a train, indicates worry about the health of a relative. If you are delayed yourself in your dream, you are about to enter an unhappy period in many respects.

DELIRIUM

Being literally delirious because of illness suggests being betrayed in matters of love, while being delirious with love or happiness indicates enhanced prospects in your work.

DELIVERING

Delivering a letter, or having one delivered to you, indicates successful projects at work; a parcel is a sign of relationships with someone else needing clarification; and a telegram, expenses to be watched carefully. Delivering a message by hand means you will be impressed by initiatives taken by a new colleague at work, while delivering a secret message signifies that you will experience a disappointment in the field of business. Delivering flowers is a symbol of trust in the future.

DEMOLISHING

Dreaming about something being demolished has a dual meaning. It indicates inner anguish and unhappiness, but can also symbolize renewed hope after a painful but necessary decision.

DEMOTION

Dreaming about being demoted, or taking a step backwards in one's career, indicates insecurity and an over-sensitive attitude: try to have more confidence in your abilities or you will end up in a state of depression which will be almost impossible to get out of. If you choose a job which is below your capabilities in the dream, it suggests you should not be put off by a minor failure at work; while if you demote someone in the forces to a lower rank, you can expect a period of emotional difficulty.

DENIAL

Denying you have done something in a dream has different meanings depending on whether or not you are being truthful in your denial. If you are, you should accept the advice and help being offered to you; while if you are lying, you are not displaying enterprise or intelligence in your dealings with others.

DENTURES

Like teeth, dentures are not a favourable sign in a dream. Any dream involving false teeth is an indicator of major crises on the way, emotional instability and unhappiness in love.

DEPARTURE

Friends departing in a dream in fact signify possible visits by old acquaintances; relatives departing mean temporary setbacks; and a

Do only human beings dream?

Experts on the subject of dreams believe it is possible to show with a fairly high degree of certainty that animals such as mammals and birds do exhibit symptoms of dreaming while they are asleep. Many of us will have heard a household cat or dog mewing, barking or growling in their sleep, or possibly displaying signs of pleasure or fear. It is now thought that there is every likelihood that animals have sufficient material in their memories to form the basis of dreams.

The fundamental difference between ourselves and other species is that they are unlikely to be able to distinguish between events which happen in reality, and dreams, so things that happen in their dreams form part of their active memory.

Studies have brought many interesting facts to light about the way animals sleep. Lizards, for example, often stretch out completely motionless and with their eyes closed, suggesting they sleep in much the same way as we do, with all their muscles relaxed. Snakes sleep, too: although they keep their eyes open, their pupils disappear beneath their eyelids. Fish rest (or sleep: we are not yet sure) by staying upright in one position, and keeping

themselves there using slight movements of their fins. Carp appear to be the only fish which lie on the river bed, though whether this is simply to rest is not yet known.

husband or wife departing means things between you and your partner are being straightened out gradually and permanently. Dreaming about deciding on a departure date for a journey indicates that you have ambitions and ideas which are too lofty. If an actual dream departure is on a train, there are very bright prospects for the future; if by a plane, legitimate hopes and aspirations for the future; and departing by car means new burdens and responsibilities to be taken on if you are not to become too dependent on

DIAMOND   Combine the meanings of 'diamond' and 'queen' for this image.

others in your work. If you depart somewhere by yourself, you will soon receive an interesting suggestion; while if you go with a friend or loved one, you will resolve your present financial difficulties.

DESERT

A desert to be crossed indicates a difficult period of your life. A clear sky above suggests the problems will be temporary in nature, but if there is a sandstorm, you may have to fight for some time to overcome your adversities. An oasis in a desert suggests temporary respite from problems, and a mirage a happy distraction.

DESK

A desk is something of a warning signal if it appears in a dream. Dreaming about sitting at a desk, or seeing someone else at one, suggests you should avoid fruitless discussions and hurried decisions and keep your mouth firmly closed for the time being.

DEVIL

A dream in which the devil appears is, without exception, a sign of danger. Seeing the devil in a dream means major temptations to be avoided, and speaking to him means possible harm or damage has already been done. If you dream about being the devil yourself, a difficult time is on its way and you will have an uphill struggle to regain composure and tranquillity.

DIAGNOSIS

A diagnosis is an auspicious sign. Diagnosing an illness actually means your love for someone is growing, while a favourable diagnosis – the doctor telling you there is nothing wrong – indicates security in your job.

DIAL

The dial of a watch or clock in a dream signifies new interests and initiatives being taken, while a sundial indicates major long-term successes in your work. Using a compass dial to try and find your way indicates a period of well-being due to the success of some of the projects you are involved in in your work. It also suggests that things are working well in romantic relationships, but you should avoid getting unnecessarily jealous of your partner.

DIAMOND

Despite its positive connotations in real life, in dreams a diamond is not a favourable indication. Being given a diamond means short-lived illusions; buying one, financial problems; and giving one, hypocritical behaviour by people dear to you. Dreaming about finding a diamond heralds family unhappiness.

DICE

One or more dice in a dream are a symbol of knowledge being put to good use. Playing any game involving dice, though, means uncertainty and illusion in your life.

DICTATING

Dreaming about writing down a classroom dictation is a sign of a reflective frame of mind. Dictating letters to a secretary denotes a lasting friendship. Dictating your memoirs means you are very ambitious, and dictating a will means you will get unhappily involved in someone else's dispute.

DIET

Being on a diet after an illness symbolizes pointless anxieties and a feeling of resignation. Dieting to get thinner, on the other hand, indicates good fortune in business, and being on a vegetarian diet in a dream suggests that you have trustworthy friends.

DIGGING

Dreaming about digging a ditch means you need something new and different to happen in your life, while digging a hole symbolizes debts to be repaid as soon as possible. Digging a well indicates differences with members of your

DICE   You are making the most of your knowledge if you dream of dice.

DOCTOR   A doctor in a dream brings good luck and good health.

family. If you are involved in digging for some kind of precious metal or stones, you are subconsciously aware that there is hostility towards you at work.

DILIGENCE

A hard-working or diligent woman in a dream denotes great enthusiasm for a suggestion made at work, while a diligent man symbolizes a long-awaited solution to an emotional problem. Being diligent in your studies means that the sacrifices you are making at present will be appreciated and rewarded by someone who is important in your life.

DINING

The precise meaning of having dinner in a dream depends on the circumstances. Dining at home means you will soon be involved in new projects and initiatives. Being invited to dinner at someone else's house may indicate a journey. Eating out at a restaurant denotes a certain amount of sadness at the way things are going in your love life, while having dinner on a train or aeroplane suggests deep-seated desires and longings that are not being fulfilled.

DIPLOMA

Receiving a diploma or similar award in a dream is a pleasant omen, suggesting pride in one's hard-won successes.

DIPLOMAT

Dreaming about a diplomat indicates travels and change, and if you dream about receiving one you should be ready for a major piece of good news.

DISASTER

Disasters in dreams actually signify their opposite: good fortune and prosperity. If you are in love with someone, seeing or being a victim of a disaster in fact indicates that weddings bells will be ringing before long.

DISH

A silver dish in a dream symbolizes unexpected changes or moves, while a gold one shows ambition being crowned with success. An aluminium dish suggests emotional excitement or agitation, and a china plate is a symbol of a tranquil, peaceful life. A dish which is oval indicates an emotional episode in which your aspirations prove to be overambitious; and if the dish is round, you are being unreasonable in your dealings with others. Buying a plate indicates success in business; but if you break one, you can expect financial problems.

DISPUTE

Dreaming about a legal dispute shows you are agitated and dissatisfied at present, but others are not aware of the fact. A union dispute suggests immoderate behaviour and lack of responsibility on your part. A personal dispute or disagreement indicates you are in a combative frame of mind and are taking things out on other people.

DIVORCE

This dream in fact means the opposite of what one might expect. If a married person dreams about getting divorced, it usually indicates that his or her marriage is a strong one, without the jealousy and unfaithfulness of some marriages.

DOCTOR

A doctor who appears in a dream indicates good health and fortune.

DOG

Most dreams involving dogs mean that we can expect agreeable events to occur as the result of a friend's actions. But a growling dog in a dream indicates that a friend cannot necessarily be trusted, and a dog that bites someone means you are making things difficult for yourself by being obstinate. A barking dog signifies imminent danger and a howling dog also warns of impending misfortune.

DOG-CATCHER

Dreaming of a dog-catcher who pursues and finally catches a dog warns that a sudden loss of freedom is in the offing, but if the dog escapes, there is a possibility of unpredictable events in your love life.

DOLL

A doll made of paper or cardboard in a dream is a sign of rivalry in love, while one made of wood shows that you are experiencing a period of unhappiness. A plastic doll indicates jealousy from your partner, and one made from some kind of fabric shows you are going through an experience which may prove useful. A doll which walks or talks suggests that you should take care not to become unnecessarily involved in disagreements with a new acquaintance.

DOLPHIN

Despite its connotations in real life,

DONKEY   For a girl, donkey dreams predict a kind but not wealthy husband.

a dolphin in a dream actually indicates anxieties and preoccupations, dangerous journeys, projects failing or a friend being ill.

DONKEY

A donkey appearing in your dreams is a favourable sign, showing that although you have problems at present, you will overcome them if you are patient and show sufficient humility. If a girl dreams about a donkey it means her future husband will be a kind, determined man, although he will not be well-off.

DOOR

The front door of a house in a dream symbolizes good fortune in love; if it is open, it means you will find harmony with your partner, but if it is closed you could find him or her to be a major disappointment. The most favourable sign of this kind is a door which is half-open, as this indicates a long, emotionally satisfying relationship. Opening a door means new acquaintances at work, and closing it indicates the need for a major change of course before it is too late. A door being slammed means you will be the object of petty, slanderous gossip concerning your private life.

DOORBELL

If you hear a doorbell ring in your dreams, take great care before you make any decisions. If you ring a doorbell yourself, you are very clear in your mind about the way you see your life developing.

DORMITORY

A dormitory or ward in a hospital in a dream heralds visits from relatives, while a school or college dormitory indicates that you are subconsciously mulling over several plans for the future.

DOUBLE BASS

As with the dreaming of many musical instruments, the appearance of a double bass in a dream is a favourable sign, showing that your personality is calm and composed. Learning to play the double bass signifies that you are both original and imaginative, while hearing someone else playing it indicates a forthcoming proposal or suggestion which you would be well advised to take up.

DOVE

A dove in a dream is a double-edged symbol. A dove cooing or at rest, indicates happiness on the domestic front and a long and happy marriage, but if it is in flight a loss of money is in prospect. A dead dove means a project will prove to have been a waste of time.

DRAGON

Although many unpleasant animals, such as insects and reptiles, have negative implications in a dream, a dragon is a harbinger of spiritual and material wealth.

DRAPES

To dream of brightly-coloured drapes or of banners used to decorate a festive occasion indicates that a period of sadness is in the offing. Funeral drapes or shrouds in a dream suggest that your projects at work will peter out in mid-stream. However, you should not let yourself get discouraged by their failure because far more favourable opportunities are on the way. Drapes, or altar-cloths, in a church indicate that you are going through an emotional relationship which your partner does not know about.

DRAWER

If you dream about opening a drawer, this indicates that some money you have lent is about to be repaid. Closing a drawer means you have a

DOOR   Opening and closing doors point the way to change in your life.

complex, introverted personality. A full drawer means there are dangers just around the corner, but if it is empty, this suggests that you will take up new interests and pastimes.

DRAWING

Seeing a drawing in a dream can have various meanings depending on what is being drawn, but in general it indicates health, sociability, and warmth and sympathy from those around you.

DREAM

Interestingly enough, it is quite common to dream about having a dream, and usually it indicates a period where things are going your way. Dreaming about having a nightmare in fact signifies that you have a financial status which is in many respects enviable, and if you dream about having a pleasant dream this suggests that new developments will happen at work.

DRESSING

If you get dressed with a great deal of time and care in your dream, it shows that you want approval and respect from others in real life, but if you carelessly throw on your clothes it indicates that you will soon resolve a hostile situation. Putting your clothes on inside out in the dream is a sign of good luck.

DRESSING UP

It is not at all unusual to dream about dressing in the clothes of the opposite sex: if you are a man dressing up as a woman it indicates jealousies and disagreements with a loved one, while if you are a woman who dreams of dressing up as a man, this suggests that you may have a selfish, presumptuous personality. If you dream of wearing any other kind of fancy dress this shows that you are hiding your feelings from those around you.

DRAGON   Dreaming of a dragon means spiritual and material riches.

DRILL

An electric drill in a dream symbolizes a state of depression which cannot be shaken off easily, while a hand drill suggests that you are being careless and unthinking in your relations with others. Buying a drill means you are spending time with people who will harm you in the long run. Drilling a hole in a wall indicates that you should not shy away from the burdens being placed on you because your career may depend on them. Drilling a tunnel suggests that you are gradually overcoming the shyness which has made it difficult for you to form relationships with others in the past.

DRINKING

Having a drink from a crystal-clear fountain in a dream indicates future health and happiness. Giving a drink to someone who is thirsty shows that you are by nature a generous and kind-hearted person. Drinking milk or wine signifies health and happiness, but drinking

DRINKING   Indulging in a glass of wine, milk or clear spring water is a sign of health and happiness.

dirty or muddy water means you are getting involved in matters which are not really your concern. Drinking a toast can have various mean-

51

ings depending on why the toast is being drunk – a wedding, a birthday, a business function – but in general it signifies the arrival of either an unexpected but very welcome piece of news or a guest who is equally so.

DRIVING

If you dream of someone else doing the driving, then your dream has hopeful implications, but if you are driving a car or other vehicle, you can expect to lose, or spend unnecessarily, a large amount of money. Driving a car in a dream means differences of opinion with those dear to you, and driving a lorry indicates that you will shortly find a solution to a major problem which has been worrying you. Driving a tractor means that you are feeling very secure about your future, and riding a moped or motorbike is also a sign that you feel you are in control of your life and where you are going.

DROPSY

Suffering from dropsy in a dream signifies that you will face a danger caused by water in some form and so you would be well advised to take great care if you decide to go swimming or plan to take any sea voyages in the future.

DROWNING

To dream that you are drowning means that you are experiencing major problems and worries which are threatening to overwhelm you. However, if you manage to keep your head above water in a dream, or if someone else comes along and rescues you, this means that in real life you can rely on either yourself, or friends and acquaintances, to help you get through these problems in one piece.

DRUG

Dreaming about taking a drug of any kind, whether medicinal or narcotic, means you have too many illusions and fantasies and need to come down to earth. Dreaming that you are 'high' on a drug of any kind means that there is a potentially dangerous situation just around the corner. Buying drugs suggests you are putting money into something which will give you a poor return, but selling them indicates major financial gains.

DRUNK

Seeing someone drunk in a pub in a dream shows that you are in poor physical condition. Getting drunk yourself indicates that small gains are heading your way. To dream of a drunk in the street suggests careless

spending on your part, while seeing a drunk lying on the ground means your health may be at risk. A sleeping drunk is a symbol of your excessively hard work, while to dream of a drunk who is singing indicates that you have little self-confidence in your skills and abilities. Getting 'high' or 'drunk' on a piece of music, a sunset, a painting or something similar in a dream indicates that you have a considerable degree of sensitivity.

DUCK

Seeing a flight of ducks in a dream means an improvement in your personal finances. Ducks swimming on a pond or a lake are a symbol of success for anyone with their own business. A pair of ducks symbolizes a marriage in the near future.

DUEL

A duel in a dream suggests either risks to your health or damage to your standing with others. People duelling with swords suggest that you will have romantic adventures of some kind, while a pistol duel indicates a possible reconciliation with a loved one.

DRIVING   When you drive a car yourself, it reflects disagreements and loss of money.

DUNG

Dreaming about manure or dung is a good sign for anyone who is poor, but is less so if you are well-off. If you dream about spreading manure on a field or garden this indicates that your hard work will make you rich. If you dream of falling into a dung-heap this suggests that you will have an unexpected windfall.

DUST

To dream of coal dust is a sign of industriousness and conscientiousness bringing their own just reward, while to dream of gold dust shows that you may be underestimating the virtues of people you work with. Getting dust in your eyes in a dream means a major change in your relationship with your partner, while dusty furniture denotes minor irritations which are being caused by your employers. A dusty road signifies the need for compromises.

DUCK   A swimming duck signals success for anyone with their own business.

DUSTBIN

Although a dream involving a dustbin might not seem particularly auspicious, putting anything into a dustbin suggests help from someone who is important to you, while emptying one is a symbol of success in the face of problems. Opening a dustbin indicates that you are involved in a pleasurable relationship, while putting the lid back on one means that you must reflect carefully before you make a decision as you are now at a crossroads.

DUTY

Taking on any kind of duty in a dream suggests that your work is about to undergo a major change which will have an effect on your lifestyle. If the duty is an unpleasant or onerous one, it means you are extremely self-confident at present, and that if you choose the right moment to make a decision, it will prove to be very advantageous. To dream of undertaking a pleasant duty suggests that you are deluding yourself and are likely to come down to earth with a bump the moment an obstacle gets in your way.

Dreams that you can't forget

Dreaming about death suggests that you are involved in a conflict within yourself. Even children dream about death, and adults often wake up and remember scenes of killings, bodies, or tombs. In some periods of a person's life, when they are experiencing changes which affect their physical or mental well-being, these dreams can become particularly important: death can represent liberation from feelings, responsibilities and situations which can have a negative effect on the person's life.

So death in a dream does not foretell the death of a real person, but simply the death of a part of the dreamer: a departure or separation from something that is troubling them, and which they are still unable to escape from in their conscious lives because they have not yet come to terms with it.

It is hard to forget a dream involving death: we tend to wake up feeling oppressed and perhaps frightened. It is only when we start to think through the dream and analyze it that we begin the process of catharsis, of freeing ourselves from the inner conflicts we have not yet managed to resolve. Some of these symbols are not only personal to us, but part of the

collective unconscious, the system of myth and ritual which we all share in. In Jung's words, they are "symbols of transformation".

DWARF

Meeting a dwarf in your dreams is not a sign of good luck: you are likely to be attracting petty jealousy and malicious gossip from those who dislike you. But there is no cause for alarm if you dream about being a dwarf yourself: this actually indicates a new strength of purpose on your part where previously you have been irresolute and incapable of dealing with problems in your working life.

DYING

Seeing someone else dying in a dream indicates that you need to look after yourself and slow down if your health is not to suffer. If someone is dying and makes a will in a dream this indicates that there will be arguments and disagreements within your family. Therefore, on the whole, dying – in whatever manner and whether it is you or someone else – is not a favourable sign in a dream.

DYNAMITE

As in real life, the appearance of dynamite in a dream suggests danger. It warns of the emergence of potentially serious troubles which could get out of control if you are not extremely careful.

EATING   This generally points to health and happiness.

EAGLE

If you dream of this beautiful bird soaring through the air it shows that you have high expectations of yourself and will one day see your ambitions realized triumphantly. If the eagle is wounded or dead, however, your reputation will suffer.

EAR

Straining your ears to hear what someone else is saying in a dream indicates a decision which needs to be made; washing your ears heralds the beginning of a connection or relationship which will prove to be a profitable and happy one. Any dream in which ears play an important part suggests you should be breaking off from someone who has let you down badly or who is acting unpleasantly towards you.

EARRING

A pair of golden earrings in a dream is a symbol of temporary problems, while silver ones suggest that unpleasant judgments are being made about you by your detractors. If the earrings are made from diamonds or some other precious stone, your energies are below their peak and you are displaying a certain amount of laziness. Buying earrings is a sign of extravagant ideas; losing them indicates that you are experiencing a bumpy period in financial matters. Finding an earring means you should avoid gambling, while wearing them shows you need to put more effort into your work.

EARTH

Red earth in a dream reflects your own shyness and anxiety, while yellow earth is a symbol of false

EARRING   Dreaming about diamond earrings? Try harder at work!

information. Black earth denotes gloom and depression. If you dream about picking up some earth, your physical strength is outstanding. Kissing the earth means that you will have disappointments in emotional matters.

EARTHQUAKE

A distant earthquake in a dream signifies a sudden, unexpected change, but if the earthquake is closer, this indicates that you will experience difficulties for quite a while. If the earthquake is prolonged, this suggests that you are worrying unnecessarily about a friend's health, but if the tremors are over quickly, this shows that you are nervous and irritable.

EATING

Most dreams involving eating symbolize physical and spiritual health, though the precise meaning depends on what is being eaten and how it is being eaten. Eating standing up suggests that you are doing things too hurriedly and not giving them enough thought. Eating with your hands indicates that you feel very angry and disillusioned with your partner. Eating in secret indicates both a nostalgia for the past, and also ill-humour.

ECHO

Dreaming about an echo indicates that you will receive a favourable response to a proposal, either from a would-be lover who is proving elusive or, less romantically, from a business acquaintance.

ECLIPSE

A solar eclipse indicates a shadow being cast over almost every aspect of your life. This will threaten the happiness of your relationship with your partner, your safety if you happen to be travelling anywhere, and also your future career. An eclipse of the moon, on the other hand, is a harbinger of good fortune, particularly if you are engaged to be married.

EDGE

The appearance of the edge or brim of a container, such as a bowl, in a dream symbolizes the postponement of a journey which would have had an important effect on your career. The edge of a cliff or precipice symbolizes new emotional encounters. If you dream about filling a container right up to the brim, it signifies that you are an optimist who faces up to obstacles calmly and thoughtfully.

EEL

Dreaming about an eel indicates either finding work, or changing jobs, at some time in the very near future, but the job may be difficult and your new boss may be hard to get on with. A dead eel symbolizes getting the upper hand over someone who is trying to create problems for you.

EGG

Easter eggs in a dream symbolize an important statement or report being made at work. Fresh eggs mean opportunities are being presented to you on a plate, but rotten eggs indicate that things will be going against you. If you buy eggs in your dream, you will be able to make good use of the extra financial resources which are coming your way.

EGG   Fresh eggs are a good sign: your projects could hatch soon.

ELBOW

Dreaming about breaking an elbow indicates that you adapt easily to new surroundings and circumstances. A swollen elbow in a dream means that you will have an unpleasant experience, but a grazed elbow reflects your lasting affection for someone.

ELEPHANT

A dream about an elephant is a favourable indication, suggesting strength, health, and also a possible association in the future with somebody important.

ELF

An elf, goblin or similar creature usually has bad implications in a dream, indicating that your relationship with a loved one is in danger. It also signifies vendettas and rivalries at work.

ELM

This tree is not an optimistic sign in a dream. An elm which is in leaf symbolizes loss of money, while if the tree has shed its leaves it suggests that you could run into personal enmities which may cause a bad situation for you. An uprooted elm signifies family arguments and a harmful influence in your rela-

"Although I am a man, I dreamed I was pregnant..."

The meaning of dreams about death, which we have already looked at, is not greatly different to that of dreams about birth. Very often, in males as well as females, being pregnant in a dream means the same as dying: it shows that a period of change and transformation is about to begin.

The fact that it can happen just as easily to male dreamers as it can to females shows how we often need to go beyond a literal interpretation and start looking at the content of a dream in broader symbolic terms. Analysis has shown that this type of dream symbolizes a need for greater maturity and for change. The new life signified by the pregnancy in this dream is in many ways similar to life after death, something which transcends human existence. It is our true essence, a rediscovery of ourselves.

Dreaming about pregnancy thus shows a process of transformation in the dreamer: like any other dream of this type it affects all the most important facets of our psychological development and every phase of our lives.

Do our dreams always remind us of this process of constant change? There are a number of factors: first, the dream needs to be correctly interpreted, so that the message being sent to us by our unconscious is understood on a rational level and also lived out in a profound, involving way, so that the message is not wasted, but becomes part of the self.

It is not at all unusual for a man to dream he is pregnant: it shows a need for constant change and development.

tionship with your partner which will lead to poor communication and jealousy. A very tall elm tree means you are being over-enthusiastic about someone or something.

EMBALMING

Despite its unpleasant implications, dreaming about embalming is often a pleasant sign. An animal being embalmed in a dream is a sign that your health will improve and a bird being embalmed means that you can look forward to unexpected windfalls. A person being embalmed means you will show great courage in adversity.

EMBARRASSMENT

Being embarrassed in a dream indicates that you must put forward concrete proposals where these are required at work, while embarrassing someone else means that negotiations which you are undertaking are now coming to an advantageous conclusion. Being embarrassed by the generosity of others in your dream means you are an intelligent, practically-minded person.

EMBRACE

The exact meaning of this dream depends more on the person being embraced than the action itself,

though to dream of an embrace shows that you are being open and receptive. Embracing a friend indicates that pleasant news is on the way, but embracing an enemy is a sign of betrayal. Embracing members of your family means that you will shortly be given a secret which you must not disclose.

EMPLOYER

The appearance of an employer with whom you have good relations in a dream means that you will be shortly embarrassed by an unexpected piece of news. If you see your own employer in a dream, it means you

are too emotional and impressionable. If you are summoned to your employer's office, there is an excellent prospect of success in a new project you have embarked on. An angry employer in a dream shows that you have misplaced confidence in someone.

ENCLOSING

Enclosing a piece of land in a dream signifies that you have an irrational fear of being led into a trap, as well as many temptations to overcome. Enclosing livestock or animals in a field means losing something you were particularly attached to. Building a wall round something means that you will soon have to face unpleasant news. Enclosing something in a letter in a dream suggests that the real reasons for a generous action of yours may be more selfish than they appear.

ENCYCLOPEDIA

Buying an encyclopedia in a dream indicates sound business sense, and looking something up in one means you are highly motivated, particularly in the intellectual field.

ENEMY

As in real life, the appearance of enemies in dreams can lead to unhappy consequences for you, but to dream of an enemy is not necessarily always a bad sign. If your

EVENING   Dreaming about evening has implications for your love life.

enemies are afraid of you in the dream, it means that you will soon have a decisive encounter with someone very important. But to argue or to fight with these enemies means that you will make mistakes through ill-considered actions; while getting the upper hand over them means that you will have an unexpected and unfortunate experience, and humiliating them indicates that you will buy something which will turn out to be a mistake. Putting your enemies to flight shows that you are in a difficult predicament which has still to be resolved; pardoning them suggests that you tend to be contradictory.

ENVELOPE

Dreaming about an empty envelope signifies that your present depression is unlikely to last for much longer. An envelope full of money in a dream means you are hard-working and tenacious. A sealed envelope means you are very busy.

ENVY

Envying someone in a dream actually means that you respect, or even love, that person. Likewise, if in the dream, someone else envies you it means that others appreciate and respect you in real life.

ESCAPE

This is an ominous subject for a dream: watching an escape – perhaps from prison – means that you show a lack of scruples which will eventually involve you in losing money, and taking part in an escape suggests that your ambitions will not succeed. Running away from something you are afraid of in a dream means you will make a hasty decision which fortunately will prove to have been the right one eventually.

EVENING

A moonlit evening in a dream symbolizes complications in love. A dark evening suggests your oversensitive and childish behaviour will damage your relationship: if you do not change your ways you will lose the affection of the person you love. Passing a pleasant evening with one or more other people in a dream indicates that you can look forward to happier times.

EXAMINATION

Revising for an examination in a dream suggests that you are a well-balanced, conscientious person. Undergoing a written exam indicates difficulties in your everyday life, while taking an oral one shows that you are proud of yourself and ambitious. Passing an examination in a dream shows that you have self-control and discipline; failing an exam, or not being able to do any of the questions, indicates that you need to think more carefully before you rush into things.

EXCREMENT

Curiously enough, the appearance of excrement in a dream is, according to popular tradition, a harbinger of good fortune. The presence of human or animal excrement in a dream is likely to bring you success in almost everything you do, particularly where financial matters are concerned.

EXCURSION

The meaning of this dream depends on the type of excursion and the modes of transport used. A trip into the countryside in a dream signifies that you will make a certain gain or profit, while a seaside excursion means that you will come into an unexpected income. An excursion into the mountains indicates that you will be travelling in the near future. A railway excursion suggests that your desires are being realized. An excursion on a boat means that you will soon have an unexpected visit, while travelling by bicycle suggests that you are spending too much.

EXECUTION

An execution in a dream has a dual meaning. Watching an execution signifies that something in which you are involved will have a surprising outcome, whether for good or ill. If the executed person is guilty, you may find enemies in unexpected places, but if the person is innocent, your health may be in danger.

EXERCISE BOOK

The appearance of a lined exercise book or notebook in a dream shows that you are worrying about an old person, while one with squared paper shows that you are being obstinate and tenacious. Dreaming of a new one with no writing in it indicates that you are a firm, decisive person, but dreaming of a used one shows that you might be being anti-social at the moment. If you dream that you buy an exercise book, your present loyalty and courage will be soon amply rewarded. If you write in one, you will be unfairly criticized by someone; if you tear one up, you will have heated arguments with the person you love.

EXPERIMENT

Dreaming about doing a scientific experiment in a laboratory means there are hidden dangers to be

EXPLOSION   An exploding building means that the dreamer is possibly ill.

avoided. If the experiment is successful, it indicates that you have physical resilience, but if it goes wrong, perhaps causing an explosion, your successes will be short-lived.

EXPLORER

Dreaming about an explorer on his travels suggests that you fear what the future might hold. An explorer who is lost or injured in a dream means you are worried about something. If it is you that is doing the exploring, your dream shows that you are an imaginative person with a great spirit of adventure.

EXPLOSION

This can have different meanings according to the type of explosion. A bomb or mine exploding signifies well-deserved recognition for your achievements, while an exploding building shows that you are in dubious health. An explosion of emotion, such as rage or happiness, indicates you have great powers of concentration but are also a contented and relaxed person.

EXTRACTION

The extraction of a tooth, or a painful object like a splinter, in a dream indicates that you are undergoing some kind of physical suffering at present.

EYELIDS

This dream indicates that you are at a very difficult stage in your life: you are in danger of losing your partner's love and respect because of repetitious and pointless arguments. But if you can bury the hatchet and sort things out rationally you should be able to save the situation. Fluttering your eyelids at someone in a dream means you have breadth of vision and great generosity, while drooping eyelids indicate naiveté and childishness.

EXPLORER   An explorer – like Marco Polo – reveals a fear of the future.

FALCON

The meaning of a falcon in a dream can change depending on the circumstances. If it is flying without hindrance in the sky, this indicates that you have great ambitions which will eventually be fulfilled, but if it is plummeting downwards to catch its prey, there are dangers in store for you. If the falcon is tethered or being used for hunting, it means that someone close to you may have a few surprises up their sleeve.

FALLING

This is one of the most frequent experiences in dreams. It indicates some kind of loss, especially in love or money matters. If you dream of falling out of bed, this indicates that you are highly sensitive to your environment and the behaviour of others, while falling into something unpleasant such as a dung-heap indicates new prospects at work.

FAMILY   Dreaming about a family gathering heralds important news.

FALSIFYING

Falsifying or forging documents, money or someone's signature in a dream is a sign of major difficulties ahead.

FAME

Dreaming that you are famous simply means that you have a great desire to be famous in real life and to use your abilities to achieve public recognition.

FAMILY

Dreaming about your own family suggests that there is important news on the horizon, while dreaming about any large family means that you are in a comfortable financial state but that you will have to make major sacrifices of some kind in the future. Dreaming about abandoning a family indicates problems with your finances.

FAMINE

A famine in a dream actually indicates prosperity, well-being, strong friendship and lasting love.

FACE

Dreaming about seeing your own face in a mirror means that a secret project in which you are involved is about to come out into the open. If you see a happy, smiling face, it indicates happiness in your daily life, and conversely, if the face is sad, you will be sad yourself. The face of someone you know in a dream indicates an invitation to a celebration, perhaps a wedding or a christening, while one you do not recognize means there are upheavals or travels in prospect. A man's face in a dream shows that you have confidence in the future, but a woman's face signifies that you are beset by doubts and worries about the future.

FACTORY

Seeing a factory in a dream indicates that you are in good health and are satisfied with your job. Working in a factory in a dream means that success and well-being are on the way.

FAIRY

A fairy is invariably a bearer of good tidings if it appears in a dream, indicating riches and good fortune.

FAN

Buying a fan in a dream – whether of the old-fashioned variety which you hold, or of an electric kind – indicates that you are wasting time daydreaming, while selling a fan reveals that you have had a sudden injection of new energy for a task in hand. Using a fan suggests unpleasant relations with someone at work, while breaking a fan indicates that you are engaged in important family discussions.

FARM

Seeing a prosperous, well-tended farm in a dream signifies good financial prospects: you will soon make a profit as a result of an astute business decision. If you own a farm yourself in the dream, you will be helped in your work by people who have more expertise than you, while if you are working on a farm, you will enjoy an advantage or benefit

FAN   Using a fan suggests tricky relations with a work colleague.

that your colleagues do not have. Selling a farm indicates that you are likely to have unpleasant disagreements with a new acquaintance. A farmhouse on fire in a dream reveals that you have enthusiasm and energy.

FASTING

If you voluntarily go without food for a long time in your dream – perhaps as an act of penitence – it means you combine a vivid imagination with a decisive personality; however, if someone else forces you to fast, it reflects uncertainty in your

FARM   If a prosperous farm appears, money matters look promising.

life. If you stop eating because of illness in the dream, this shows that you have a low level of physical or mental stamina, while if you dream of being too poor to buy food, this signifies that in real life you will experience change for the better.

FATHER

Seeing your own father in a dream indicates that you should follow advice given to you by an older person; while embracing your father means that you ought to take up sensible suggestions which are being put to you by others. If your father appears healthy in the dream, you will shortly benefit from someone's support, but if he is ill, your faith in yourself is waning. If your father dies in the dream, it means you will come to occupy a responsible and respected position in which you will feel happy. To dream of a benevolent father shows that you are subject to passing enthusiasms, while to dream of a bad one shows that you are in good physical health.

FATNESS

Dreaming about being fat indicates poor health, physical weakness, and anxiety. If you are in love it can also mean that there will be deceitfulness and a possible breakdown in relations with your partner.

FAWN

This example shows that you cannot trust appearances in a dream: despite its pleasant connotations, the appearance of a fawn in a dream is a sign of imminent danger, and if you are in love, it indicates that your partner might be being unfaithful.

FEATHERS

The appearance of white feathers in a dream is a sign of happy, long-lasting friendships, but black ones suggest there may be a loss of money on the way. Generally, however, dreaming of any kind of feathers indicates that you will be

fulfilled in love. Buying feathers means possible irritations and friction with people at work, while burning them signifies an upturn in financial matters. If you dream about sleeping on a feather mattress or pillow, you will achieve an important goal you have set yourself.

FESTIVAL

Taking part in a festival, such as a street carnival, in a dream suggests that you are going through a stage of dissatisfaction and impatience. Any religious festival such as Christmas or Easter indicates that you have a spiritual side to your nature which is not being allowed to express itself.

FEVER

A dream involving a fever in fact indicates the end of a period of ill health and the beginning of renewed energy and vitality. If you are ill when you dream about a fever, you will get well very soon.

FIGHT

Taking part in a fight in your dreams suggests you have many enemies, but if you emerge victorious it reflects the fact that they are powerless to do anything against you. Getting stabbed in a fight symbolizes failure. Being in a fight is an unfavourable dream for anyone in business, travelling, or in love.

FESTIVAL   Dreams of Christmas or Easter suggest suppressed spirituality.

Dreams of water

In many of the popular creation myths of antiquity, water is the most important element, for it is the origin of all life. Many myths have been handed down to us in which water is depicted as a fertilizing, life-giving substance: some peoples believed that two babies were plucked from the waters of a lake to begin the human race, and Venus, the goddess of love, began her life in the waves of the sea. Many of the heroes of ancient myth took night-time journeys across the sea to discover their true selves. In the Bible, Moses was found floating on the water as a child, and christening with water is used to purify and cleanse people.

Freud believed there were strong links between dreams about pregnancy and about water: as well as reflecting a desire to have children, they can also show that the dreamer wants to return to the warmth and protection of his or her mother's womb.

In dreams, water can mean renewal taking place as we mature and grow. For this reason, it occurs frequently in the dreams of teenage children, who themselves are undergoing a physical and spiritual rebirth, with many major changes in their personalities.

Water symbolizing change is also frequently found in the dreams of old people, where it reflects a realization that they are changing as they grow older. In these two instances we can see how dreams about water can encompass the two opposing concepts of birth and death. Water is a symbol of living energy: water is life.

Water flowing either gently or noisily in a dream often signifies change in our lives.

FILM

To dream of camera film shows that you have made a malicious remark to someone who respects you a great deal. If you dream of watching a film in a cinema, this means that new opportunities are on the way: you should try and give your utmost to these new projects because they could be important to your future career. A broken or torn film symbolizes a secure, unassailable position at work and reveals that you have plenty of scope to improve your prospects there.

FILTER

To dream of filtering something generally indicates that you are patient but given to temporary enthusiasms, though the precise connotations of the dream depend on what is being filtered. A coffee filter in a dream indicates that favourable opportunities are on the way, and a photographic filter suggests you are viewing life through rose-tinted glasses and only seeing what you want to see.

FINANCIER

Dreaming about a financier or banker indicates an important meeting or appointment. If the financier lends you money, it indicates you are very serious in your ambitions.

FINDING

Finding things is a common theme in dreams. Finding money, a purse or a wallet indicates new and exciting relationships with the opposite sex, while finding a document or piece of paper means you are being decisive and confident in your actions. If you dream of discovering someone else's secret – for example, that they are guilty of a crime – this indicates that you yourself wish to hide secrets from others.

FINGER

A finger is a good omen in dreams: it indicates good health and happy relations with your partner. If the finger has rings, you can look forward to future gains and profits.

FINISHING

Finishing a piece of work in a dream suggests that you are going through a period of stagnation. If you dream of finishing a painting, then you have just been through some unpleasant wrangles with the person you love. Try to be patient and understanding, or you will end up breaking off a relationship that has a lot going for it!

FINISHING POST

If you dream of running a long and exhausting race and finally see the finishing post in the distance, this means you have been overly timid and indecisive at work recently: you need to have more faith in yourself and to assert your rights both at work and in other situations. If you stand up for yourself you won't have cause to regret it.

FIR TREE

Finding yourself in a grove of firs in a dream is a favourable omen, indicating that you will be successful in business. If the firs are growing close together, this means that you are facing difficult problems, but not insuperable ones and these can be overcome.

FIRE

A fire in a grate in a dream symbolizes energy and health. A

FIRE   If you are in love, this scene suggests your desires will be fulfilled.

FIR TREE   *Standing among fir trees means a prosperous business venture.*
FISHING   *Going fishing in a dream augurs well for the immediate future.*

large, warm fireplace in a room indicates good fortune, wealth and – for those in love – the realization of their desires. Putting a fire out, on the other hand, means there are problems for you in prospect – as does being burned by a fire. An artificial fire or an empty fireplace warns you of deceptive appearances in real life. A big spreading fire, such as a house or bush fire, tells you that events, and perhaps your own feelings, are getting out of control.

FIREMAN

The fireman in a dream is a symbol of good news; you can expect news from a distant place which will help you to fulfil a plan which you have been nurturing for a long time. Calling up the fire brigade in a dream indicates that you have received useful information at work, while watching firemen in action means that you will win a personal battle after a great deal of hard effort. Seeing a fireman riding a fire engine is a sign of overambitious ideas, while seeing one on a ladder shows that you have great confidence in yourself.

FISHING

To dream of a fisherman on a boat indicates that new horizons are opening up for you while one on a river indicates that your ideas can now be put into action. A sea fisherman is a symbol of new business or romantic relationships. A sub-aqua fisherman indicates the arrival of interesting news, and a pearl fisherman reflects disappointment and worry caused by the failure of a work project. If you dream about going fishing with a rod, you will soon be made an attractive suggestion which you will greet with a great deal of enthusiasm, while if you go fishing with a net, current business matters will have successful results and considerable financial benefits. A fishing line in a dream is a warning of a possible risk, perhaps from a potential enemy, or to your health.

FLOODING   The extent reflects the gravity of your financial problems.

FISHMONGER

Dreaming of a fishmonger in a shop or market is always a good omen: you have just embarked on a new initiative at work and you can count on the trust and support of everyone else involved. A fishmonger weighing his wares in a dream means you are short on initiative and others may find you boring; a fishmonger unloading fish means that good fortune will go with you for a long time to come. Being a fishmonger yourself indicates that you have made mistakes which can be put right, but only by making major sacrifices.

FLAME

Lighting a flame in a dream indicates an adventurous frame of mind, but putting one out indicates competition and rivalry. A candle flame in a dream reveals indecisiveness with regard to a proposal, while a gas jet means a craving for freedom.

FLAUNTING

In dreams, as in real life, ostentatious behaviour often leads to unpleasant consequences. If you dream of flaunting your wealth, this means you are attracting ill-will from someone close to you, while dreaming of flaunting your beauty indicates that you are prone to petty-mindedness. Flaunting your talents in a dream means you will waste a large sum of money. Boasting about your courage means that you will face dilemmas and difficult decisions caused by disagreements with someone you love. Boasting about your friendships, or name-dropping, shows that your hopes are temporarily being dashed.

FLEAS

These tiny insects are capable of causing a disproportionate amount of irritation in real life, and in dreams they suggest minor annoyances and problems or petty ill-will. Squashing fleas in a dream portends a success.

FLESH

The appearance of the flesh of a chicken in a dream indicates a lost opportunity, while that of a turkey shows inconstancy and unfaithfulness in emotional relationships: you need to try and change this unpleasant side of yourself or you will find yourself abandoned by those who really matter. Dreaming of the flesh of a fruit, such as a mango, means you will come up against delays and annoying obstacles which will impede the success of a project you have been particularly involved in.

FLIGHT OF BIRDS

A flight of swallows in a dream is an omen of unexpected, and not necessarily pleasant news; a flight of gulls indicates recent bold, daring behaviour. A flight of ducks symbolizes an unbelievable stroke of good fortune, and any other large group of birds is likely to bring pleasant news of some kind.

FLIGHT OF STAIRS

A flight of stairs in a dream is an indication of your well-founded aspirations for some scheme; if it is particularly steep, it reflects difficulties which will be easily overcome in your work environment. If you climb a flight of stairs in your dream, you will achieve a major success at work, but if you go down one, it is because you need to sort out a few problems if you want to continue an important emotional relationship with someone. Falling down a flight of stairs means the premature failure of a financial undertaking.

FLOATING

A large area of water in a dream usually signifies danger of some kind. However, a much more favourable sign is if someone or something is floating on the water, because it indicates that you will overcome future obstacles. Similarly, floating can also herald success and major financial or other gains.

FLOODING

A flood is an ill omen in a dream. If all the land as far as the eye can see is flooded, this suggests that you are facing major financial worries, while if only a field is flooded, then your money problems are much less troublesome. A house or other building which is flooded symbolizes temporary ill-health or unhappiness or small setbacks in love.

FLOOR

A wooden floor in a dream is a sign of warmth or sympathy being reciprocated; a marble one, difficult times with a loved one. A tiled floor indicates that you are a delicately constituted and easily influenced person. A clean floor means you are anxiously awaiting the arrival of an old acquaintance, and a dirty one means you will soon recover a sum of money. Washing or sweeping a floor shows an untroubled, cheerful frame of mind.

FLOUR

Flour is invariably a good luck sign in a dream, indicating abundance, comfort, health and strength. Making flour into pastry in a dream foretells happy family news.

FLOWER

Different flowers have different connotations in dreams, though generally they foretell a period of happiness or good fortune which then – like flowers – withers and dies. Dried or dead flowers indicate obstacles and illnesses, but brightly-coloured, fresh flowers hold out better hopes for the future. A bouquet in a dream indicates an impending marriage. Arranging flowers reflects improvements in your life, and picking them and placing them in a vase the further additional good fortune of financial or other gains.

FLUTE

Listening to most musical instruments like the flute is a better sign in dreams than playing them yourself. The sound of the flute in a dream bodes well for the future and indicates that the birth of a child is in the offing.

FLY

This is one of those exceptional insects which do not foretell good fortune in a dream. The fly is a symbol of envy, jealousy and resentment from people who occupy a less favourable social position than one's own. Trying to swat a fly shows that you are likely to experience a major worry about something.

FLYING

Flying is one of the most common things that happen in dreams and it can have various meanings. Flying across the sea means you are far too conceited and confident for your own good, while flying over an abyss means insufferable, annoying behaviour on your part. Flying at a very low level indicates setbacks in love.

FOETUS

Dreaming about seeing a foetus alive inside its mother's womb indicates that new enterprises or activities will be highly successful. A dead foetus, on the other hand, reflects lost illusions.

FOG

Just as in real life a fog casts a thick, silent mantle over everything and stops us seeing the things around us properly, so, in a dream,

FLOWER A vase of flowers means you will soon be better off financially.

a fog shows that you have an introverted, mysterious personality which could cause problems in relations with those around you. If you dream of the kind of fog which is so thick that you can hardly see your hand in front of your face, there may be unseen dangers lying in wait, but if the fog lifts in your dream, you are being over-careful.

Getting lost in a fog in a dream suggests that the suspicions you have about somebody are unfounded.

FOLDING

Folding clothes in a dream indicates a period where things keep going wrong, particularly in emotional matters where your lack of commitment will lose you the trust of the

FOREST   Becoming lost in a forest may be alarming, but it predicts success.

person you love. Folding a newspaper or something else made of paper in a dream means that you will achieve all your desires.

FOOD

Dreaming about food can have different implications depending on precisely what the food is. If there are large quantities involved, or you eat too much, this shows that you hold ambiguous or unclear intentions in regard to a person or project, while if there is not enough to eat, a period of tranquillity and prosperity is on the way.

FOOTBATH

Washing your feet in a dream indicates that you are repentant for a misdeed in the past, but there is no need for you to feel guilty because you will be able to explain the reasons for your action to others and they will understand why you acted as you did. Washing your feet in the sea suggests that others may be somewhat mystified by an action of yours whose precise meaning is not clear to them and which could harm your interests at work. A hot footbath is a sign of your enthusiasm for new projects, and a cold one reflects a peaceful and uneventful period in your life.

FOOTPRINT

A man's footprint in a dream indicates a stern, unbending personality, while a woman's signifies that you have achieved a difficult but very important victory. An animal's footprint suggests unfulfilled ambition. If you see a footprint in the snow in your dream, you are about to enter a period of inner conflict and indecision. Dreaming of a footprint in the earth indicates a complicated and burdensome life fraught with difficulty. Following someone else's footprints suggests that you have limited ambitions, and tracing them out on a piece of paper indicates that you have mental blocks which are making it difficult for you to maintain a sense of balance in your life.

FORBIDDING

Dreaming of forbidding a meeting to take place indicates that you need to be more flexible and adaptable, while to dream of banning a procession suggests that you have confused ideas. Forbidding or sabotaging a hunt meeting in a dream will bring you good luck and an upturn in your business affairs. If you forbid a relation to get married in a dream, you are entering an uncertain and prickly period from the emotional point of view.

FOREST

Dreaming about going through a forest indicates a risky enterprise, but getting lost in one actually means that a project is guaranteed to be the success that you were hoping for.

FORTRESS

Attacking or laying siege to a fortress in a dream signifies high morale and optimism; seeing a fortress full of soldiers means you currently are running a great risk by doing something which is difficult and dangerous. An abandoned fortress symbolizes a state of deep fatigue.

FOUNTAIN

Clean water always indicates good fortune in a dream, and this is also true of a clean fountain. A fountain

which is dirty or has dried up indicates bitterness and troubles, and one that is working suggests abundance and good health. Dreams which involve drinking from a fountain are a symbol of love being reciprocated.

FOUNTAIN   Only one with clean, sparkling water reflects good fortune.

FOX

The fox is a wily, sly and fast-moving creature, and in dreams signifies someone you dislike, possibly a passing acquaintance, or a rival in love. So if you dream about a fox, you need to take a close look at the potentially harmful activities of those around you.

FREEING YOURSELF

The meaning of this dream depends on what you free yourself from. Freeing yourself from people who are annoying you indicates a need for independence, while freeing yourself from a promise or obligation heralds a difficult time in which careful reflection is required. Freeing yourself from chains or

Difficulties in interpreting dreams

As we all know, some dreams are very common, and some very unusual. Dreams about falling or running away might be included in the first category; an example of the second, recorded by researchers, is a dream about the plant saxifrage. The dreamer described it as follows: "I saw a rock-dwelling plant. It was winding itself round a tombstone and gradually breaking away the stone with the strength of its roots."

This dream would seem to symbolize the person's desire, possibly already realized, to break away from the past, from their heritage and their social background and a reluctance to tolerate any obstacle to this goal.

Of course, not every dream about a saxifrage plant would necessarily have such a profound meaning; similarly, a dream does not have to feature saxifrage for that meaning to apply. It might simply serve as a warning: we are feeling stifled by certain responsibilities or limitations and need to act calmly and decisively to get them into perspective and, eventually, to get rid of them altogether. In broader terms, such a dream could simply show that by nature you have an ability to overcome opposition and obstacles, through patience, perseverance and the courage of your convictions.

escaping from prison shows that you have great energy, and ridding yourself of parasites indicates short-lived problems.

FREEZING

Ice is not an auspicious sign in a dream, and being frozen indicates unhappiness and lack of success. Frozen hands mean an acquisition of doubtful benefit, and frozen feet indicate that something is slipping out of your control. Dreaming of frozen food or of taking it out of the freezer indicates lack of communication with those around you.

FRIEND

Dreaming about a friend is usually a good sign. Dreaming about a distant friend indicates that good news is on the way, and a friend showing you

affection in a dream, perhaps by embracing you, means either a success at work or happy family events. A friend who dies in a dream is in fact a sign that a marriage is in the offing.

FROG

Seeing or hearing frogs in a dream means that fate is smiling on you. They indicate new close friendships, a good harvest for the farmer, and that an unmarried woman will meet a good husband.

FRONTIER

Being on the border between two countries in a dream means that you are very good at adapting to diffe-

FRUIT   A bowl of fruit points to health, wealth and happiness.

rent situations, but crossing over it means you have a sentimental side which is not doing you any good.

FRUIT

The meaning of this dream depends on the type of fruit involved, but in most cases it is a favourable sign. Dreaming about a bowl of fruit shows that you are, or soon will be, enjoying excellent health and prosperity, and a happy domestic life. Bitter or rotten fruit is a sign of discord or sadness.

FRYING

The meaning of this dream varies with the type of food being fried. Frying fish suggests that you are gambling with the future, and frying eggs indicates a reserved, introverted personality. Frying meat signifies enthusiasm; potatoes, malicious gossip; and vegetables, difficulties of all kinds.

FRYING PAN

The appearance of an iron frying pan in a dream foretells of a pointless waste of energy and strength, while a steel one means a decision needs to be made. If the pan has butter in it, your health is particularly good; while if there is oil in it you are being negligent and putting yourself or others at risk. Buying a frying-pan in a dream means you should be more careful at work, and washing one means you are about to rebel in the face of an impossible situation.

FUNERAL

Like death, a funeral in a dream indicates the very opposite of what it seems to. It actually signifies health, and a marriage in the offing (not necessarily yours). Although the colour black often has negative connotations in dreams, it does not signify anything ominous or unpleasant when seen in this context.

FUNNEL

Using a funnel in a dream indicates an ability to extricate yourself from the most complicated of situations. A glass funnel suggests that you

have the gift of the gab which may get you into trouble, and a plastic one indicates minor problems of a temporary nature.

FUR

Buying a fur of any kind in a dream tells you that you are about to get bogged down in major problems caused by people who are envious of your success. Putting on a fur coat or similar item in a dream means that you will get involved in a very important relationship at work, and giving someone a fur as a present shows that you are wasting time on risky activities. A white fur symbolizes lost friends, a black one ideas which are not feasible, and a brown one emotional conflict. A fur in a shop window means that your plans are well thought out and should succeed.

FURNITURE

Dreams in which furniture plays a prominent part foretell a period of happiness. If you dream about buying new furniture you will shortly receive encouraging news which will remove any doubts you may be having with regard to the feasibility of a plan at work. Old furniture in dreams symbolizes constancy in love.

GAME

Playing in a game of any kind in a dream indicates heated, possibly violent arguments with your partner. Winning a game means that hopes connected with your profession are not being realized, and losing one, getting the upper hand over your enemies. Selling games in a shop in a dream suggests you are deluding yourself that someone loves you when they do not: don't run away with your illusions or you will make yourself very unhappy. A game which you win by a wide margin indicates differences with older people, and a friendly game indicates unstable relationships with the opposite sex.

GARAGE

Dreaming of a garage with many new cars suggests that an older

GARDENER   Loved ones may pose problems if you dream of being a gardener.

person will help you over an obstacle which you thought was insurmountable, while if the garage contains old cars that need repairing, you will gain a great deal by co-operating with someone else.

GARDEN

A well-kept garden full of flowers in a dream signifies a good harvest for the farmer, advantageous deals for the businessman, happiness for lovers, and good news for people in general. But an abandoned, overgrown garden indicates a period of confusion and difficulty.

GARDENER

Seeing a gardener at work in a dream signifies business success, while talking about a gardener means an unexpected gift is on its way. Dreaming about being a gardener yourself suggests that you are having problems with someone you love.

GARLAND

A garland of flowers in a dream promises either good news or short-lived pleasures. Having a garland on your head is a symbol of success attained in the teeth of slanderous remarks and petty jealousies.

GARLIC

Dreaming about eating garlic is a hopeful sign that you shall find something valuable which you have lost.

GARLIC   Dreaming of garlic means you may find a lost item.

GARMENT

A man's garment in a dream indicates that your support and help are needed by an old acquaintance, while a woman's shows that you are behaving in an irrational and irritable way. Mourning clothes in a dream indicate a serious loss; new clothes symbolize financial worries, and old ones, your seriousness of intent for some project or ambition.

GARTER

The significance of a garter in dreams relates to your love life. If a man dreams about a garter it shows there is a particular woman he desires, and if a woman gives her garter to a man, it is a token of eternal faithfulness.

GATE

An open gate in a dream indicates that major changes are forthcoming in your life, while a closed one signifies that various difficulties must be dealt with. Dreaming about a wooden or iron gate indicates the opportunity of a sparkling social life and involvement in projects you particularly enjoy. A gate made of bronze, gold or similar metal suggests that you must be more careful in your actions.

GATHERING

A reunion of former classmates in a dream is a sign of pleasant encounters, while a car rally indicates a slow and difficult ascent of the career ladder. Any other gathering of people in dreams means there are trials and tribulations to be overcome. If you attend a gathering at a friend's house in the dream, there is a period of happiness on the way, while a gathering of children –

GATE Anticipate a lively social life if you dream about an iron gate.

perhaps a party – shows interesting news in prospect. Gathering objects together means you will be used and then abandoned by the person you love.

GEM

Contrary to appearances, a gem is not a pleasant thing to dream about. Any dream involving finding a gemstone, stealing one, or being given one, indicates coming unhappiness and depression. Losing one, on the other hand, means unexpected gains. A fake gem in a dream indicates malicious gossip is circulating about you.

GHOST

To see a ghost walking around in a dream indicates coming setbacks and financial worries, while a talking ghost signifies that you have dangerous illusions. If the ghost is wearing white, you will enjoy good health, but if it is dressed in black, there will be bitterness and recriminations caused by your partner's unpredictable behaviour. If you don't run away from the ghost and it then goes away, you can expect good fortune in love and in business matters.

GIANT

A giant appearing in a dream is a sign of danger, but if you kill the giant or get the better of him in any way, you will be able to overcome the difficulties that presently lie in your path.

GIFT

Receiving a gift in a dream is not a good omen, suggesting that in real life you should take a long, hard look at the giver of the gift in the dream to see if you can trust them. Giving someone else a gift on the other hand, is a sign of your great pleasure at an unexpected personal success. The act of buying a present in a dream symbolizes your discouragement and depression at an emotional upset which you had not expected. Giving a useful present means you will be involved in a major setback, while if your present

GIRL   Dreaming of a pretty girl is a positive sign on the emotional front.

is a decorative one you will have to take a very important decision shortly. If you give an expensive present, you will soon find yourself in a situation which is favourable to your plans and ambitions. Giving or receiving a gift of money in a dream signifies ingratitude from people around you, and a gift of flowers shows that you have a sensitive mind.

GIRL

The appearance of a beautiful girl in a dream signifies romantic fulfil-ment, while an ugly one means you are spoilt for choice in some area of your life. A laughing girl in a dream symbolizes unexpected expense, and a crying one, major financial problems. If the girl is asleep, you will meet with an obstacle in your work which you had not anticipated; if she is studying, you have bright prospects for the future. If the girl is ill, there will be new conquests on the romantic front, and if she is dead, you will be let down by someone who is dependent on you.

GLADE

A glade or clearing in the trees in a dream foreshadows a pleasant sur-prise. If there are flowers in the glade, there will be an unexpected and not particularly pleasant jour-ney to be made, while if it contains animals, good fortune and a strong will are indicated. If you dream

about eating a picnic in a glade, there is a large amount of money coming your way, and if you go to sleep in one, you should keep a tight rein on your actions if you do not wish to damage a relationship irretrievably.

GLASS

Dreaming about glass in general, and things made of glass, means that you may have to lower your sights with regard to a risky project you are involved in. Coloured glass in a dream suggests friendships that may not be trustworthy. Cutting yourself on glass indicates a forth-coming break in an emotional rela-tionship. An empty drinking glass signifies vanity, but if it is full of wine or anything else, you have a vivid imagination which you may well be able to put to good use.

GLOVE

The meaning of this dream depends on the type of glove and also on what it is made of. Ski gloves are a sign of problems solved, and boxing gloves indicate contacts to be made. White gloves symbolize important people you may have met recently, while black ones are a sign of failure. Leather gloves indicate melancholy

GLASS   A full glass of wine – or any drink – suggests a lively imagination.

and dissatisfaction; wool gloves, matters being brought to a success-ful conclusion; and rubber gloves show that you have important choices or decisions to make.

GOAT

Dreaming about a goat indicates adversity being overcome through your powers of patience (but not if the goat is a black one). A goat perched on a high rock or mountain signifies wealth.

GOD

This is always a comforting, reas-suring subject for a dream: seeing God indicates happiness; speaking to him, well-being; and praising him, a strong sense of moral respon-sibility. Praying to God in a dream is a sign that you have solved a problem.

GODPARENT

Dreaming about someone else being a godparent signifies happiness and the recognition by someone of a kind deed that you did in past. If you dream about being a godparent to a relative, you need to be astute and decisive if you are to take advantage of a favourable opportun-ity being offered to you. If you dream of being a godparent for a friend, you are going through a good period in your life.

71

GOING MAD

Going mad in a dream signifies that the very opposite is true in real life: it indicates that you are very intelligent, have a secure business and are in good health. Going mad through love in a dream means there are changes in the offing.

GOING OUT

Going out of a house in a dream symbolizes separation from someone you love; going out of a church means something you are involved in coming to an end, and going out of a hospital, slow but inexorable progress in your career. Leaving a theatre means you will suffer an emotional crisis in the near future but will emerge stronger for the experience.

GOOD LUCK

Paradoxically, good luck in a dream indicates bad luck in real life. Winning a competition, inheriting a large sum of money, or finding something valuable all indicate that a somewhat black period of your life is just beginning; the good news is that it won't last long.

GOOSE

Dreaming of a large, fat goose is a sign that new, definite proposals are being made to you, perhaps at work. A goose flapping its wings indicates good fortune. If a man dreams about a goose fighting with others, he should be careful, because the woman in his life will turn out to be argumentative and jealous.

GOSPEL

Reading the gospel in a dream bodes well for the future: it shows that since your reasons for loving someone are sound and your feelings for them are genuine, you will soon be able to persuade them to spend the rest of their life with you.

GRAIN

The appearance of a grain of sand in a dream indicates a shifting, unstable situation; a grain of salt shows boredom. A grain of pepper signifies physical strength and vigour, and a grain of wheat or other cereal means time being lost or wasted. Grain growing in a field or drying in the sun indicates financial well-being and strong, secure relationships. Sowing or harvesting grain both indicate that you are in robust health.

GRANARY

A full granary is a favourable thing to dream about, indicating either present or forthcoming wealth and abundance; but if it is empty, it shows you are worried or insecure about something at the moment.

GRANDPARENTS Dreams featuring your grandparents are promising. Those on your father's side suggest you have a good business sense; those on your mother's side reflect a gentle but persuasive nature.

GRANDPARENT

If you dream about talking to your grandparents, it suggests that advice being given to you is both sound and useful. Dreaming about your grandparents on your father's side indicates sound business acumen, while those on your mother's side indicate gentleness combined

GOOSE Dream-visions of fat geese indicate that new ideas are prominent at work.

with strong powers of persuasion. Dreaming that your grandparents have died is a sign that your business affairs – but not your health – are at risk.

GRAPEFRUIT

Picking grapefruit in a dream indicates that you are excited about a new financial project you are involved in; buying grapefruit shows recent practical successes; and peeling them foreshadows a difficult situation which it will be hard to extricate yourself from. You need to keep calm and use all your common sense to stop things getting out of hand.. If you dream about giving a grapefruit to someone, it means you are about to make great strides in your work, and if you are selling

GRAPEFRUIT   Peeled grapefruit suggest a difficult situation.

them it means there will be problems within your family.

GRAPES

Dreaming about sweet grapes indicates an unexpected meeting with someone, while sour grapes also mean sour grapes in real life. White grapes indicate that you are embarking on ambitious projects, and black ones signify a temporary setback. If you dream about picking grapes, a very happy period in your life is about to begin.

GRASS

Grass is a pleasant omen in a dream, for it indicates prosperity and good health. Cutting the grass bodes less well, however, for it indicates that you are in danger of being beset with financial problems in the near future, and grass which has gone yellow and dried up signifies that somebody's health could change for the worse.

GREEN

Dreaming about a green field suggests that a welcome invitation may be in prospect; green cloth signifies projects which you are enthusiastic about. Green clothes in a dream indicate your involvement in long and complicated negotiations or discussions, and a green plant signifies that you have gained well deserved recognition. Green, damp wood means you are being too extravagant and letting your imagination run away with you.

GRINDING

Dreaming of grinding or milling grain of any kind (apart from pepper!) indicates prosperity and happiness; it signifies also that you are the type of person who derives great pleasure from the simple things in life. Grinding pepper, on the other hand, symbolizes a worrying piece of news.

GROCER

Going into a grocer's shop in a dream means that your actions or initiatives have a good chance of success. Being a grocer yourself reflects annoyance and disagreements within the family, and buying groceries means a calm state of mind. If the grocer's is closed, it means you can expect a project you were involved in to come out right in the end.

GROUP

Dreaming about a group of people indicates that you will shortly be disillusioned about something; a group of animals of any kind means that there will be very pleasant family news arriving shortly.

GROUP   A group of people in a dream warns of impending disillusionment.

GROWING TALLER

Someone else growing taller in a dream indicates a fear of what the future may have in store, but you yourself growing shows that your self-confidence and self-respect are increasing daily. A house or other building growing taller means that financial improvements are on the way, and a plant or tree getting bigger also suggests a state of prosperity.

GUARD

A night-watchman in a dream signifies the possibility of a theft or other crime, while a military guard at the gates of a barracks or elsewhere means that you are being illogical in your behaviour at the moment. Being on guard yourself indicates an imminent loss of money.

GUESSING

Dreaming of getting the answer right in a guessing game indicates favourable opportunities and invitations; guessing the future in a dream indicates that you have come back to earth after a period of illusion; and guessing what someone else is thinking suggests misunderstandings with the person you love most.

GUILT

Dreaming about being guilty of some misdeed is not necessarily an ill omen; more often than not it reflects improving prospects. Dreaming about other people being found guilty of something wrong indicates – if it is a man doing the dreaming – unusual or unaccustomed situations, while if it is a woman, it shows that you are being unusually over-sensitive and intolerant.

GUITAR

In common with other musical instruments, a guitar can have two different meanings in a dream. If it is you that is playing the guitar, the dream is an unfavourable one, since it indicates unreliable, whimsical behaviour, but if you listen to someone else playing the guitar, it means you are in the process of overcoming difficulties successfully.

GULF

Dreaming of a gulf, either of water or empty space, symbolizes a sad parting from someone you love,

though the parting might be avoided if you gave them more care and attention.

GULL

Seeing a gull in flight in a dream indicates a danger being avoided or overcome, but if the gull is trying unsuccessfully to fly, or is injured, there is a minor illness on the way.

GUN

Carrying a gun in a dream signifies your present problems and troubles. A loaded gun in a dream is a symbol of misfortune, and an unloaded one of your recent cantankerous behaviour. A double-barrelled rifle foretells worries and conflicts to come, and a machine gun indicates that you feel weak and drained of strength. Using a gun to hunt with in a dream shows that you are putting off decisions.

GUST

A gust of wind in a dream stands for the imminent arrival of unpleasant news and also indicates your fear of facing up to the future. Seeing something being blown away by a gust of wind means you are being domineering and possessive in your relationship with your partner and should avoid getting things out of proportion unless you want to lose your love and respect.

GYM

Dreaming of an indoor gymnasium indicates a respected position in society and material prosperity, while dreaming of an open-air gymnasium indicates an unexpected trip abroad where you will meet people who will broaden your horizons and allow you to overcome some of your prejudices. Exercising in a gym means that your relationship with your partner will be a lasting and faithful one.

HABIT

Dreaming about a habit, either good or bad, means you are trying to get out of an uncomfortable situation; if you get rid of the habit in your dream, your affairs will return to their previous orderly state.

HAG

Seeing a hag or a witch in a dream brings ill luck and is a symptom of a highly-strung, restless frame of mind. Seeing one riding on a broomstick means there will be a scandal which will harm your image and put

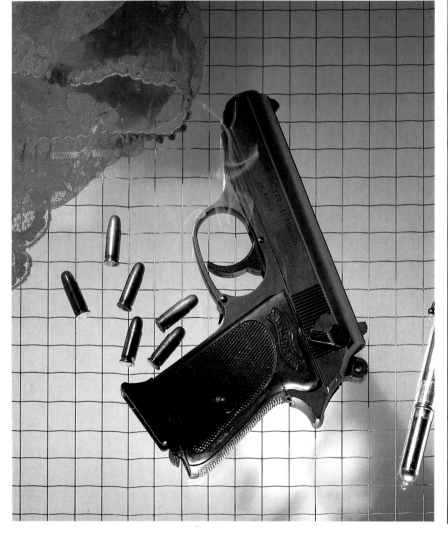

GUN   An unloaded gun suggests you have been bad-tempered and irritable.

74

your job at risk; if the hag talks to you, your reputation is being impaired by someone you know.

HAIL

Hail is not a promising subject to dream about, for it indicates a sad and overemotional state. Being hit by hailstones means your present state of melancholy is unlikely to last much longer. In general, hail is a symbol of losses in business, arguments between lovers, and bad harvests for farmers.

HAIR

Dreaming about having long hair is a sign of good health, while short hair indicates liveliness and enthusiasm. If your hair starts going white, it means you are getting weak physically. Black hair in a dream is a sign of contacts with old acquaintances being renewed, and blond hair suggests you should be getting on with an onerous task instead of thinking about it. If you dream you have a beard, you should accept advice in the spirit in which it is being given.

HAIRDRESSER

A men's hairdresser in a dream signifies that you are the subject of gossip for people around you, and a ladies' hairdresser is a sign that you feel strongly about someone else but they do not love you, so you need to dampen your enthusiasm unless you want to be disappointed. Going to a hairdresser means you are about to get involved in something exciting but risky, and being a hairdresser yourself suggests differences of opinion, or more major disagreements, between yourself and members of your family.

HAM

The appearance of uncooked ham in a dream indicates that you will have to make an unexpected change of plan, while cooked ham, signifies resignation and gloominess caused by a mistake which has cost you dearly. If you dream about eating ham, you will have annoying arguments with people at work, and if

you buy it, you will receive insincere praise from someone who is envious of your achievements. Selling ham means you are feeling uncertain and insecure.

HAMMER

The significance of a hammer in a dream varies according to what the hammer is made of. A metal hammer means that something will go wrong at your place of work, where a failure to agree about something is causing delays and setbacks. A wooden hammer or mallet means you should calm yourself: you are being too irritable and touchy.

HAIR   You are well and healthy when you dream of having long hair.

HANDS

Hands have always been regarded as an eloquent way of expressing one's state of mind and one's emotions in a way in which words are not able to. A woman's hands in a dream are a sign that a brief feeling of depression will cloud your thoughts at work and in love, but everything will sort itself out once you have received help from someone dear to you. A child's hands indicate financial success. Dirty

HARVEST   Dreams of harvesting corn suggest that you are reaping the rewards of past endeavours.
HANDS   These usually explain the current emotions of the dreamer.

hands indicate that a relative may be facing a risk which is putting them in some danger. If the hands are clean, a matter which is important to your career will be resolved happily.

Handbag

If you dream about finding a handbag with money in it, you can expect good luck, in love if not in business matters. If it is empty, it suggests that you dislike routine and prefer it if something new and interesting is happening all the time. Losing a handbag indicates indecisiveness, and buying one, being extremely busy.

Hanging

Tradition has it that if you dream about seeing yourself hanging from the gallows, it indicates a step upwards in the social scale. But seeing someone else being hanged indicates a temporary or long-term lack of money.

When 'dreaming with one's eyes open' isn't simply a figure of speech

Many studies have been carried out on the phenomenon of dreaming with one's eyes open: the most interesting have been in the Soviet Union. Between 1956 and 1957, 400 long-distance lorry drivers were asked to write down any dreams, visions, or strange images they were able to remember at the end of each journey. Of the 400 drivers, 240 recorded actual dreams they had had, usually after seven hours or more at the wheel. In 27 cases, these dreams had occurred at a stage where the drivers were so tired they had had serious problems in controlling their vehicles.

The first conclusion to be drawn from this evidence is an obvious one: dreaming with your eyes open happens when the brain becomes overloaded with toxins created by fatigue, and tries to switch off briefly, in what the Soviet researchers called a 'dreaming pause'.

Dreams of this kind are not the same as hallucinations. In most cases, the dreamer is starting to succumb to the stress of staying awake, and tends to take refuge in an idyllic situation of one sort or another ("I thought I was in the middle of a field"; "I was on the banks of a river"; "I was outside my parents' country cottage"). But this is interrupted by an alarm signal set off by an in-built desire to survive: the person is brought back to reality with a jolt ("All of a sudden I was attacked by a dog"; "I was falling into icy water"; "My mother slapped me hard in the face").

'Dreaming with one's eyes open' occurs when the subject is extremely tired and in the waking equivalent of a trance-like state.

HARE

Dreaming about a hare is a sign of good luck: if it is running towards you, close friends will soon be coming to see you, and a girl who dreams about a hare is likely to be on the verge of meeting her husband-to-be. A hare being coursed, on the other hand, means serious risks being faced.

HARMONY

Hearing harmonious sounds or pleasant music in a dream is a sign of a long and happy life, and has favourable connotations for everyone.

HARP

If you hear a harp playing in your dream, there is good news on the way: either an unexpected reconciliation, or an association with an important person.

HARVEST

Harvesting potatoes in a dream indicates that you are taking on a laborious but profitable task; picking apples or other fruit indicates a happy life in which most things are going your way. Harvesting grain of any kind reflects the fact that you are now reaping the fruits of work you did a long time ago.

HAT

If you dream about putting on a hat it indicates unexpected gains, while buying a new one means there may soon be arguments between members of your family or even the loss of friends. A dirty or patched-up hat means that you will undergo an unhappy emotional experience.

HAY

Hay is a hopeful indicator if it appears in a dream. A haystack, or hayloft full of hay, indicates an unexpected stroke of good luck, but if the hay is wet, there are troubles in prospect for you.

HAZELNUT

Hazelnuts are usually an optimistic indication in a dream, showing lasting health, while if you are in love, your partner will be faithful, kind and loving. But if the nuts are just empty shells, or they have been partly eaten by insects or worms, their significance in the dream changes radically: they indicate hopes being dashed, and petty-minded behaviour from people around you as well as jealousy and arguments with your partner.

HEALTH

A healthy man in a dream foreshadows a brilliant career full of satisfactions, but a healthy woman suggests bitterness and resentment for a misdeed in the past. Eating a healthy meal in a dream means that your feelings towards your partner now are not the same as they used to be.

HEATING

Heating a house in a dream symbolizes profound, but short-lived emotions. Heating a bed using an electric blanket means a worrying physical weakness, and heating up food suggests pressing financial needs. Warming your hands in front of a fire means you are letting your imagination run riot, and warming your feet means you tend to be indifferent towards the joys and misfortunes of others.

HELL

As you might expect, hell is an ill omen in dreams. If you dream about going there, or even of just seeing it, misfortunes, illness and monetary losses are in prospect. Escaping from hell, on the other hand, is a sign of good fortune in times to come.

HERD

A herd of animals grazing peacefully in a dream symbolizes a large material or financial gain. A herd of cows suggests lasting friendships, and a herd of goats is a mark of good luck. Tending a herd of animals indicates minor difficulties with

other people, and dreaming about a herd which has broken up, and some of the animals are lost, means you have worries on your mind at the moment.

HIDING

Hiding anything in a dream indicates you are shy and introverted and tend to give your partner too little space to develop within your relationship. More particularly, hiding money suggests nervous tension and susceptibility to the influence of others. If you hide from something you are afraid of, you have secrets which are not particularly well kept and prejudices which you need to overcome.

HILL

A hill in a dream symbolizes a difficulty to be overcome. Dreaming you are standing on top of a hill means you have already put these difficulties behind you, while climbing up one indicates fatigue.

HILL A hill in a dream warns that present problems should be tackled.

HOARSENESS

A hoarse voice in a dream indicates new interests and new stimuli at work, but the dream is also telling you to change some of your plans. If you hear someone singing hoarsely in the distance it means you are good at choosing the right friends and are sure of yourself and your abilities, but if you are trying to sing or talk yourself and your voice is hoarse, an advantageous financial venture will end successfully.

HOLLY

Because it is an attractive but prickly plant, holly in a dream indicates that disappointments and annoyances are on the way.

HOMAGE

If someone pays homage to you in a dream, it indicates that you are sometimes a conceited and selfish personality which makes people see you as unreasonable and even rude. You are likely to receive a comeuppance which will make you think twice about the way you have been acting. If you render homage to your father, you will receive unasked-for advice, while if it is to your mother, you can expect a period of peace and tranquillity. Paying homage to someone who is important in a dream shows that you can expect faithfulness from your partner.

HERD   A herd of cows symbolizes the security of life-long friendships.

HOMICIDE

If you dream about committing a homicide, you should avoid a temptation which would harm your reputation, no matter what the cost to yourself may be in terms of emotional turmoil. If you kill someone on purpose, you need to have another look at some of your opinions, because they may prove to be wrong. If the death is accidental, you are in excellent health and your worries about possible illness are unjustified. Planning a murder of any kind in a dream means you are intolerant and excessively talkative.

HONESTY

An honest man in a dream is a sign that new horizons are opening up at work, while the appearance of an honest woman means you need to defend either your own or someone else's interests at all costs. If it is a relative that displays honest behaviour, it indicates that you may be someone who is easily led and who is without any distinctive personality of their own. An honest servant indicates an unusual degree of firmness and organizational ability. If you are honest yourself, it means you can expect to make a new, and quite unusual acquaintance. An honest tradesperson means you are being too complacent and this trait could develop into vanity.

HONEY

If honey appears in one of your dreams, it is a highly optimistic sign. Eating honey symbolizes fitness and health, prosperity and happiness. You have a chance to become more independent in your work, while in love things are going well and your partner is being more kind, attentive and affectionate than usual. Runny honey indicates financial advantages of some kind, and thick honey suggests temporary worries.

HONOUR

Honouring someone else in a dream, perhaps at a celebration of some kind, brings good luck: you will find that someone you hardly know thinks much more highly of you than you have realized. Honouring someone who is dead indicates that better times on the way. Losing your honour or reputation is a sign that you are depressed and confused and need help and understanding. Defending your honour, or someone else's, is a sign of violent emotions. Giving your word of honour means an important personal success.

HOOK

Hanging something from a hook in a dream indicates generosity and sociability, while injuring yourself on one indicates that someone close to you is not happy with your behaviour. A fishing hook shows that you have a secret passion for someone you have known a long time. Screwing a hook into a wall means you are obstinately carrying on with projects which others would have given up on. Banging one into a rock to help you climb a mountain means you will be praised for a generous gesture to a friend.

HORNS

Horns are usually a sign of good luck in dreams. A bull's horns indicate calm confidence, and a goat's rapid progress in your career. Having horns yourself is also a favourable sign, showing strong will power.

HOROSCOPE

Reading your horoscope in a dream indicates a happy event which will cheer you up considerably, while writing one means you have strong resources of character to fall back on, and an equally strong will. If the horoscope is a good one, it indicates that you are in a nervous and restless frame of mind because of a failure to agree on something at work and your consequent inability to take action. An unfavourable horoscope in a dream, curiously enough, means that a hope you have been nurturing will come to fruition. Reading someone else's horoscope indicates arguments with your partner.

HORSE

A dream involving a horse is always a good sign, unless the horse is black all over, in which case mourning or grief is indicated. Riding a horse is a sign both of independence and happiness, though if the horse manages to unseat you, plans you have made are likely to go wrong. Finding a horseshoe in a dream is an extremely good omen.

HOSPITAL

An ordinary hospital in a dream indicates a depressed, melancholic person, while a field hospital in a war means you are missing someone who is a long way away, and any other kind of military hospital reflects a worrying piece of news. A psychiatric hospital indicates stormy family relationships. If you see any kind of hospital, you are probably being stricken by worries which you need to overcome, and if you go inside one for any reason, whether as a patient or visitor, your health is on the mend and you are being exceptionally decisive. Coming out of a hospital indicates a solution being found to a long-standing problem.

HORSE   Riding indicates happiness, but if you fall, your plans may be dashed.

HOSPITALITY

Giving hospitality to a relative in a dream indicates unexpected expense, while if it is a friend you entertain in your dream, you can expect a business agreement which will not only be advantageous, but will also free you from the dependence on others which you dislike so much. Giving hospitality to an enemy means you are nervous and irritable because of a delay in receiving important news, and you should be careful not to express your feelings to people you do not know very well, or you will get involved in heated and pointless discussions.

HOUNDS

Following the hounds in a hunt in a dream means that research or similar work you are involved in is unlikely to be productive; while if you are attached, your partner may not trust you totally and you should look for ways to reassure him or her in this regard.

HOUR GLASS

An hour glass in a dream means that you should calm yourself and avoid rushing into anything, including major decisions: always think before you act.

HOUSE

There are many different meanings to the symbol of a house in a dream, depending on what type of house it is and where it is. Building your own house reflects confidence in your own abilities and the likelihood of success in something you are doing, while moving house indicates worries relating to money. A house in the country indicates peace and tranquillity, and an empty house, a low income. A new house indicates a busy social life.

HUBBUB

If you dream about being in the middle of a lot of noise and confusion, you need to make an important decision straight away, and not let yourself be distracted by other people.

HOUNDS   Following hounds suggests your partner mistrusts you.

HUDDLING

Huddling in a corner in a dream is a sign of arguments about money or material objects, and huddling behind a door suggests that you have problems which are very hard to sort out. Huddling under a table indicates financial worries. Being huddled up in an armchair means you will be briefly shaken by some unexpected news, and being curled up on a bed means your feelings will be hurt by the assertiveness of the person you love. Curling up on the ground means being constantly worried by problems, and huddling up with cold means you have an obligation to carry out.

HUMILIATION

A man being humiliated in your dream indicates an important decision which is likely to change your emotional situation in a big way. A humiliated woman suggests good relationships within your family and with those close to you.

HUMMING BIRD

This tiny bird is a bearer of good fortune in dreams, indicating successful trips to foreign countries. A flock of humming birds is as good a sign as one can get in several respects and means that you will receive more than your fair share of good luck and money.

HUNCHBACK

Tradition has it that meeting a hunchback in a dream will bring pleasant news not long afterwards, and if you manage to touch the hunchback you can expect good luck and personal success. Being a hunchback yourself, on the other hand, suggests your health is not as good as it might be.

HUNGER

This is the classic example of a dream signifying its opposite: if you, or other people, are hungry, it means both good luck and a healthy financial situation. In fact, strange as it may seem, the more intense the hunger, the more fortune is likely to smile on you.

HUNTING

The meaning of this dream depends on what it is that is being hunted. Hunting a hare is a symbol of worries and troubles ahead, while a fox-hunt means lack of trust from someone close to you. Hunting a deer or a game-bird denotes intrigues involving someone you are in love with. If you are the one being hunted in the dream, it means that you are worried either by your responsibilities or some problem that you are reluctant to face.

HURRICANE

Tinea Ballater, the famous expert on dreams, says in one of her books, "I wouldn't wish this dream on anybody." In fact it is one of the worst things you can dream about, indicating that an extremely shaky period lies ahead in which, if you put one foot wrong, the result may be disastrous.

HUSBAND

If a woman dreams she has a husband when in real life she is not married, it indicates that she is not yet ready to get involved in relationships which tie her down in any way, while if she is married and dreams about her husband, marital quarrels are in the offing. Dreaming about someone else's husband suggests that you may show a lack of seriousness about important matters, though if you are not married yourself it indicates that a meaningful and lasting relationship is in prospect.

HYMN

Dreaming about singing a hymn means you are exceptionally brave and courageous, while listening to hymns means a journey of some kind is not far off.

HYSTERIA

Dreaming about someone who is hysterical means you should take care not to be forced into anything against your will, while if it is you having hysterics, it indicates that you should follow the advice of someone close to you.

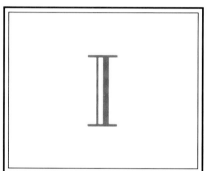

ICE

Ice is not a good omen in a dream. If you see a vast expanse of snow and ice, or find yourself in the middle of one, it invariably signals either danger or difficulties of some kind. An icy road or path symbolizes restlessness and waiting for something new or interesting to happen.

ICE CREAM

Eating an ice cream in a dream suggests that you have secure relationships. The various flavours can mean different things: a fruit-flavoured ice cream signifies a repayment of money; a coffee flavour, influential friendships; vanilla, illusions, and chocolate, being sensible.

ICICLE

If you dream of seeing icicles hanging down from the eaves of a roof or a window, it indicates that you will

ICE Danger and difficulty lie ahead when you dream about ice.

find a great deal of common ground with someone and there will be a happy outcome to the association. Eating an icicle shows a need for new sensations and experiences.

IDIOT

If you dream about saying or doing something stupid, it actually means the opposite of what one might expect: if you are likely to be the kind of person who succeeds in almost everything you do. Dreaming that someone else is an idiot means that you have friends who are particularly intelligent.

IDOL

If you dream about worshipping an idol – whether it is a pereson or an object – you are about to meet with a major disappointment. A wooden idol means you need to be careful; a silver one indicates moodiness; and a gold one symbolizes jealousy.

IMITATING

Any kind of imitation in a dream has negative connotations. Imitating a person, a voice or an action indicates a personality which is rather mysterious, prone to jealousy, and not very lucky.

INCENSE

The smell of incense in a dream indicates love and well-being, while seeing the smoke of incense means that your hopes can be put into practice. Unburnt incense symbolizes false praise and untrustworthiness.

INFIDELITY

If you dream that either a friend, or your partner, is being unfaithful to you, there is no cause for alarm: it actually indicates quite the opposite. But if you dream about being unfaithful yourself, there are very strong temptations in your path, so you should get ready to resist them.

INGOT

A silver ingot in a dream indicates that a great deal of effort is being put into solving a problem at work, while a gold one shows an important agreement being reached. An iron bar suggests you are embarking on new, exciting projects at work. If your dream involves stealing an ingot, you will not be able to avoid an onerous responsibility or duty.

INHERITANCE

Inheriting something from a relative in a dream indicates the fact that you are worried about someone else's health, while if someone else inherits something, you may well lose a sizeable amount of money soon. If you dream about dividing an inheritance with other relatives,

The hidden warning in dreams about fire

Fire is a sign of natural energy. In almost every race, throughout every period of history, fire and the sun have both been regarded as sacred. Fire is a symbol of transformation and purification; the gradual change from old to new. The sun represents light and life, fertility and the richness of nature, but it can also stand for drought and death. It is a powerful, but ambiguous symbol.

In religious ritual, fire has always had an important place: there is the flame on the tomb of the unknown soldier; the Olympic torch; the use of fire to dispose of the dead; and in churches we burn candles on the altar.

This wealth of symbolic imagery is used by the unconscious to tell us that a period of purification and renewal is in prospect together with a certain amount of painful reflection; just as fire both warms and purges, so it can hurt us if we get too close to it. Fire also indicates that we have considerable reserves of instinctive and mental energy to help us through what may be a very difficult time.

When we dream about fire getting out of control and destroying things, it indicates that we have contravened the normal rules which society imposes and feel guilty about it. This type of dream is a warning not to get things out of perspective and overestimate their importance, just as the fire itself has got out of control.

So tradition is right to ascribe as much importance to dreams about fire as it has. In folklore, fire is a positive sign when used in the service of man, to keep us warm or cook our food, and a negative one when it becomes an enemy to be fought against or fled from. This is

Purification and renewal, calling on the energies that lie within, are indicated by dreams of fire. It may also be time for home truths.

another example of how modern psychology has upheld beliefs which came into being centuries before psychology became a science: this linkage of old traditions and dreams is a phenomenon which many experts believe is much more common than we might think.

INN   This image signals poverty and an unfaithful partner.

you are being much more emotional and highly-strung than usual: but if you keep calm, many of your problems will solve themselves. Losing or squandering an inheritance means that you are apprehensive about an important event.

INK

A dream which involves ink in any way is a foreboding of loss or separation, particularly if the ink gets spilt. An ink stain is a sign of possible illness; the larger the stain, the worse the illness will be.

INKWELL

The exact meaning of an inkwell in a dream depends on the material it is made of. If it is expensive – gold, silver, cut glass – it indicates adversity to be overcome, as well as shyness. If it is made of plastic or a similar material, it reflects indecisiveness. A full inkwell is a sign of a faithful lover, and an empty one of irritable, jumpy behaviour.

INN

This is not a very fortunate dream; usually it indicates poverty, and dreaming about staying in an inn means that there may be a major business failure on the way with a consequent loss of money. Where lovers are concerned, this dream can mean their partner will go off with someone else.

INNKEEPER

An innkeeper in a dream, like the inn he lives in, signifies ill-fortune, and, in particular, jealousy directed at your partner which will lead to fruitless arguments and misunderstandings.

INSANITY

Being insane yourself, or seeing someone else who is mad, in a dream suggests that you are going through an unhappy period in virtually every respect. In your relations with the opposite sex, painful arguments will place a long-lasting relationship in jeopardy, and possibly ruin it for good. At work, you are having trouble finishing a job which initially seemed to be perfectly simple. Being cured of insanity, however, indicates improvements in your health.

INSPIRING

Inspiring someone else with an emo-

tion, or being inspired yourself, in a dream can have various meanings depending on the emotion aroused. If it is sympathy or pity, there are surprises on the way, and if it is hate, then your merits and abilities will be recognized. If it is horror or

disgust, your freedom to manoeuvre is indicated, while love signifies short-lived happiness.

INSTRUMENT

Most musical instruments in dreams are a sign of happiness and harmony, though there can be subtle variations in meaning from one instrument to another. The appearance of a medical instrument such as a scalpel in a dream indicates obstacles being created by members of your family, and a navigational instrument such as a sextant means you need help and understanding following a mistake you made at work.

INSULT

Dreaming about being insulted yourself means you have emotional problems and your partner has just betrayed you in some way. Insulting someone else indicates an unhappy period which may be ended by a

INSTRUMENT   The appearance of navigational instruments reveals you need a helping hand.

major change or upheaval in your life, such as changing your job or moving home.

ISLAND   A wooded, tropical island promises good things on the horizon.

INTERROGATING

If you interrogate someone else in your dream in an attempt to find out the truth, it suggests you are not good at forming lasting relationships with people around you. If it is you that is being interrogated, there is a pleasant surprise, involving a journey, in the offing.

INTERVIEWING

Interviewing an entertainer of any kind in a dream means there is a pleasant meeting coming soon, while interviewing a politician denotes a rebellious personality. A job interview in a dream indicates a major change, not necessarily connected with your career, and any interview involving a woman indicates that you are highly-strung and nervous, possibly because an underlying problem remains unresolved.

INTRIGUE

There are various ways of interpreting this subject in dreams, but all of them are unfavourable. An intrigue involving lovers indicates that an emotional relationship will not last long, and a political intrigue signifies that you are indulging in pointless gossip. Taking part in a plot of any kind is a warning sign to the dreamer, while refusing to be involved in one indicates that your suspicions about someone are unfounded.

IRON

Rusty iron in a dream symbolizes great physical strength; molten iron shows a satisfying love life; and beaten iron indicates an irritable, gruff person. Any object made of iron is likely to bring good luck with it. An iron for pressing clothes indicates that minor problems need solving before they get bigger.

ISLAND

It is quite common to dream about being on a desert island, and this indicates your present boredom and loneliness. An inhabited island, on the other hand, indicates that interesting new developments are underway in some aspect of your life. A tropical island covered in palm trees foretells hopeful prospects, but if there is no vegetation on it, it means that things are going wrong because you have not treated them seriously enough.

ITCHING

Itchy feet in dreams, as one might expect, signify a yearning for new opportunities and new places to live; itching hands indicate that

IVY   One of the best dream images, predicting success and happiness in all.

money is on the way. If your nose itches, you should be careful because you are at a stage in your work where you could easily make mistakes, and you should therefore think very carefully before you do anything.

IVORY

Ivory has always brought good luck, whether you actually own it or you dream about it. This is particularly so for business people, travellers, and lovers who dream about ivory. A girl who dreams about something made of ivory is almost certain to marry a man who is kind and gentle and who will help her build a happy family life.

IVY

Ivy is a symbol in dreams of your assertiveness being put to good use, as well as of your faithfulness and tenacity. It promises total dedication in matters of love, loyalty in business affairs, and all-round success in life.

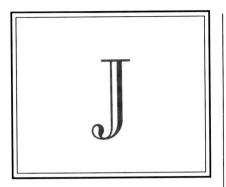

JACKAL

Dreaming about a jackal is not an optimistic sign. The animal symbolizes an enemy waiting for a weak moment to attack, though if you move carefully, you can turn things against him.

JACKET

If you dream you are putting on a jacket, it indicates that you are keeping a danger at bay, so if you dream about taking one off, the danger is likely to catch up with you. Dreaming about a new jacket is an indication of financial problems, and an old one, a serious suggestion being made.

JADE

Precious stones normally symbolize success in dreams, and the colour green shows that you are undergoing a long, difficult task involving much hard thinking. Dreaming about jade therefore indicates a success, most likely an intellectual one, being obtained after lengthy strivings.

JAM

Despite its sweet taste, jam does not as one might expect, indicate sweetness in a dream. But it tells you a lot about the state of your emotions at the present. Eating jam on your own, possibly straight from the jar, shows your present sadness and loneliness and indicates that it is likely that you will have an argument with someone dear to you. However, eating jam in the company of other people means new friendships which will turn into long-term, trusting relationships, and making jam foreshadows your getting married.

JAUNDICE

A dream involving jaundice is a warning to look after your own health, and can also presage lack of money and unhappiness. For lovers, it can be a sign of unexpected unfaithfulness.

JEALOUSY

The appearance of jealousy in a dream is a sign of worry and anxiety. Being jealous yourself means happiness in matters of the heart, while being the cause of jealousy means you are repressing strong emotions. Dreaming about being jealous of someone at work means setbacks in love.

JAM   Making jam suggests your wedding day is not far off; eating jam reflects loneliness.

JELLY

Jelly of any kind in a dream is synonymous with lies and deceit. If you dream you are eating jelly, there will be unhappiness in your family, though fortunately it will not have any damaging long-term consequences.

JESUS

If you have the good fortune to dream about Jesus, there is a long period of physical and spiritual well-being in prospect. If you talk to him, or he talks to you, this indicates that you are full of hope for the future.

JEWEL

Jewels in dreams are a sign of success, and are a particularly favourable sign when dreamed of by

lovers. Any dream where you have lots of jewels, or someone gives them to you, is an omen of healthy profits for those in business, good harvests for people who work on the land, and pleasant, safe journeys for seafarers.

JEWELLER

Dreaming of a jeweller, goldsmith or silversmith at work means that a person dear to you is in particular need of your help and advice, while dreaming of a jeweller in a shop shows that you are making important decisions in a rational, careful frame of mind. A jeweller buying jewellery means that a personal

JELLY   This dream tells a tale of lies, deceit and unhappiness.

Sexual symbolism in dreams

Many dreams that are sexually based use ancient symbols for the male and female organs instead of depicting them directly. Very often, too, the dreamer expresses his or her desires through images which take the place of the sexual act itself. Even if we are unaware of this symbolism, the feelings we have in the dream, and after we wake, are akin to sexual desire.

It is rarely possible to interpret this kind of dream in simple terms. Although human behaviour is rooted in instincts of a very basic kind, dreams are a complex combination of instinct, rational thought, and imagery which can help us to a better understanding of who we are and why we behave the way we do.

For example, dreaming about a spear landing in the ground is not simply an oblique way of referring to the sexual act. The fact is that the combination of the man-made spear, and the earth which we did not create, shows the human being fertilized and enriched by its environment. Although the connotations are sexual, there is a less obvious message in the dream. If all dreams were interpreted simply in terms of man's most basic instincts, they would give only half the picture, for dreams also reflect how we have matured and grown psychologically from being creatures governed by our most basic needs to rational yet multi-faceted human beings.

dilemma will go on troubling you for some time to come. An honest jeweller means that you need to put back the finishing date of a project you are involved in if you want to make sure it works out properly. A dishonest one, on the other hand, means you will receive an offer which is very advantageous and will add to your prestige at work.

JOCKEY

A jockey is always an auspicious person to dream about, especially if he is actually riding in a race, and most particularly if he wins, for this signifies that your hopes and desires are about to come true. However, it is a bad portent if he falls off his horse, for this foretells the failure of an enterprise.

JOY

Quite simply, joy in a dream means joy in your everyday life: it indicates good health and success in everything you do.

JUDGE

This is a dream which bodes ill for the future: there are obstacles and difficulties waiting just round the corner and you may be involved in an argument, or someone may accuse you of something you are not guilty of. If you keep your cool, though, everything will turn out for the best.

JUG

Like dreaming of bottles, this dream also depends on whether or not the jug is empty, in indicating whether it will bring good fortune or bad. A jug full of milk indicates *joie de vivre*, and one full of coffee indicates heated, perhaps angry exchanges with someone.

JUGGLER

A juggler is a pleasant omen in a dream: it means that a potentially profitable opportunity will shortly come your way, and that you should grasp it with both hands.

JOCKEY   A jockey in a race promises fulfilment of your wishes, especially if he rides a winner.

JUG   Dreaming of a jug full of milk indicates that life is full of happiness and joy at present.

JUNGLE

Dreaming about a jungle full of dense trees, plants and creepers is a warning to the dreamer. If you get lost or stuck in the jungle, there are major problems lying in wait for you, but if you manage to make your way through the vegetation without too much trouble, you will also overcome difficulties in your real life.

JURY

If you see a jury in your dream, it is a promising sign, but this is not the case if you are part of the jury yourself.

JUSTIFYING YOURSELF

This is a dream which reflects inner conflicts, a difficult personality, and disappointing experiences. No matter what you are trying to justify, or who you are doing the explaining to, your outlook is one of unhappiness and gloom.

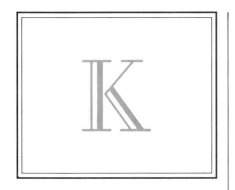

KETTLE

A kettle in a dream symbolizes the danger of being cheated or deceived by someone you thought that you could trust. A boiling kettle indicates that you need to widen your social horizons, while a copper kettle is a symbol of material and spiritual riches.

KEY

If you dream about losing a key, there is a difficult situation on the way. Finding one is a token of good fortune. For lovers, a key symbolizes the key to their partner's heart. A bunch of keys indicates profitable business dealings.

KICK

The precise interpretation of this dream depends on what is being kicked. If it is a ball, good news and good luck are in prospect, but kicking a person indicates that you are repressing conflicts which need resolving. Kicking an animal shows that you need to get your thoughts in order before you make an important decision.

KILLING

Killing your father, or someone else killing him, in a dream means you will have to make sacrifices, while your mother being killed indicates unpleasant remarks or actions from people close to you. Killing your lover means you may be involved in arguments with him or her which could ruin the relationship for good. If it is your husband who is killed in the dream, it indicates that you are

KING   A crowned king suggests that business is booming.

a naive, impressionable person; while if it is your wife, it shows that you are harbouring unjustified suspicions and jealousy about her which you should take pains to correct in your mind.

KING

A king seated on his throne in a dream suggests there is a danger of someone cheating you. A king being crowned is a symbol of business matters going well, and one holding a sceptre shows your increasing energy and strong force of will. A king standing beside his queen symbolizes initiatives you have taken

being successful. If the king is a young man in your dream, you will be criticized and abused behind your back by a colleague at work who dislikes you, but if the king is old, you will enjoy a major personal success.

KISS

This usually symbolizes happiness in dreams. Kissing someone means the emergence of a new love affair, while being kissed by your own partner indicates sincerity and genuineness in the relationship. Kissing a dead person is a sign of a long and happy life.

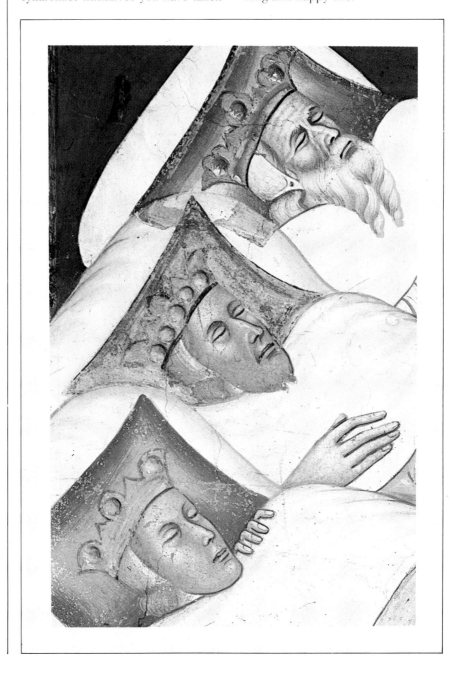

KITCHEN

A large, bright, tidy kitchen in a dream is a symbol of harmony within your family. The newer and cleaner the kitchen, the more auspicious the dream.

KITTEN

Although a kitten is normally a good omen in dreams, this is not the case if it bites or scratches anyone: for it shows that your partner is deceiving you in some way, and if you marry him or her, it will be an unhappy marriage.

KNEADING

Kneading dough is usually a pleasant subject for a dream. If you are making pastry, it suggests optimism on your part, while if you are making bread, financial gains are in prospect, and if it is cakes, the dream symbolizes your ambition. Kneading something that is not edible indicates a desire for revenge.

KNEE

A swollen knee in a dream is a sign of your business or financial affairs being at risk, while a cut or grazed knee means that you will soon undergo a long journey. A bandaged knee means you should take things easy for a while.

KNEELING

Kneeling down to pick something up in a dream means you are good at taking advantage of opportunities, while kneeling in church indicates that your wishes will be coming true. Kneeling down beside the bed of a sick person indicates a family illness in the not too distant future.

KNIFE

An ordinary table knife is a favourable sign in a dream, indicating new conquests and successes. But any other dream involving a knife (a kitchen knife, or one covered in blood, or being sharpened), indicates possible danger and the need for great caution.

KNOCK DOWN

Knocking down an object such as a wall or other obstacle in a dream indicates that you are enterprising and go-ahead, but if you dream about knocking down a human being or animal, perhaps in your car, it is a sign of your present mental or physical tiredness.

KNIFE   Beware! A kitchen knife in a dream warns of imminent danger.

LABEL   A label on a bottle is an indication of a practical mind.

KNOCKING

Hearing someone knocking on the door in a dream means that fortune is about to smile on you. Knocking on a door yourself indicates a feeling of nostalgia and desire to recreate the past, or of missing something or someone you once had; knocking on a window signifies a dispute between partners.

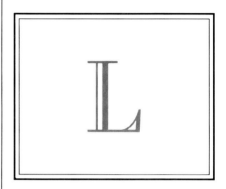

LABEL

Dreaming about the label on a bottle means you are sensible and practically-minded. Putting a label on something is a sign of your maturity, and putting a label on a suitcase means that you, or someone close to you, are about to take a long, pleasant journey. Labels in a museum or art gallery signify staidness and conformity.

LABORATORY

This dream is a sign that you are in some kind of danger. This could involve your health (exhaustion, overwork), your state of mind (major depression), or your relationship with your partner, perhaps through a lack of mutual understanding. However, these problems in store will probably only be temporary and will soon be resolved.

LABOURER

Seeing a man involved in any kind of heavy work in a dream, such as pushing a wheelbarrow or unloading things from a lorry, has pleasant connotations: a fortunate coincidence is on the way, and will bring you both money and respect. If the labourer is having a rest, your working life is stagnating because you are lacking in willpower and enthusiasm.

LAKE

This dream can have both negative and positive aspects, depending on context. It is an optimistic one if you dream of a large, calm lake with clear waters, as it symbolizes future happiness and success. However, if the water is rough, or dirty, there is a difficult period of your life just

ahead. Crossing a lake in a boat indicates that you have risen in the estimation of others; jumping into a lake suggests that you are undergoing pain or severe unhappiness.

LANDSCAPE

Most landscapes in dreams hold out the promise of happiness, and tranquillity in love. If you dream of a

LAKE   A large, calm lake symbolizes happiness and success in prospect.

pleasant landscape, you are very wise and all your decisions are well-considered and promptly put into action. If the landscape is empty or unattractive, you will suffer a disappointment in matters of the heart which will leave a bitter after-taste for a long time. Dreaming of a seascape means you have a need for solitude, and a mountain landscape indicates that the past plays an important part in your life and that you spend a lot of time thinking about it.

LANDSLIDE

Observing a landslide from a safe vantage point some distance away in a dream indicates that you are sensible and intelligent, but get-

LANDSCAPE   Look forward to a happy, harmonious future after dreaming of a beautiful landscape.

ting caught up in one indicates that there is cheating and deception between yourself and someone close to you.

LANE

Dreaming of a long country lane

which stretches across the countryside indicates that a lengthy burdensome task will soon be bringing its own reward. But if the lane is very narrow, it means that you must make some necessary concessions or compromises, while if the lane is blocked off, it means that you are troubled by personal dilemmas and doubts. If the lane is dark or in some way frightening, you have major financial problems at the moment.

LAUGHTER

A man laughing in a dream is a symbol of new knowledge or skills gained from a new project at work, while a woman laughing symbolizes your introversion and unsociability. A child's laughter means pleasant news from a long way away. If something you do or say in your dream makes other people laugh, you need to face up to some fundamental differences between you and your partner.

LAUNDRY

Doing your laundry by hand in a dream indicates considerable physical strength. Hanging it out to dry indicates your psychological strengths. If the washing comes out clean, good fortune is indicated, but if there are dirty marks on it, there are problems in store.

LAW

Any dream involving the law means that there is the danger of something unfavourable happening in your financial or business affairs. You should not take risks, such as lending anyone money or signing any guarantees, at least not for the time being.

LAWYER

If you dream about being a lawyer, it indicates that your strength and

Dante's dream

We have already seen how important dreams have been in the literature of all lands and epochs. The *Divine Comedy* opens with a dream: the vision of the poet, Dante, who finds himself in a dark forest and meets in succession a leopard, a lion and finally "a wolf whose limbs were so thin that he resembled a carcass".

The opening lines of the *Divine Comedy* are well-known:

> Halfway along the highway of our
>   life on earth
> I found myself in the middle of a
>   dark forest
> Straying from the proper road,
> Ah! I cannot express what it was
>   like, how harsh
> This forest was, how hostile and
>   how fearsome,
> So much that I am afraid even to
>   think of it!

Guido da Pisa, who was one of the very first commentators on the *Divine Comedy*, noted how human life was, according to Aristotle, "divided into two equal halves, consisting of light and darkness, of sleep and wakefulness. Thus, when Dante speaks of being *halfway along the highway*, he is referring to sleep, and the famous opening scene of the poem shows that Dante is dreaming when he enters the forest."

Dante's own son agreed with Guido da Pisa's interpretation, as do many critics today.

Like many of his contemporaries, Dante used the vision, or dream, as a literary device, to explain his meaning. The *dark forest* symbolizes the poet's situation: he has lost the ability to make any kind of proper judgment.

energy will bring considerable benefits and successes. If you are
defending someone else, it means
you may have lost the trust and
respect of other people, but if you
are prosecuting them, you will be
helped out in some way by a woman.
If the lawyer in your dream is
someone else, it indicates a feeling
of guilt about something you have
done.

LAZINESS

Just as in real life, laziness in
dreams does not produce favourable
results. Being lazy at home means
you are being overambitious, while
being lazy outdoors or in the countryside means unwelcome news is
on the way. If you dream of spending time stretched out on a beach in
the sun, you ought not to make hasty
judgements about someone who is
offering you their help because they
probably know more about the problem you are tackling than you
yourself.

LEADING

This dream may take several forms.
Being ahead of others in your
studies signifies unexpected melancholy on the horizon, while excel-
ling on the sports field shows that
you have a very highly-developed
sense of observation. If it is art in
which you are ahead of other people, you have ideas about the future
which may be over-ambitious and
impractical. If it is in your work,
you have a strong will-power and are
likely to experience friction with
your partner because of it. If it is
cultural matters that are involved,
you need to overcome prejudices in
the field of love.

LEAF

Like flowers, leaves in dreams bring
good fortune when they are green
and healthy, signifying things going
your way, faithfulness in love, and
harmonious family relationships.
Fallen or dried-up leaves are a sign
of difficulty and illness.

LEARNING

Learning how to do something in a

dream is a favourable sign, provided
it is easily learned. Learning to read
indicates new business prospects,
and learning to write signifies that a
secret will be revealed to you.
Learning to sing means temporary
sadness, and learning to dance,
getting involved in a new activity.
Learning a language indicates
reaching agreement with older people, and a musical instrument,
superficial feelings of attachment to
someone.

LECTURE

Giving a lecture in a dream is a sign
of new developments and novelty in

*LEAF   Fresh green leaves signify that
life is treating you well at present.*

your life. Going to one indicates that
you will shortly be acting unwisely
and this will cause others to criticise
you.

LEGACY

As you might expect, this dream has
an entirely favourable significance.
It suggests a pleasant surprise,
possibly a gift of money, a visit, or a
wedding.

LEMON

To taste the bitter juice of a lemon

LIGHTNING A lightning flash in a dream announces good fortune.

in a dream indicates your current problems and jealousy. Dreaming about lemons on a tree means a trip to a foreign country, with the likelihood of a marriage to someone who lives there. Eating lemons in a dream means that you are not looking after your health, and that, if you are involved in a relationship, there will most definitely be an argument, in the near future, between you and your partner.

LENT

If you dream about giving something up for Lent, it means you will make a great deal of effort to achieve a success, but that the result will repay the trouble, and even misery, of getting there. If you dream that you persuade someone close to you to observe Lent, you will easily overcome the obstacles you thought were insurmountable.

LEOPARD

This dream is a favourable one, foretelling a trip overseas in the near future, and indicating that although there may be problems during or after the trip, these should not be insuperable. It is also possible that your stay in the country might turn out to be a permanent one.

LEPROSY

If you dream about having leprosy yourself, it suggests that you are already worried about a situation and that further problems might crop up to complicate things even

LEMON Be ready for a row with your partner if you dream of eating lemons.

more. It can also mean that you feel guilty about your behaviour towards someone. Dreaming of others with leprosy suggests you have enemies.

LETTER

Writing a letter in a dream reflects the fact that everything is going well from an emotional point of view. Getting one, not surprisingly, indicates news being received from a long way away, and putting one in a post box suggests that you have few problems at present. An anonymous letter signifies dangers to come; a black-edged one (paradoxically) indicates joy; and a love letter means there are problems in your way, but they can be solved.

LIBRARY

A library in a dream is normally a favourable indication – whether it is a public or a private library – for it shows that the dreamer has a strong sense of responsibility, as well as self-confidence.

LICE

Despite their unpleasant connotations, lice are a good sign, signifying pleasant news.

LICKING

Licking your lips in a dream is a sign of your greed and lust, and licking your fingers means you have complexes and phobias to overcome. Licking an ice cream symbolizes unexpected joys to come; a spoon, pleasant new developments; and a plate, unexpected problems in matters of the heart.

LIGHTHOUSE

A very bright lighthouse shining through the night in a dream indicates that you are free to choose from a number of exciting opportunities ahead of you. If it shines constantly, it signifies strength of will, but if it goes on and off, it shows that you have repressed feelings about somebody.

LIGHTNING

Lightning momentarily turns night into day, and is therefore a healthy sign in dreams: seeing it flash indicates long-lasting good fortune. A tree, a house or anything else being struck by lightning means that you can look forward to the fulfilment of your plans for the future.

LIGHTNING CONDUCTOR

Because lightning is a favourable omen in a dream, anything which gets in its way is the opposite. A lightning conductor on the roof of a house means that unpleasant accusations from people you know are in the offing, although you should not get too worked up about them because right is on your side. Although the situation might seem nasty, it will eventually resolve itself in your favour. A lightning conductor mounted on a church means you are embarking on something which is too risky and is certain to fail. If the lightning conductor is on a bell-tower, you will soon be at the centre of a dispute or difference of opinion.

LILY

Lilies are a symbol of purity, and are therefore a good sign when dreamed of by someone who is in love. A white lily signifies happiness for anyone who dreams about it, but a red one shows a burning desire for money. A dead or withered lily symbolizes misfortune, though it will only be short-lived.

LINGERING

To dream of lingering in conversation when you should be doing something else can have various meanings. If you are talking to males, the dream signifies a happy relationship, and if it is women, you can expect at least one new friendship in the near future. If you are lingering in conversation with friends, it can indicate either recent heated but friendly discussion, or violent arguments. Lingering in conversation in a pub indicates a lack of loyalty to someone.

LILY   Pure white lilies suggest happiness for anyone in love; red lilies suggest greed for money.

LION

A lion is generally an animal which brings good luck, and if you dream about one it indicates a personal success or gain, although not necessarily a financial one. If the lion is roaring because it is enraged, you are anxious about the jealousy of someone close to you. Fighting with a lion means a fight or argument in real life.

LIONESS

Dreaming about a lioness is also a hopeful sign in dreams, especially if she is lying down with her cubs, in which case your family relationships will be happy ones.

LIPS

Dreaming about licking your lips indicates greed and envy, and chapped lips mean your health may be at risk in some way. Kissing someone on the lips means your moods

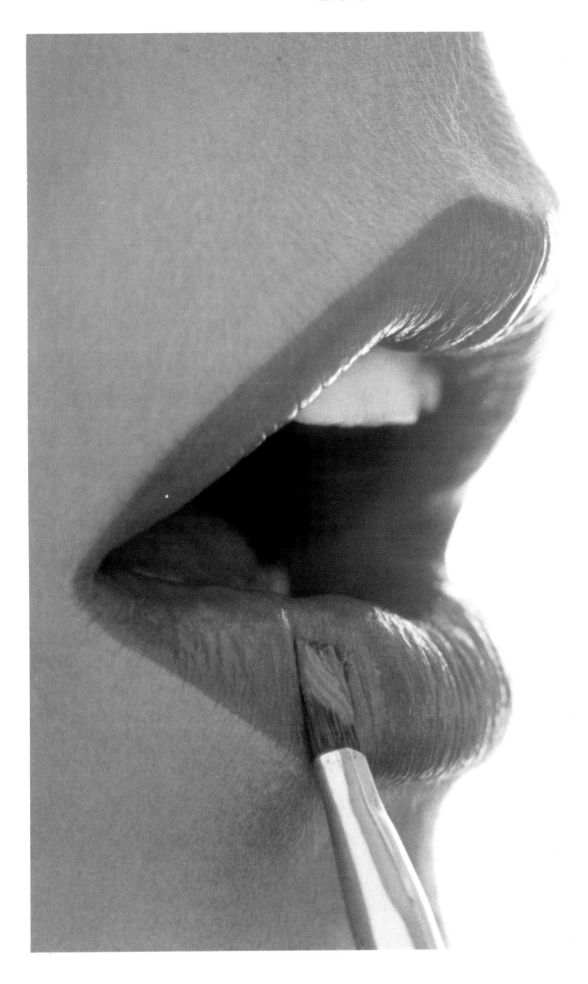

change easily, with a lot of emotional high and low points. If you dream about somebody with a hare lip, your future is very uncertain.

LIPSTICK

This is obviously a dream with strong feminine connotations, and if you dream about yourself or someone else wearing it, it suggests a certain amount of vanity and selfishness on your part. Choosing a lipstick in a shop is a sign of future financial difficulties, and paying for lipstick suggests that you should be less enthusiastic about something at home or at work. Giving somebody a lipstick as a present means you have confidence in yourself and your abilities.

LIST

Dreaming about a shopping list foretells great pleasures and satisfactions to come, while a guest-list means you are meticulous and pay a great deal of attention to the finer details of your work. Any other list indicates a need for caution in money matters and decision making.

LIPS, LIPSTICK *Licking your lips suggests envy; kissing someone on the lips shows emotional volatility; and lipstick suggests vanity and selfishness.*

LIVER

Eating liver in a dream indicates that you are in the best of health. The further meaning of the dream depends on the type of liver you are eating: if it is calves' liver, you feel you are being picked on for some reason; pig's liver denotes your impressionability; and goose or chicken liver means your efforts are to no avail.

LIVERY

Dreaming of a servant dressed in livery indicates that you already have a comfortable degree of financial well-being, and also foretells more social advancement in prospect. For a young person the dream can also mean marriage to a wealthy person they already know.

LIVING TOGETHER

Living together can often cause difficulties in real life, and the same is true in dreams. Any dream involving living with someone of the opposite sex is a danger signal: someone is making excessive demands on your time and emotions. Sharing a home with someone of the same sex, however, indicates that you are heading for a possible deception in love, and if you dream of sharing with someone you do not

LOAF *Brown bread in a dream suggests imminent financial gains.*

know, you will soon have to confront many different problems which may not necessarily be of the emotional kind.

LIZARD

This is an unfavourable dream, indicating enemies lying in wait for you.

LOAF

A loaf of brown bread in a dream is a sign of major financial gains, while a white one signifies that you are forming projects for the future. A warm loaf reflects your partner putting your courage and faithfulness to the test. A stale loaf means you are about to enter a short period of discouragement and unhappiness, and an overcooked or burnt one means you should not make a fool of yourself by getting involved in something pointless and time-wasting. Buying a loaf of bread means excellent prospects on the work front, and eating one means you need to be more aware of your own responsibilities.

LOAFING

If you dream about spending time loafing around doing nothing, it indicates that your anxiety about the course of a relationship with some-

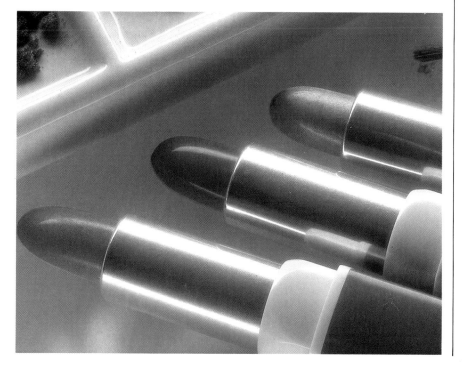

one of the opposite sex has become obvious to everyone but that you should stop worrying because these fears have no basis in reality. Seeing a woman loafing around means differences and disputes with the person you love, because of excessive jealousy, while a man loafing around means you are likely to make mistakes in your work. You could also meet with unexpected problems in your social life and with your friends.

LOCOMOTIVE

Not surprisingly, a locomotive in a dream indicates either that you are about to go on a journey or the arrival of someone you love. A moving locomotive means that a period of happiness is in the offing, but if the locomotive is stationary, you are still awaiting urgent news. A locomotive being derailed means you are feeling unsettled and anxious.

LOCUST

A swarm of locusts in a dream foretells some kind of risk or danger. Seeing a single locust eating a plant foreshadows a journey in the near future.

LOSING

Losing a watch means that you have new ideas to try out, while if you lose any other object it means unexpected changes are in the offing. Losing a bet reflects your arrogance and presumptuous behaviour, while losing a race or game means you are getting into bad habits. Losing an argument indicates a business trip is coming soon. Losing blood suggests a need to stick up for somebody or alternatively for them to stick up for you, and losing your voice means that you are wasting time in fruitless gossip.

LOTTERY

Dreaming that you are taking part in a lottery is a bad omen from the romantic point of view. It indicates risks and uncertainty about the future, or more precisely it can mean that the behaviour of your partner is worrying you a great deal, and making you very unhappy and unsettled.

LOVE

Dreaming about falling in love means that someone loves you, and will tell you so very soon. If you dream about love passing you by, it in fact means that you are shortly to fall in love and get married. This is another dream which indicates the opposite of what you might expect.

LOVERS

Dreaming about two happy lovers heralds new experiences involving the opposite sex, and a lovers' tiff foretells happiness and harmony with a partner. Dreaming about being attracted to your own partner means you are faithful to each other, but if he or she is pale and unhappy, there is the chance of one of you succumbing to an affair with someone else.

LUGGAGE

This is not a happy symbol to appear in a dream, as it indicates everyday difficulties and problems. The

LUTE   The sound of a lute may bring joyful news from a faraway friend.

heavier the luggage in the dream, the greater will be the problems in store for you: these may take the form of a debt, an injustice, someone leaving you, or an unexpected item of expense.

LUTE

Hearing the pleasant strains of a lute in a dream means that you can expect good news from a distant friend; that after an argument with someone you know things will calm down; and that your happy emotional life will help you get over any minor obstacles which may be placed in your path.

LUXURY

This is a dream which signifies the opposite to what might be expected: if you dream about living in luxury, surrounded by material goods and comforts, it in fact means that you can expect financial losses and general difficulties. As far as love is concerned, it indicates arguments and jealousy.

LOVERS   Two lovers suggest the start of a new relationship.

What use are dreams?

We know that man cannot live without dreaming, and being deprived of dreams can cause psychological imbalance and difficulty in coming to terms with reality. We also know that dreaming takes place in colour, even though it may not be remembered in colour after the dreamer has woken up: this is probably because dreams are so fleeting that only their most important features are remembered, and this may not include colours.

Why is it so important for us to dream, given that the actual meaning of the dream is often impossible to determine? Psychology has helped to answer this question: dreaming is a kind of safety valve, because it allows us to live out our desires, including those which are completely secret, as well as our hopes, our fears and our frustrations.

When we dream, we are able to free ourselves from many of the tensions that build up in our everyday lives. We can camouflage aspects of ourselves or our lives which we have trouble coming to terms with, in the form of images which are less

disturbing to us than reality itself is.

Dreams express problems, anxieties and states of mind; they recreate in symbolic form experiences we have had which have struck a particular chord in our subconscious. An event or a word whose meaning we did not appreciate at the time can be shown to us in a different form in our dreams, giving us a better understanding of its significance.

A dream is a representation of our inner world. In it every person, every image is a sign, a word in a language which we do not fully understand, but which is capable of being understood. This dream language can consist both of personal symbols, created by the person dreaming, or universal symbols, relating to the outside, material world and common to everyone because they exist in everyone.

Inside us, there is a part of our personality which we barely understand and which we give little space to express itself. At night, the Ego, the rational part of our minds, takes a back seat and our unconscious can reveal itself to us and communicate with us.

LYING

Lying to your parents in a dream indicates that you are involved in a friendship which is doing you more harm than good; lying to a friend indicates concealed hatred of someone; lying to your loved one, suggests that you have differences of opinion with them which will be easily resolved; and lying to someone you work for means that a worrying piece of news connected with work is on its way.

LYING DOWN

Lying down in a dream signifies weakness, and may indicate temporary illness or unhappiness. Lying down with someone else signifies happiness.

LYNX

Dreaming about a lynx means things are going wrong for you, especially if the lynx attacks you or someone else.

MACHINERY

Watching or inspecting any type of machinery in a dream has a generally positive significance from the point of view of work. It indicates success and progress being achieved despite problems and differences of opinion, as well as your having to take on very hard work, sometimes for not much money. If the machinery causes you fear for

MACHINERY To dream of machinery means work is going well.

some reason, it means you may be confronted by serious problems and obstacles caused by a lack of ability to get things done.

MACKEREL

These lively fish, constantly on the move are a sign of success in a dream, particularly in the business world. A dead or rotting mackerel is therefore an indicator of bad news which is difficult for you to accept.

MADMAN/MADWOMAN

Dreaming of mad people in a hospital or asylum indicates that you have recently undergone some unjustified humiliation, while mad people in the street suggest hostile gossip going on behind your back. If the mad are confined to their beds, perhaps in a straightjacket, your nerves are in shreds at the moment and your mind in pieces. Seeing a mad person shouting, or talking to themselves, means you are making an exhibition of yourself and possibly harming your interests or reputation as a result. A madman or woman laughing means it is best to put off new financial ventures for the time being, and one crying means you will receive an unexpected but welcome gift. Being mad yourself means you love someone else and that they love you; killing someone else who is mad indicates that a misdeed in the past will now catch up with you and bring unpleasant results.

MAGIC

Dreams involving magic are not as common as one might suppose, but usually they indicate the arrival of news, possibly leading to a major change – for better or worse – at work. These dreams show that although things may be happening in your life at the moment which are hard to understand – such as the loss of a friend – they will start to make more sense as time goes on.

MAGISTRATE

The idea of being up before a magistrate may not be an attractive one in real life, but as a dream it can have positive implications. If the magistrate finds you guilty, you can expect a period where very little goes your way, but if he finds you not guilty, you are going to be happy for some time. If you dream you are a magistrate yourself, it means your hard work will achieve the desired results.

MAGNET

The magnet is a symbol in dreams of power-games in relationships. Using a magnet yourself means you want others to do your bidding and bow to your will, but if someone else uses one, this person is trying to exert their influence over you in real life.

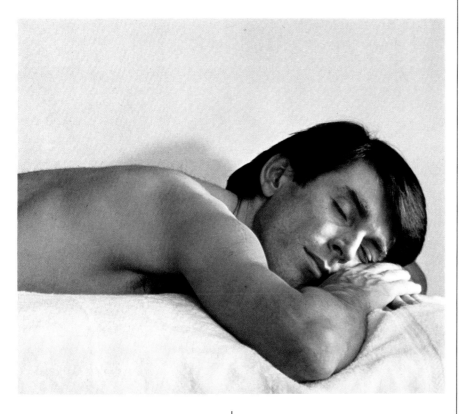

MAN   A good-looking man is a sign of health and happiness. If he is tall, though, you should lower your sights.

MAGPIE

These elegant black and white birds with their thieving nature are not an auspicious omen in dreams: they foreshadow problems within your family, which are likely to increase in seriousness in proportion to the number of magpies you see in your dreams.

MAN

An attractive male in a dream is a sign of happiness and health, and an ugly one denotes your uncertainty in emotional matters. If you dream of a tall man it means that you are setting your sights too high and you should adjust them, while a short one reveals that you have an adaptable, practical nature. Dreaming about a deaf man indicates that a secret to which you are privy must not be revealed to others, whatever happens, and a blind one reflects the fact that you are restless and lack confidence.

MANURE

Manure, surprisingly enough, is an entirely favourable thing to dream about, especially from a financial point of view: it indicates material well-being, profitable ventures, and hard work being rewarded.

MAP

Any dream which involves looking at a road map or street map suggests you have a craving for new experiences and new horizons, and that in fact you will soon go on a long trip abroad which will satisfy this need.

MARRIAGE   Going to a wedding means there is good news on the way.

MARBLE

This material usually indicates that the dreamer is an unusually cold and rational person. If it is white marble, you are well off financially, and if it is any other colour, you are worried about a younger member of your family. A glass marble, or a game of marbles, means that you are taking risks at the moment, but that they will probably pay off.

MARKET

Dreaming about a market is a favourable omen in a dream, particularly if you are unattached. This dream shows you have a high degree of flexibility which will stand you in good stead in your work, as well as an open-minded personality which allows you to form long-lasting relationships with people. If you are not in love with anyone at the moment this dream indicates that you soon will be falling in love. You can also expect some other pleasant surprise which will make you particularly happy. If you are a married woman, on the other hand, a market signifies imminent jealousy and betrayal.

MARRIAGE

Dreaming about a marriage is not the happy omen it might seem to be: if you are the one getting married, it

MARSH   Struggling across a marsh suggests tricky times ahead.

indicates resentment and friction with someone which will last for a long time; there will also be a major financial loss which will have a bad effect on your living standards and may also adversely affect your health. Going to someone else's wedding, fortunately, means there is good news on the way.

Getting married because you love someone in a dream shows an enthusiastic approach to a new project at work, while being forced to get married against your will, for example in an arranged marriage, signifies that you can look forward to a lively and eventful period in real life. Marrying someone for their money means you are behaving nervously and irritably. A secret marriage suggests you are very uncertain and confused because of a disappointment in love.

MARSH

If you dream about walking across marshland, there is a period of worry ahead and a difficult problem for you to tackle. If you get stuck in the mud, it means you will attract displeasure from others, but if you manage to get across to the other side without too much trouble, there are better times ahead. With regard

to personal relationships, dreaming about a marsh indicates that you are about to enter a difficult period when everything on the emotional front seems fraught. However, this phase will pass and leave you stronger.

MARTYR

Being a martyr in a dream indicates that you have the characteristics of one yourself, being a generous and honest person who will make great sacrifices for something you believe in. Martyrdom in dreams also shows that in the future you will be decisive enough to bring all your personal projects to a successful conclusion. Seeing someone else dying for their beliefs is a sign that

MASK   This symbol reveals an envious streak in the dreamer.

you should not start getting things out of proportion or exaggerating their importance.

MASK

Just as masks are often used in real life to conceal the truth or hide faults and defects behind a superficial attractiveness or feigned sincerity, so in a dream they suggest that you or other people are being duplicitous and secretly jealous. Putting on a mask yourself in a dream means you need to look closely at your relationship with your partner to uncover the cause of the problems you are having at present.

MASTIFF

Dreaming about a mastiff indicates a very pleasant surprise in the offing: you will find that someone who you had thought disliked you is

in fact strongly attracted to you. If a woman dreams about a mastiff, it means her partner is faithful to her, but if you or someone else gets bitten by a mastiff, one of your friends has just let you down badly.

MATCH

As with any flame or fire in dreams, lighting a match is a favourable indicator, meaning fulfilment in relationships with the opposite sex. But blowing out a match has less pleasant connotations, indicating that you will soon have to make a painful sacrifice. A box of matches in a dream is a symbol of an impending pleasant surprise, provided you are able to keep a secret entrusted to you.

MATTRESS

A mattress in a dream symbolizes peace and tranquillity of mind combined with an unusually high degree of firmness and decisiveness. If it is an old mattress, it indicates that you will be given some advice which will prove very useful in your work; if it is a new one, spiritual renewal is indicated. A double mattress reflects your desire to get your relationship with your partner on a sound and lasting footing.

MAZE

A maze in a dream is always a sign of problems, sometimes serious ones. Getting lost in a maze indicates uncertainty and indecision about which course to take in your life, while finding your way out of one means you have solved a major problem.

MEDAL   Confidence is high if you dream you are receiving a medal.

MEADOW

A meadow full of flowers in a dream indicates that your happiness and trust in your partner is being reciprocated by him or her. A newly-mown meadow indicates a worrying state of sadness and depression, and one with thick grass indicates illusions and vain hopes about the future. If you dream about walking through a field, you are set in your ways and most people would regard you as rather staid and conventional, while if you are sitting or lying in a meadow, there is pleasant news on the way. If you dream of going to sleep in a meadow you will soon experience a period of happiness.

MEASURING

The meaning of this dream depends on what is being measured. Measuring fabric means you are behaving pretentiously, and measuring an item of clothing means you are over-sensitive and selfish. Measuring land indicates faithfulness in love, and measuring the height of

MEADOW   Flowers in a meadow mean your partner returns your love.

anything means you have a tendency to superficiality.

MEAT

Any dream which involves buying meat or cooking it is a sign of your prosperity, but eating meat reflects your disagreements with someone. Frozen or packaged meat is a symbol of falsehood and deception, and rotting meat means your health may be at risk in some way.

MEDAL

Being given a medal in a dream means you are going through a period of confidence in yourself and in your potential at the moment, so this would be a good time to get started on a project you have been thinking about for some time. If it is a gold medal you are given, there is unexpected news on the way, which will please both you and your family, while a silver one means that reserving your energies for a while will stand you in good stead in your work.

MEDICINE

If you dream about taking a medicine which leaves a bitter taste in your mouth, this is an optimistic omen. You will come to realize that a predicament or person which you thought were a hindrance can actually be of great help to you. Although there will also be problems in your relationship with your partner, these will only serve to strengthen the ties between you.

MEETING

Holding a meeting in a dream indicates that you are discontented and dissatisfied because of a lost opportunity, while taking part in one means you have a strong sense of responsibility and are decisive in everything you do. If the meeting is a particularly noisy one, there is a period of contentment on the way which others will be envious of.

MELON

A melon is a very pleasant omen in a dream, predicting a time of happiness and good fortune. You will finally be able to put a stop to a dispute that has been going on for a long time, while in relationships with the opposite sex, this fruit

MELON   This heralds happiness and the end of a disagreement.

symbolizes faithfulness and the fact that you are now ready and willing to commit yourself to someone. The only negative note is in relation to health matters; someone in your family will fall ill but, as long as he or she gets proper treatment they will emerge healthier and stronger than they were before.

MELTING

This has a generally unfavourable significance in dreams, depending on what it is that is melting. Gold being melted down indicates sadness and discontent, and silver indicates that although you may not seem to have any financial problems at the moment, this may not be the case for much longer. Melting ice is a sign that you feel something is getting out of control.

MENDING

This is not a very frequent subject for dreams, but its significance is a largely favourable one. Mending a shoe or any other item of clothing means you are open-minded and have a strong sense of responsibility. Repairing a net foretells a period when everything will go your way: you will finally win the affections of the person you have set your sights on for so long, while at work you will receive a well-deserved promotion.

MENTAL HOSPITAL

This dream can indicate either good or bad news. If you dream about being admitted to a mental hospital this shows that you need to be less confused about events as things will turn out all right in the end. If you dream about visiting a mental hospital, it is likely that you will disagree with your superiors at work or even with your parents. Coming out of one indicates a break with the past which may be difficult to make, but which will be followed by a period of greater happiness.

METAL

The appearance of metal in dreams reflects the fact that the cold and hard properties of this substance are also shared by the dreamer, though different metals can mean different things and so you should also look up the separate entries for the various metals. On the whole, though, dreaming about metal indicates that you should make more of an effort to relate to people on a personal level.

MICROSCOPE

Looking through a microscope in dreams suggests that you are trying to peer into the truth that lies behind appearances: in other words,

you are suspicious of someone and of what you see as their insincerity, but this over-sceptical state of mind is making it hard for you to see everything else in perspective. If you try to take life a little less seriously, you will realize that your suspicions were unfounded.

MILKING

Generally speaking, to dream of milking an animal symbolizes prosperity and abundance, though the precise meaning of the dream depends on what animal is being

milked. If it is a cow, there are unexpected financial gains on the way, but if it is a goat it indicates that there is a slightly childish side to your character, and your whimsical behaviour could damage your reputation.

MILL

Seeing either a windmill with its sails turning, or a watermill with its wheel revolving, in a dream means that an important project you were involved in at work will be a success and will bring you both job satisfac-

Nightmares and fantasy animals in Flaubert's dreams

One of the most famous writers to draw inspiration from his dreams was Gustave Flaubert. He normally slept only five hours a night, but he said "the sixth hour of my sleep is given over to dreaming". He would reach for his notebook when he woke up, to record his dreams, and he would refer to this notebook while he was writing his novels and stories.

In his *Temptation of Saint Anthony*, Flaubert recounted some of the events that had happened in his dreams. Odilon Redon, the famous painter and engraver who illustrated the book with a series of beautiful lithographs (example shown at right), observed: "If you had not known that Flaubert conceived this book in his dreams, you would have been afraid of him and his wild imagination."

Redon was not exaggerating. Judge for yourself by reading an extract from the *Temptation*:

"Endless ranks of terrifying animals appeared: the Tragelaphus, half goat and half ox, the Myrmicoleo, whose rear part was that of a lion, and whose front was that of an ant, with its genitals back to front; Aksar, the python, sixty cubits long, which struck fear into the heart of Moses; the giant weasel, Pastinaca, which kills trees with its smell; the Presteros, which turns anyone who touches it into a gibbering idiot, and the Mirag, the horned hare which lives on islands in the sea. The Fulminant Leopard has a belly that has been ripped apart by the force of its roaring; the Senad, or three-headed bear, which tears its

offspring to pieces by licking them, and the dogs of Sepo which spill blue milk onto the rocks from their teats . . ."

tion and the respect of others. If the mill is derelict or simply not working, both your work and your relationship with your partner are stagnating at the moment, and if you do not make an effort to change matters the situation could get worse.

MIME

Using gestures to express what would normally be said in words is not a favourable omen in a dream. It means you have just met someone who, as time goes on, will prove unworthy of the trust you have given them. Nor are things going particularly well in your relationship: your partner is going through major problems and will be relying on you for help and support.

MIRROR   A large mirror reveals that the dreamer has an impulsive nature.

MINE

A mine or a quarry serves as a warning in dreams: it foreshadows a period of many uncertainties, risks and doubts in your life. Therefore you need to use all your rational and analytical skills to avoid making mistakes, as these could be particularly harmful to you at the moment. The dream can also indicate an unhappy break in relations with someone of the opposite sex. A mine of the kind used against enemy troops and ships indicates that hidden dangers may be lying in wait for you.

MIRROR

A large mirror in a dream suggests that you have a changeable, flighty kind of character: take care, because your eccentric behaviour could upset your partner. A small mirror, on the other hand, means you are unjustifiably frightened or shy of doing something.

MISER

Dreaming either that you see a miser, or that you are one yourself, indicates that you have to confront a wide variety of problems: your financial future is shaky, you will become involved in minor affairs without your partner's knowledge, and your plans and ambitions will not be successful.

MIXING

Mixing any kind of cake or pastry in a dream indicates a short-lived infatuation, and mixing a salad suggests that your health may worsen for the short while. Mixing drinks, such as cocktails, means that you are filling your head with unrealistic ambitions and ideas. Mixing cement means that a relationship which is slight at the moment will become a lot closer as time goes on.

MONEY

Provided it is not present in excess, money in your dreams is always a harbinger of good luck. If you dream about giving away money, it shows that you can expect a period of financial stability and prosperity, while if someone gives you some money in a dream there will be a major new development such as the birth of a baby or a significant success at work. Finding money is a very common theme in dreams, and it indicates a change for the better in your work or in your relationship with your partner.

MONEYBOX

An empty moneybox in a dream indicates that a difficult and time-consuming task lies ahead of you which will be exceptionally successful if you keep at it until the end. If you dream about buying a moneybox, your patience and honesty will eventually get you over some minor difficulties in your private life, particularly where children are involved.

MONKEY

The monkey is an inauspicious sign, indicating that you are surrounded by lies and deceit.

MONSTER

Not surprisingly, meeting any kind of monster in a dream is not a favourable indicator: it means you are going through a time when you are particularly depressed and pessimistic and this is making it difficult for the people you meet from day to day. Seeing a monster in the distance indicates emotional disagreements with someone, and being attacked or chased by one reflects your being disheartened by the failure of something you were involved in.

MOOD

Paradoxically, being in a good mood in a dream suggests that you are tired and unhappy in real life; you should try not to get too wrapped up in yourself and not to be so difficult with your partner. If you dream about being in a bad mood, you can expect major problems involving the law in some way.

MOON

Dreaming about the moon, which is a symbol of peace and harmony, is a very hopeful sign, particularly from the romantic point of view. The particular phase of the moon is also very important to the dream's interpretation. A crescent moon can indicate mental confusion and problems with your partner, though the latter should easily be overcome. A half moon indicates a hazardous journey, and if you see a full moon in a cloudless sky, a period of great happiness is in prospect, with the chance of a new relationship with someone of the opposite sex.

MOSQUITO

Mosquitoes bring good fortune in a dream if they are flying high up, but if they bite you this indicates your feelings of jealousy and enmity toward someone. If you hear them buzzing, it means there is unpleasant gossip going on about you.

MOTH

A moth flying around outdoors in a dream is a good omen, but if it gets trapped indoors you can expect some minor problems; fortunately, these problems will be overcome without too much difficulty and will soon be behind you. A moth fluttering around a light symbolizes short-lived conquests in love – as one would expect! A dead one indicates that there are hidden dangers facing you.

MOTHER

It is very common to dream about your own mother, and for that matter any other relatives. The dream indicates that you are having difficulties with your partner – although this

MOTHER   Dreaming of motherhood suggests short-term romantic problems.

state of things will not last for long if you take the hint and sort out the problem rather than leave it to resolve itself in a less satisfactory way – and that you are turning back to your old family ties for emotional security. Seeing your mother crying means you are already anxious about something and there are more problems to come.

MOTHER-IN-LAW

The appearance in a dream of a mother-in-law that you get on well with actually indicates gossip and arguments within your family. An elderly mother-in-law in a dream is a sign of your flexibility and adaptability. If you argue with your mother-in-law in a dream, you will make an interesting new friend, while if you patch up your differences with her and endeavour to

reach a better understanding with her in future, there is pleasant news on the way.

MOTORCYCLE

This dream can have a wide variety of meanings. If you dream that you see a motorcycle you are about to succeed where others have failed; buying one means you will eventually receive the fame or, perhaps, notoriety you deserve; and selling one means recouping or being repaid some money. Driving a motorbike suggests the possibility of obstacles and difficulties at work, and falling off one indicates a generally unstable financial situation. Seeing or taking part in a motorcycle race means that help from an unexpected quarter will extricate you from a difficult predicament.

MOULD

Dreaming of the moulds used for making food dishes, such as jellies, indicates your lack of enthusiasm about something. Dreaming of the kind of mould that grows on cheese, on the other hand, means that although things have been stagnating over recent months, you have now taken action to remedy the situation and make life more interesting.

MOUNTAIN

This is a favourable sign to dream of in most cases. If you dream about being at the top of a mountain, or a high hill, everything will go well from the point of view of work, and you will soon be rid of any hindrances or obstacles standing in your way. Coming down from the summit of a mountain means you are being too timid and too melancholic, and both these traits could land you in trouble in your everyday life.

MOURNING

As is often the case when death or misfortune occur in dreams, mourning is, paradoxically, not a sign of a bereavement in real life. Wearing mourning dress in a dream foreshadows an unexpected but very happy event, and dreaming that

your family is in mourning suggests that the dreamer has abilities and qualities which bode well careerwise and emotionally.

MOUTH

Although the meaning of the dream can vary depending on the exact circumstances, the mouth usually signifies trouble of one kind or another. An open mouth indicates a recent argument, and a closed one your unjustified fears about something. A laughing mouth suggests that you are facing an awkward situation, and a crying one signifies your current behaviour is reckless. If the mouth is grimacing, the dream shows your present lack of flexibility in both your private and professional life. However, if the mouth is toothless, the dream indicates that you should be making a great deal more effort to come to terms with a situation that you do not, at the present time, understand.

MOUNTAIN   To be at the summit reflects success at work.

MOVING HOUSE

Most dreams which involve someone moving house are favourable ones: your present anxiety and nervousness will disappear and be replaced by an enviable state of contentment and calm.

MOWING

The significance of this dream depends on what is being mown: if it is a field of grass, you are worried about something that is about to happen; if corn or barley is being cut long-term prospects for the future are bright although you may have to overcome a few minor difficulties. Mowing a lawn is a sign of good health.

MUD

Dreaming of mud indicates that serious difficulties of some kind may be lying in wait. If you fall into mud, intrigues or plots are being hatched against you; if you get mud on yourself or your clothes, the health of someone you know is shaky; and walking through mud means that hard times are on the way and that you will have to adjust to your new circumstances.

MULE

Dreaming about a mule suggests malice and foolishness, arguments with friends, and wasted effort. A sleeping mule shows a feeling of security, and a laden mule indicates that profits are on the way.

MUSEUM

If you dream about going to a museum, it is likely that you are going through a period of unhappiness and boredom. You ought to try to find new interests and get involved in new activities or the situation will go from bad to worse. If you visit a museum of ancient civilisations in the dream, the main cause of your unhappiness at the moment is that you feel disappointed because someone does

MUSHROOM   Expect good luck in money matters if you dream you are gathering mushrooms.

not love you as much as you thought; if the museum contains sculptures or statues of any kind, your depression is caused simply by the fact that you are working too hard. A museum of the prehistoric era, perhaps containing dinosaurs, indicates that you will meet new acquaintances who will turn out to be very important in the future.

MUSHROOM

Collecting mushrooms in dreams brings good luck, usually in connection with money. Eating them indicates a slight illness or injury. Dried mushrooms indicate unexpected obstacles being placed in your path.

MUSIC

Most people dream about music quite often, and it is invariably a hopeful sign. It suggests that you are feeling particularly relaxed at the moment, and enjoying life more than usual, with the result that you are being more sociable and outgoing in relationships with friends and partners. If you dream about playing music yourself there is an exciting new relationship in prospect which you will remember for the rest of your life. Writing music in a dream suggests you spend most of your day dreaming.

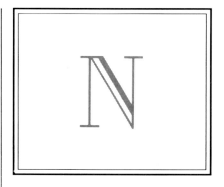

NAIL

The cheaper the metal the nail is made of, the more good fortune the dream promises. An iron nail indicates a solution being found to a problem, but a gold one reflects your worries and preoccupations. Banging a nail into something indicates brief unhappiness, and trying to pull one out means you are sensible and careful in your actions.

NAME

If you dream about someone calling you by name, you are probably feeling highly-strung and irritable; you are going through a difficult time, and you need help and understanding to get you through it. Calling someone else by their name indicates a visit from someone you had totally lost contact with. Using a false name in a dream means you should be more careful because you have been making mistakes by not concentrating on the task in hand.

NATIVE LAND

Coming home to your native land after an absence abroad suggests that a time of considerable happiness is about to begin, and you will start a relationship that will turn out to be a lot more important than you thought. At work, your hard work and dedication will receive their just reward. If you dream about leaving your native land for good, you are about to enter an intense and passionate relationship.

NECKLACE

Dreaming that you are putting on a necklace suggests either advancement in your career or an imminent marriage. Seeing one in a shop, or

round someone else's neck, denotes your present feelings of jealousy and resentment. A pearl necklace indicates that a short period of gloom and despondency is coming.

NEEDLE

Pricking yourself with a needle in a dream foretokens emotional problems involving a friend or relative. Threading a needle suggests you are involved in a difficult task which will require a great deal of patience.

NEGLECTING

Neglecting your wife in a dream indicates that things are going against you, while neglecting your husband, paradoxically, reveals your ability to provide help and support to others. Neglecting children indicates your lack of understanding and resentment; neglecting your mother means there are obstacles looming which you will have to overcome; and neglecting your father shows your involvement in something which may compromise you.

NET

A big trawling net in a dream indicates that you are not spending your money wisely, but a small landing net with a handle suggests a bumpy period in your everyday life. A net being laid out to dry suggests excellent health and self-confidence. Making a net means you have many talents and abilities, and throwing one into the water means you are being unfairly suspicious of someone you have just met.

NETTLES

Growing nettles in a dream, or allowing them to grow, means you are not in control of your life at the moment. Being stung by nettles means you are entering a period of gloom and pessimism and will feel

---

I dreamed I was lost at sea . . .

Sometimes we wake up with the very clear feeling that we have had a bad dream, and it can adversely affect our mood for some time afterwards. Nevertheless, this type of dream needs as much careful reflection as any other, for almost always it offers some kind of clarification of an issue or solution to a problem.

It is not unusual when we are uncertain or doubtful for some reason to dream about walking along a dried-up river bed, or seeing a spring or well which has dried up, just as we are about to drop dead from thirst. Because it is not a particularly pleasant dream, we wake up, and just as we do so, we hear a distant murmur of water which could save us from the situation. Our subconscious is sounding a brighter, more optimistic note, but we have not given it time to express itself fully.

Moving water, be it in the sea or in a river, symbolizes particular aspects of your personality. The strength of the soul is represented by running water: the river scours its bed and creates a constant process of renewal, just as our own minds are constantly being refreshed and renewed, and the sea reminds us that there are distant shores signifying rebirth.

Dreaming about walking towards the sea to bathe has a very clear meaning: it shows a desire to live in the subconscious. Instead of being positive about our lives and making things happen, we want to be freed from responsibility for ourselves and other people.

let down by the behaviour of someone you thought you could trust. For lovers, dreaming about nettles signifies betrayal, but not by your partner; you should not allow others to cause mischief between you because soon you and your partner will be able to find a compromise which will allow both of you the latitude you need.

NEWS

Waiting for news about something in a dream suggests that you need to change direction in some of the things you are involved in at the moment because they are not giving you the results you hoped for. Being given news in a dream indicates satisfaction in your job. If you receive unpleasant news, you can expect to have to postpone a trip abroad because of problems you had not anticipated. If it is pleasant news, try not to get involved in any uncertain or risky ventures, because they will not work out. Worrying news reflects hostility on the part of people you work with.

NEWSPAPER

Reading a newspaper in your dream means you will receive news from a person a long way away. It can also symbolize improvements obtained through perseverance. A daily newspaper means you should not let yourself be misled by appearances, and a weekly or monthly one indicates that you are working hard at the moment. Reading the sports pages means a period of contentment in the near future.

NIB

Dreaming of a pen-nib on its own means you will receive a suggestion which may not be all it appears, while a box-full of them means that you are making judgments based on bias and prejudice. To see drawing nibs means you are being patient and hopeful as you wait for the completion of a long, involved project. A used nib indicates that a love letter is on its way, and a new one foretells the arrival of good news from a long way away.

NICHE

The appearance of a niche in a wall, perhaps in a church, is not very common in dreams, but it suggests that you are an introverted, shy person who feels alone even in a crowd and tends to hover on the fringe of a conversation. If you get too wrapped up in yourself you will start creating a world of your own which bears no relation to the real one, and this could be very harmful indeed. If the niche is empty, you are also facing a very difficult task at the moment, and if it has a statue in it, you will overcome your uncertainty with the help of someone close to you.

NIGHT

Just as night has many unpleasant connotations in real life and in literature, so dreaming about the night indicates a period of crisis and indecision in a person who tends to be introverted and secretive. A really dark night means you are concealing your resentment towards someone who harmed you in the past, but a moonlit or starlit night symbolizes ambitions being fulfilled and the likelihood of an interesting discovery.

NIGHTINGALE

This is a very happy omen to appear in a dream, it foretells joy, success and riches. If lovers dream about a nightingale, theirs will be a happy marriage. If you dream about a nightingale when you are ill, you will soon be on the mend. If you dream that you hear the song of the nightingale, you can expect fortune to smile on you in business matters and an advancement in your career.

NIGHTMARE

It is not at all unusual to dream about having a nightmare. It means you are being heavily influenced by someone else's strong personality, and this could possibly have a harmful effect on you. The fact that you are not very clear in your own mind about matters at the moment is making it easier for this person to dominate you.

NOSE   The shape of the nose determines the meaning of the dream.

NOISE

If you dream about children making a noise outside your house, you should keep your cool and be patient while waiting for the news you are eagerly expecting. Any noise at night in a dream means you need much more rest and relaxation than you are getting, but traffic noise indicates success in your career.

NOSE

This is not a very common thing to dream about, but it has all sorts of interesting connotations. A bulbous nose reflects good personal relationships; and a red one, the loss of something important, probably a piece of paper; a long nose denotes impulsive actions; and a turned-up one, promises not being kept. A dirty or runny nose reflects great powers of imagination and creativity, but also difficult relations with a partner.

NUDITY

This very common theme in dreams is primarily an ill omen; if you dream about walking around nude, you are having quite severe emotional problems, possibly due to a failure at work, while sleeping in the nude means you may be cheated by someone you thought you could trust. Seeing someone else naked means you are anxious about the welfare of somebody. If it is a man you see naked, there will be setbacks in your relationship with your partner; and if it is a woman, you are stressed.

NUMBERS

Numbers very often play an important part in a dream, and their significance can be clearly defined. Any dream which involves writing down numbers reveals that you are in an odd situation caused by someone's unpredictable behaviour, and reading numbers means you are calmly confident in your hopes for the future. Rubbing out or changing a number means you are inward-looking and shy, and your relations with your partner involve little real communication. Unfortunately this only serves to make you even more lonely and gloomy.

NUMBNESS

Becoming numb with cold is a warning to take your health seriously. If the numbness is caused by fear, you will need to become aware of your true feelings before straightening out your affairs.

NUN

Most dreams involving nuns reflect a rather proud and ambitious personality. They show that you are close to achieving a result from a project at work and so should not harm this in any way by being big-headed, as you are prone to be. A young nun is a symbol of desires not being fulfilled, and an old one of an experience which could be useful at some point in the future. Dreaming about a nun who is singing is a promise of ongoing happiness with the person you love most; if the nun is dead, on the other hand, a fairly serious illness will affect someone dear to you.

NURSE

Seeing a nurse at work in a dress indicates that prosperity and important financial gains are on the way; a nurse looking after children indicates a faithful relationship with your partner. However, being looked after by a nurse means you feel unwanted at the moment. Pretending to be a nurse yourself means you will receive some news which is potentially very advantageous.

NURSE   A working nurse is a good omen, predicting prosperity.
NUDITY   A nude woman suggests the dreamer is under stress.

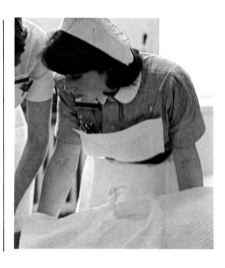

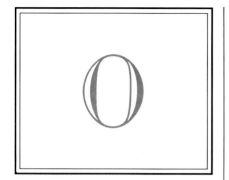

OAK

A large oak tree in a dream is a sign of your strong willpower and decisiveness, but a stunted oak indicates that you may attract enmity and hostility in the future which could be dangerous, and one which has fallen over suggests that an argument with your partner is looming. If the oak has been uprooted, differences of opinion will arise within your family. A leafy oak indicates changes for the better in your work environment, but if it is leafless, you are likely to be surrounded by people who are working against your interests. Cutting down an oak shows flagging energy, and chopping one up shows your present lack of self-control. If you climb up an oak in your dream, you are being far too ambitious, while if you are stretched out beneath one, you can expect a period of excellent health and considerable prosperity.

OAR

Using oars in a dream indicates that an important matter needs to be sorted out as soon as possible, while losing them over the side means there is bad news on the way which could irreparably damage your relationship with someone you love. If the oars are broken, or you break them, you will need to use all your goodwill to overcome a difficult obstacle standing in your way, but if you manage to use them with the necessary skill and row in a straight line, the future looks bright.

OASIS

A dream about an oasis is not always the favourable sign it might seem. Finding an oasis means you

OAK   When covered with leaves in high summer, this much-loved tree predicts positive changes at work.

are being tetchy and irritable and need to calm down and relax for a while. However, drinking from an oasis indicates that you will overcome difficulties by hard work and concentration. Seeing one in the distance means that you will undertake a new financial involvement or venture, but if you do not manage to reach the oasis, there will be minor family problems. If the oasis turns out to be a mirage, oddly enough, your hopes for the future will prove to be justified.

OATS

Dreaming of oats signifies success to the businessman, and fair weather and good harvests to the farmer. If you are travelling, or about to, this dream indicates that the journey will be successful and profitable.

OBEYING

Obeying your own parents in a dream means you have profound and genuine feelings about your partner; obeying someone at work shows that your plans within your job are slowing down and you are worried about the possibility of their running out of steam.

OBSCENITY

An obscene picture in a dream means you are in the midst of major problems; an obscene magazine indicates a lost opportunity. An obscene gesture suggests that you have psychological problems, and an obscene act means you have done something without thinking about it. Dreaming of any kind of entertainment which is obscene indicates that there will be a worrying setback in your emotional life, and reading a pornographic book shows that you are not confident enough about yourself and your capabilities personally or professionally.

OBSTACLE

Meeting with an obstacle which stops you getting on with whatever you are involved in in your dream means that there is a loss of money on the way in real life. Clambering over an obstacle suggests that an interesting suggestion or proposal will be made to you, while skirting round it shows that your beliefs are well thought out. If you dream about placing an obstacle in the path of someone you dislike, you will be unexpectedly insulted or hurt, but if you are only doing this to stop them from catching you, there is a pleasant phase of your life coming up. An obstacle course means that you feel your everyday life consists of one problem after another.

OBSTETRICIAN

If you dream about calling an obstetrician or midwife, you should take extra care because it shows you are worried and on edge following an argument with your partner, and until you can regain your former calm there is no chance of any kind of reconciliation. If the obstetrician helps with the birth of a child, you are about to make a mistake at work which will need correcting as quickly as possible.

OCEAN

Any vast expanse of water in a dream is a good omen, provided it is calm: it suggests an important pro-

OCEAN   Calm seas bring a work project to a successful conclusion.

ject at work is about to be successfully concluded, and you will also make an acquaintance, or even a friend, who will one day be very useful to you. It also suggests things are going well in terms of romance, not least because your own likes and interests are so strongly reflected in those of your partner. If the ocean you see is a stormy one, there is exciting news on the way.

OCTOPUS

Any dream with an octopus in it signifies your spirit of adventure, while an octopus being killed or caught reflects your strong sense of moral right and wrong. An octopus attacking anyone in a dream means trouble in store.

ODOUR

Sensations are often felt even more vividly in dreams than they are in everyday life, and this is equally true of smells. A strong smell means new friendships are coming which will stand you in good stead in the future, but a more delicate one means bad advice is being given to you which should not be accepted. A pleasant smell such as perfume

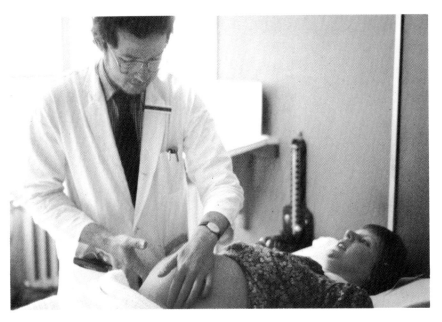

OBSTETRICIAN   This dream image means tension with your partner.

OLIVE   Eating olives indicates that an attractive offer may be made at work.

means a break with a colleague at work, while that of flowers means disorder and chaos in your life. The smell of drink signifies intense but short-lived pleasure.

OFFENCE

This is another dream which indicates its opposite: someone offending you in a dream foretells a period of happiness and inner peace. It also indicates that your boyfriend or girlfriend will give you a sign of their faithfulness and love which shows they are ready for a serious and long-lasting relationship. Offending someone else in a dream, on the other hand, reflects a low level of self-confidence which is being reinforced by problems at work.

OIL

Dreaming of oil tends to be an unfavourable sign unless you are a person who uses it regularly, such as a mechanic or a painter. Castor oil indicates your argumentativeness, and lubricating oil reflects exhibitionism and boastfulness. Vegetable oil and olive oil means things are looking very bright on the work front, but sun-tan oil shows your personality is incompatible with someone you know. An oil-well symbolizes overweening ambition.

OILING

The act of oiling or lubricating anything in a dream indicates that suspicions you are harbouring are totally without foundation. Oiling a lock means that you may face some sort of encounter involving violence.

OINTMENT

Dreaming of a medicinal ointment of any kind signifies good prospects in your work environment, while a perfumed ointment symbolizes that you are being too thoughtless and optimistic in your actions. Making an ointment means that you are, or shortly will be, getting more than usual satisfaction from your job.

ONION   Eating onions is a favourable sign, but peeling them foretells difficulties and danger.

OLD PERSON

Dreaming of an old person who is poor means your apprehension about something is unjustified; a rich one indicates future delays and hindrances in your life; a sick one shows your adaptability to your surroundings; and a dead one means financial benefits are in prospect for you. Seeing an old person who is drunk means you are feeling uncertain and insecure, but if the old person is a hunchback, you will be fortunate and successful in matters of romance.

OLIVE

Dreaming about olives growing on a tree foretells future prosperity, while picking them yourself foreshadows success at work. Seeing someone else picking them, however, indicates that problems are looming for you. Buying olives indicate strong emotions of some kind, and eating them, an advantageous offer being made to you at work. Green olives in a dream signify your good health, but black ones show that you are caught in difficult relationships at the moment. An olive tree signifies work-related doubts and worries, and an olive grove shows that your health has not been good, but is now on the mend.

OMELETTE

Making an omelette in a dream means you are trying hard to save money, and eating one signifies a gambling loss. An omelette with onions in it shows that you will have to make a temporary move; a ham omelette signifies that you will make influential friends; and one with cheese means you are spending time with people who are a harmful influence on you.

ONION

This is a dream which can be both a good and an ill omen; eating onions indicates unexpected gains of some kind, but peeling them means dangers and problems ahead.

OPENING

Opening a door in a dream means you are receptive to new developments. Opening a lock suggests you will make a find or discovery in your own home. Opening a safe suggests you have no secrets from members of your family. If you open a tin, it suggests that something you have recently done will have unexpected repercussions, and opening a box means you will be rewarded for your patience.

OPERATION

Being operated on in hospital in a dream means you like to have the attention of others focused on you all the time, but operating on someone else yourself means you are a generous and caring type of person. Performing a heart transplant means you will succeed in all your plans, and brain surgery means you have still to overcome a major obstacle. Watching almost any kind of operation indicates weakness of character.

OPINION

Dreaming of disagreeing with an opinion shows you have unpleasant thoughts about something, but if you agree with what someone else says, this shows that you are a forceful, decisive person in real life. An unfavourable opinion being expressed means that either you or someone you know well is being obstinate in relationships with a partner, but a favourable one means that any ill-humour you are experiencing will not last very long.

OPIUM

Using any kind of narcotic drug in a dream tends to bring ill-fortune. Taking opium indicates thoughts which are confused and lead nowhere. Selling opium means you are taking on responsibilities which are too great. Seeing other people smoking opium means that you are worried about some setback in your relationship with your partner. Dreaming about an opium smuggler signifies a loss of both money and prestige.

ORACLE

Dreaming of turning to an oracle to find out what the future holds in store suggests that you are confused and disoriented by an unexpected and unpleasant event. However, if you can return to your usual calm state you will soon get over these problems. Being an oracle yourself suggests you have an inbuilt fear of what the future holds for you.

ORAL

An oral examination in a dream means an unexpected event which will dispel any remaining doubts you have about the strange behaviour of someone very close to you (consisting mainly of interfering in matters which are none of their concern). If you dream about taking a medicine orally, it means you are very upset about being separated from someone dear to you, though relatives are providing a certain amount of consolation.

ORANGE

Oranges in a dream signal danger of some kind: this may take the form of a crime, a loss in gambling, or an injury. To lovers, an orange is a symbol of coldness and indifference. The colour orange in dreams indicates passion.

ORATOR

Dreaming of an orator standing on a platform means disagreements and disputes with important people, while if they are in church, you are being critical of a friend, perhaps justifiably. A person making a political speech shows that you have to explain some aspect of your behaviour to the person you love. Making any kind of speech yourself means you have a grievance which you are keeping close to your chest.

ORCHID   A person who dreams of these flowers is lucky: he or she has faithful and loving friends.

*ORNAMENT Expensive ornaments
mean problems may be in store.*

ORCHESTRA

Conducting an orchestra in a dream suggests that you will have problems involving the opposite sex caused by a journey which will take you a long way from home. Playing in one shows that you have finally found the solution to a long standing financial problem. If you are playing a stringed instrument, your energetic and extrovert personality will help you to overcome obstacles which up to now have been insurmountable. If the orchestra is accompanying a ballet or opera, you have been setting your sights too high, and you are about to find this out to your cost.

ORCHID

Dreaming about orchids shows you have faithful friends who will be of great help to you in your hour of need, and giving them as a present means you will shortly experience unexpected pleasures. Growing orchids reflects the fact that unfamiliar circumstances or surroundings are causing you a certain amount of confusion. Buying them heralds a quiet, worry-free period in your life which will allow you to devote more time to the one you love. Orchids in a vase mean you are going to have to be a little less ambitious.

ORGAN

Dreaming of an old organ shows that there are grounds for renewed hope where romance is concerned, while a modern electric one foretokens the arrival of some income which you had not expected. A church organ means that plans made a long while ago will have to be revised. Listening to an organ being played means that you are putting a great deal of effort into your work, and playing it yourself means that a problem which has occupied your thoughts and taken up your energies for a long time will be resolved in the best possible way.

ORNAMENT

This is a dream which mean the opposite of what it ought to logically. The more attractive or precious the ornament, the more problems there are in store. Ornaments which are cheap and tasteless suggest you have comparatively few worries to exercise you at the moment, but if they are more expensive you are going through many different inner struggles.

ORPHAN

The figure of an orphan in dreams generally reflects unhappiness and misfortunes. A child that has lost both its parents indicates that you have serious worries about the future, while if it has lost only its mother, there are family problems on the horizon, and if it is without a father, you are gradually being overcome by sadness. If you dream about being an orphan yourself, it indicates promises not being kept. Welcoming an orphan into your home and looking after them means the conclusion of a particular project at work.

OSTRICH

This curious flightless bird is a good sign in dreams: it indicates good news on the way if you observe one, and social advancement if you manage to catch one. An ostrich being kept in a zoo signifies misunderstandings at work or home suddenly being cleared up.

OUTRAGE

Being outraged by something in a dream shows you are about to take a major step forward in your work, and doing something outrageous, possibly offending other people, means that you are still finding it hard to get over the dislike you feel for a former friend.

OVEN

An oven which is on in a dream brings good fortune, but if it has been turned off, arguments are in the offing. An oven with bread in it is a particularly good sign, but an oven in a crematorium symbolizes a success in love which has only been obtained by flattery.

OVERCOAT

Putting on an overcoat in a dream means an unexpected profit or gain is on the horizon, but buying a new one means family arguments or the loss of a friend. A dirty or torn coat means you have been, or are about to be, disillusioned about the nature of someone's feelings for you which you had believed to be more romantic than they really are.

OVERSEAS

Dreaming about any foreign country means you are somewhat childish and unreliable and unless you can get rid of these traits you will lose the respect and trust of those dear to you. Making a short visit overseas indicates insincerity on the part of yourself or someone else, and if you dream about emigrating, it is an indication that you wish to escape the interference of those around you.

OWL

According to tradition, an owl is a bird of ill omen in a dream, bringing with it illnesses and financial difficulties. If you see or hear an owl hooting in a dream, the outlook is even worse.

OXEN

If you dream about a herd of oxen there is prosperity on the way; oxen grazing in a field are also a good sign, indicating that business is going full steam ahead. Oxen signify marriage and children if dreamed about by lovers. Oxen with very long, sharp horns denote forthcoming problems and difficulties.

OYSTER

An oyster in its shell symbolizes jealousy and argument with your partner, while one with a pearl in it indicates worry caused by a mistake made at work. Buying oysters means that your health has suffered periodic deterioration in recent times and you need to keep a close eye on it. Fishing for oysters symbolizes a time of unusual sadness; prizing them open means your financial future is assured and most of your future life will be spent in relative comfort. Eating oysters shows conflicts within your family caused by their inability to understand something you are doing.

PADLOCK

The precise meaning of this dream depends on the state of the padlock. If it is open, it shows a happy, carefree state of mind, but closed, it indicates laziness, which will cause you a lot of problems unless it is cured pretty soon. A broken padlock means a solution to a work problem is about to present itself.

PAGEBOY

A pageboy bearing the train of a prince or a bride in a dream indicates that things are currently going your way in love and in work. You should try and profit from this

PAINTING   Materials and subject determine the dream's precise meaning.

favourable situation while it lasts. If the pageboy is trying to entertain his master or mistress in some way, it suggests you will be receiving an unexpected visit. Someone dressed in pageboy costume, for instance at a fancy dress party or a carnival, indicates impatience and jealousy.

PAGODA

If you see a pagoda in a dream, it indicates creativity and imagination, while going into one means you will shortly find the solution to a problem which has been troubling you for some time. Coming out of a

OXEN   When in love, oxen mean marriage and children in prospect.

pagoda means you must not forget to carry out the duties entrusted to you by someone else, or you are likely to incur their displeasure. If you see a house built to look like a pagoda, it indicates you are about to embark on a risky venture.

PAIN

Any dream involving pain indicates that you are experiencing small, short-lived problems and irritations. If your eyes hurt in the dream, it is

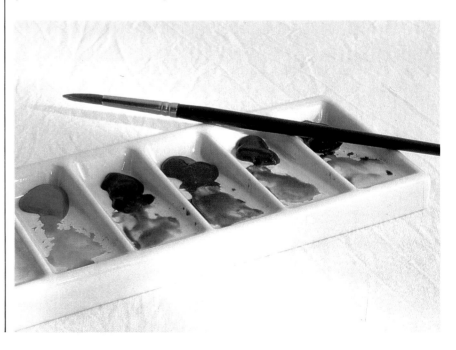

because someone in your family is ill or off-colour; an earache heralds the arrival of unwelcome news; and a headache means that for a while things will go against you to a certain extent.

PAINTER

Dreaming about a painter exhibiting his work should be regarded as a warning: you are at a vital stage in your work, and involved in important projects which will be fundamental to your future career. You should not be discouraged if everything is not working out in your favour, because things will turn out all right eventually. A painter at work shows you will undergo a period of anxiety for no particular reason, while if it is a painter of the decorating variety, a much-needed compromise will be reached.

PAINTING

The significance of a painting in a dream varies with the materials used and the subject of the painting. An oil painting suggests there are difficulties ahead, and a watercolour signifies pride. A still-life painting shows that you are admired by other people, and a landscape means you are at peace with yourself. A seascape is a sign of depression, and a portrait or figure painting indicates short-lived victories.

PALACE

A palace being built in a dream means a change of plan, while one being knocked down indicates tyrannical, overbearing behaviour. If it falls down, a romantic liaison will come to an end. A glass palace is a symbol of a heavy burden to be borne.

PALM TREE

The palm tree is a very auspicious symbol to dream of, indicating success, prosperity and happiness. It is also a favourable omen for anyone who is in love. A date palm means

What value does science attribute to our dreams?

Is it possible to predict what is going to happen by analyzing our dreams scientifically? As we know, from the earliest times man has placed great importance on the interpretation of dreams and used them as indicators of the future and of current behaviour and moods. Now, science has taken an interest in the phenomenon of dreams.

"Recurring dreams are particularly important," explains Hans S. Singer. "Because they show the psychological development of the subject up to now, and his fears and phobias, they can be used to determine what his behaviour will be in certain sets of circumstances. It is in this sense, and only this sense, that dreams can be regarded as an indicator of what is going to happen in the future."

In other words, recurring dreams show what the weak and strong points of our personality are, and can partly foretell what our reactions will be to certain stimuli. The psychologist, the modern-day fortune-teller, can analyze the messages that come from dreams we have repeatedly, and subsequently use them to map our behaviour.

"The old saying that man is the maker of his own destiny contains a great deal of truth," says Dr. Singer. "Many of the situations we find ourselves in are a result of our own choices and behaviour. So a good analyst should have no trouble in establishing what course we are

likely to take in making our own future by his being able to 'read' our dreams."

PALM TREE   Dreaming of palm trees is a favourable sign for anyone in love.

there is interesting news on the way, and a coconut palm means the situation between you and your partner will soon return to normal. An oasis of palm trees signifies new hope where romance is concerned.

PAMPHLET

Handing out pamphlets in a dream indicates that you are having a very short-lived experience of being 'high'. Being given a pamphlet shows that you have clear, well thought-out ideas; printing them indicates that you have new interests, and reading one reveals a morbid curiosity. Political pamphlets suggest jealousy from someone close to you, and religious ones indicate hasty judgments.

PANCAKE

Pancakes always bring good fortune in dreams: sweet ones indicate your thoughtfulness and kind nature, and savoury pancakes indicate favourable arrangements just around the corner.

PANORAMA

A mountain panorama in a dream denotes inconsistency and restlessness, while viewing a panorama with a lake means that you have recently formed friendships that can be counted on. A great expanse of sea means you are being hypersensitive: be careful, because this state of mind could go from bad to worse and make it almost impossible to deal with even the most minor of problems. Stopping to admire a panoramic view, and perhaps taking photographs of it, means you are in superb health and are feeling zealous and enterprising.

PANTHER

Dreaming of a panther in a forest or jungle indicates strong emotions, while one in a cage denotes victory over enemies. A wounded panther means you will find yourself at the centre of a confused situation and not be able to get out of it, while a tame one indicates a lively, adventurous personality. A hungry one suggests that your enterprising attitude will be recognized and rewarded at work. An attacking panther indicates difficult inner dilemmas, while a fleeing one shows that you have struck a blow against someone who is making life difficult for you.

PANTOMIME

Watching a pantomime in a dream is a warning that you are surrounded by people who lavish praise on you and claim to be friends when you are around, but in reality will take any opportunity to harm your interests. You should take more care in choosing the people you associate with, and base your choice not on their social position, but what you instinctively feel about them. A pantomime also suggests that any minor disagreements with your partner at the moment will be speedily resolved.

PANTS

Unlikely though it might seem, a pair of pants or knickers in a dream is very much a symbol of good fortune. Women's knickers mean there is a change for the better on the way, and men's pants mean an advantageous offer will shortly be made to you. Buying a pair of pants reflects satisfaction with the way your life is going; taking them off means you have a slightly off-beat imagination; and washing them marks the beginning of a very successful and profitable project.

PAPER

Dreaming about paper in any form usually indicates worries of some kind. If the paper is clean, it indicates a small amount of money being lost, but if it is dirty or torn, the loss may be rather more significant. However, notepaper signifies trust and sincerity, while toilet paper brings good fortune. A folded piece of paper means that a small disappointment is a strong possibility in the near future.

120

*PARAPET   A parapet on a bridge
suggests the arrival of guests.*

PARACHUTE

Dreaming of a parachute wrapped up in its bag means that you face a choice between two potential relationships: you should put a great deal of careful thought into which you choose, because it will be a deciding factor in the way things go in the future. Making a parachute jump means you are feeling very self-confident and very much aware of your abilities, but if you see someone else making one, you should take care of yourself because your health may be at risk. An opened parachute denotes an inbred sense of optimism.

PARADE

A military parade in a dream means you are being too exuberantly extrovert and should calm down and approach your problems with more decisiveness and rationality. If you dream about taking part in any kind of parade, you will get involved in a daring and risky venture. Dressing up to take part in a parade means a change of environment would be helpful if you are to get over your current emotional problems.

PARADISE

This dream is naturally a pleasant augury for the future: going to paradise means you will be protected and supported by someone who has a great deal of influence, and being there suggests the possibility that a venture at work, which has previously failed, will now be tried again. Seeing your own father in heaven means you are careful and rational in everything you do, while dreaming that your mother is there means that there will be a sudden change within your family. Dreaming about an earthly paradise – perhaps a tropical palm-lined beach – indicates long-lasting and secure financial prosperity.

PARAPET

The parapet of a bridge in a dream indicates guests arriving; that of any other building means a period of gloom and tedium: try to shake yourself free of your current apathy and get involved in a project at work which offers you a chance to get moving again. Leaning over a parapet symbolizes a very pleasant meeting with someone you have not seen for a long time. Throwing yourself over a parapet in an attempt to kill yourself means you will experience problems as a result of your partner's jealousy.

PARCEL

Dreaming of sending someone a parcel means you can expect a piece of news soon, but receiving one indicates you have already received news and it is not particularly good. Refusing to accept a parcel which arrives suggests you are being firm and decisive; opening it means that short-lived problems lie ahead. If the parcel contains newspapers, you will be put out by a friend's behaviour; if it is books, your current relationship with your partner is about to become cold and unsatisfying. If there are sweets in it, a difference of opinion you have with someone is about to turn into an argument, while if it has cotton wool in it, it indicates that you hold clear, precise opinions.

PARCHMENT

If you dream about an old piece of parchment, you should be careful because one of your friends is becoming jealous of your successes and will soon turn against you, trying to harm your reputation by spreading malicious gossip. An ancient Egyptian parchment with hieroglyphics on it reflects an eventful, satisfying life.

PARDON

If you are in love with someone, asking someone else's pardon in a dream means that there will be worries and setbacks in your rela-

*PANCAKE   Pancakes are the
harbinger of good fortune.*

tionship with your partner because of unfounded suspicions and fears; you need to clear the air by discussing things calmly and reasonably, or you are likely to lose the person involved. If you dream about granting someone else a pardon, you are reacting unreasonably and impulsively to a situation.

PARENTS

If your parents are alive and well in your dream, it means that a person close to you has just experienced a major success, and even if your parents are dead this, paradoxically, indicates a piece of very happy news. If you actually see them in the process of dying, on the other hand, it means there is a misfortune of some kind on the way.

PARK

A public park in a dream reflects satisfaction and fulfilment in relationships and at work, and a private one indicates that you are making friendships that will never be broken. A national park means that you or someone close to you have burnt their boats in a particular situation, or are just about to do so.

PARK   Dreaming of a public park suggests relationships of all sorts are good at the moment.

Going for a walk in a park on your own suggests you should set your sights a bit lower and not be so selfish, while if you walk with someone else, the current state of your affairs cannot continue in their present state for much longer – a radical overhaul is necessary. Getting lost in a park means that an error of judgment could compromise your position at work.

PARLIAMENT

Dreaming of a sitting of parliament indicates that unpleasant gossip and slanderous remarks are being made about you, while if the building is empty it means that a long-standing bone of contention between you and another person has to be cleared up if a much valued relationship is to develop in the way you want it to. If you dream about being a member of parliament, you will meet someone new at work who will turn out to be important and influential. Being a visitor at a parliamentary sitting means good career prospects.

PARLOUR

Dreaming of a parlour where guests are entertained shows that a change is about to take place in a very complicated situation, although things may not be resolved in your favour. A beauty parlour means you should not worry over-much if your partner is not giving you their usual care and attention, because things will soon be back to the way they were before. A massage parlour means difficulties at work which can only be overcome by someone with the right experience.

PARRICIDE

A parricide, someone who has killed a parent or near relative, is a sinister figure who is likely to bring ill-fortune if dreamed about. If he is sentenced to death or prison at his trial, there will be arguments and unhappiness involving your partner, but if he is found innocent, you should control your impulsive nature or you will come off worst in a difficult situation at work.

PARROT

Dreaming you hear a parrot talk indicates your state of worry and perplexed thought. A parrot on a perch means an unstable situation at work, and one in a cage suggests endless bitterness and envy on the part of yourself or someone else.

PARTRIDGE

Like other game-birds, a partridge is not a favourable omen, for it indicates difficulties and obstacles to come. Hunting partridges indicates your attempts to find out the truth of a situation or intrigue, and eating one means difficult relationships with those close to you.

PASSING

Dreaming of passing through a field indicates your susceptibility to unpredictable outbursts of anger. Passing someone you know in the street without recognizing or greeting them means you are putting your own needs before other people, but if you do acknowledge them, you are likely to be a charitable and kind-hearted person. Passing a building without going inside indicates that you do not pry into matters which do not concern you and also that you can keep a secret. Passing an examination means you are particularly worried about what the future holds in store for you.

PASSPORT

Applying for a new passport in a dream means things will go well where romance is concerned, and showing it as you cross a border indicates future financial successes. Losing your passport means you can expect disappointments from the opposite sex, and finding one means you are worried about the health of a member of your family, but there is no need for anxiety because things are far less serious than they seem.

PASTRIES

Seeing pastries in a dream means a pleasant surprise, but eating them reflects a feeling of melancholy and dissatisfaction caused by a series of failures at work. If you do not manage to put the past behind you, you will end up being burdened by additional problems caused by your own frustration and be far worse off than you are at present. Offering pastries to a guest means you do not know what to do about your partner's behaviour, but if you make them yourself and they turn out successfully, you can expect a few minor problems connected with someone of the opposite sex.

PATROL

A patrol of soldiers in a dream shows money being repaid or regained, while a police patrol means luck in sport or gambling, and faithfulness in love. If you dream about being stopped by a patrol of soldiers, perhaps at a road-block, you have considerable grounds for satisfaction in your relations with the opposite sex.

PASTRIES   A pleasant surprise is on the way if you see appetizing pastries in your dream.

PATROLLING

Patrolling the streets of a city in a dream, perhaps in a police car, means you are original and imaginative in your ideas. If it is daytime, you will be the object of the criticism and gossip of others, but if it is night, you are being over-romantic in your relations with your partner and unless you are more down-to-earth you will lose his or her love. Patrolling a forest indicates that pleasant and exciting events are on the way.

PAY

Receiving a weekly wage in a dream reflects a decision taken in too much of a hurry, while if it is fortnightly, you may be showing excessive wastefulness or extravagance. Being paid monthly is a sign of laziness. If you dream about being paid in advance, before you have done the work, it means that

one false move at the moment could cause you a serious loss, possibly of money. Having your pay docked or reduced indicates, paradoxically, a feeling of personal and financial security.

PAYMENT

Dreaming that you have a payment due, which you have not yet made, shows in fact that you are a responsible, thoughtful person who takes their responsibilities seriously. Paying for something you have not bought means you need to change your tactics if you are to achieve your aims, while someone else paying you means that you will face obstacles and delays.

PEA

Peas in a pod in a dream show that a decision has to be reached as quickly as possible. Dried ones indicate your lack of willpower, and frozen

123

ones, the need to look very closely at a suggestion being made to you. Eating peas means you are entering a period when your physical and mental strength will be at a low ebb and you will possibly experience depression; while shelling peas indicates that many of your hopes will come true soon and lead to happiness and prosperity. Planting peas means there will be obstacles to the smooth running of your relationship with your partner.

PEACE

Feeling at peace with yourself and others in your dream means that you are quite the opposite in real life: you are being plagued by doubts and suspicions which will take a long time to go away. A period of peace after anything from a minor quarrel to a major war in a dream means that you are entertaining impossible, unrealizable hopes. Peace which is broken, perhaps by a loud noise, indicates anger and irritability.

PEACOCK

This magnificent bird has long been a symbol of pride and vanity though in dreams it can also show that you are particularly aware of someone else's beauty at the moment.

PEAR   Pears on a tree mean the dreamer is kind and considerate.

PEAK

The peak of a mountain or hill in a dream represents an obstacle to be overcome or a challenge to be met square on. If you reach the top of the peak in your dream, you have solved your present problems and things are going to be much easier from now on.

PEAR

Dreaming of pears hanging from a tree shows that you are sympathetic and understanding. If they are bitter, a sad and unexpected piece of news is on the way, while if they are ripe, they represent happiness at the success of a project at work. Picking pears in your dream denotes long-term health, and eating them means that your relationship with your current partner will be very happy and rewarding and last for a long time. Rotten pears symbolize decisions taken too hurriedly, and cooked ones show insulting, malicious behaviour by someone who dislikes you.

PEARL

Buying pearls in a dream indicates significant problems with money, and selling them means a betrayal which has made you very downhearted. If your dream involves putting on a pearl necklace, the outlook for the time being is not a very bright one. Not only will a long-standing relationship come to an end, but you will fail to take advantage of an opportunity offered to you at work.

PEDAL

The pedals of a piano in a dream indicate a tendency to posing and artificiality: try to be yourself and not to take on airs and graces. If the pedals of a car feature in your dream, you are being ambitious and decisive at work in the hope that your abilities will be recognized, while the pedals of a bicycle show that you are down-to-earth and realistic, without any pretensions to grandeur. The pedals of an organ show that you have a distinctive personality.

PEDESTAL

A wooden pedestal in a dream means helpful advice and support being given to you by a friend which will help you to get out of a difficult situation unscathed. A marble pedestal shows a turbulent relationship with a partner who can be very vain and conceited when they want to be. Getting onto a pedestal, perhaps to make a speech, means you should avoid making decisions in too much of a hurry or you will miss out on a golden opportunity. Getting off a pedestal suggests that there will be a new relationship with someone of the opposite sex.

PEN

Dreaming of a silver pen shows a combative spirit; a golden one foretells pleasant news concerning a relative. A ballpoint pen suggests there is hidden resentment among people around you. A fountain pen symbolizes an important letter on its way, and an old-fashioned quill pen means you are too shy and too pessimistic in your outlook.

PENCIL

Pencils appearing in a dream are normally connected with love and romance. An ordinary black pencil shows you should be careful who you entrust your romantic secrets to, and to be especially so with those people you have only met recently, while a coloured crayon suggests new ventures in the realms of love. A gold propelling pencil indicates the future possibility of a lack of understanding between you and your partner, and a silver one indicates that you feel secure.

PENDULUM

Dreaming of the steady swing of a pendulum in a clock symbolizes the fact that you are reliable, while if it has stopped, many of your current hopes will bear fruit.

How to interpret childrens' dreams

Experts on child development have found that dreaming begins in the first few months of life, and plays a formative part in the process of learning.

Of course, it is not until the child is first able to talk that scientists have access to their dreams through the child's brief, but significant description of what happens in the dream. These dreams are easier to interpret than those of adults, because they mostly reflect simple needs and desires: a home, parents, brothers and sisters, food; any aspect of their daily lives can appear to them in dreams, in pleasant or unpleasant form depending on the child's home environment.

Children's dreams often also contain clear references to fairytales, and to religion: Catholic children, in particular, often dream about Jesus and Mary, and Protestant children not infrequently dream about the devil. There is a great deal of faith in transcendental values, concepts which the child has no experience of but which it believes in. Children also dream about ill-defined fears and dangers which can often lead to their waking up in bed crying or falling out of bed. They also dream, just as adults do, of falling and aimlessly searching for something they have lost.

Sometimes children display aggressive tendencies in dreams, or see their parents dying, perhaps in a car or train crash. These images are fed partly by the beginning of the Oedipus complex, and partly by incidents they read about or see on television.

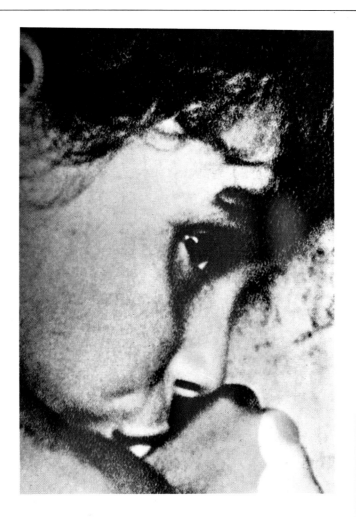

Some experiences tend to be repressed, which may explain why some adults regress to their childhood in dreams. It is important to come to terms with these experiences because, as Jung states, they contain the germ of the individual's destiny and purpose in life.

PENETRATING

Penetrating a barrier such as a wall in your dream indicates your engagement in lengthy, time-consuming but enjoyable activities connected with work. Getting through a hedge means annoying behaviour by someone in your family and tensions in your relationship with your partner. Penetrating a jungle or forest without difficulty means a period of financial security will follow after you have solved your current problems; if you have difficulty doing so, it means you will do something which you will regret immediately afterwards.

PENITENCE

Undergoing any act of penitence in a dream, such as wearing a hair shirt, means a healthy social and financial position, while making someone else perform one means you are uncertain what to do next in your relationship with your partner, but you need to act quickly to save the situation. Feeling penitent in a dream for something you have done in the past indicates a sense of guilt in real life as well.

PENSION

If the pension you dream about is the guest-house variety, it means you are worried by how gloomy and despondent you are feeling, and you should be careful not to get even

more wrapped up in your problems, because then things will start getting greatly out of proportion. Being paid a pension, or going to the post office to cash it, both mean there are problems in the offing involving your family.

PEPPER

The appearance of black or white pepper in dreams indicates your great enthusiasm for a financial venture which looks as though it is going to be a success, but you must be careful, because this optimism

PEPPERS   Dreaming of fresh peppers suggests a tentative proposal.
PEPPER   Unground peppercorns put a spotlight on current financial ventures. Take care to look before you leap.

could turn out to be counter-productive and you could lose out on another, more fruitful opportunity. If the pepper is already ground, you will enjoy good long-term health, but if you have to grind it yourself, you have lots of energy to spare and now would be a good time to take action on a project you have been planning for some time. Putting pepper on your food presages major differences of opinion in an emotional relationship.

PEPPERS

Green peppers in a dream indicate useful precautions being taken; red ones, sociability and human warmth. Fresh peppers mean a very tentative suggestion being made, and dried ones, hard work being rewarded. If the peppers are small ones, you will have an unenjoyable encounter with someone you have not seen for a long time, and if they are cooked, you are feeling very confident. Eating peppers means short-lived problems, and buying them, unforeseen rewards.

PERMISSION

Asking for permission to do something is not a particularly good sign in a dream: in your work, you will get out of your depth in a large, complicated project and end up making costly mistakes. If you give permission to someone else to do something, it suggests you are bottling up your bitterness at someone for what they have done to you recently. If you refuse someone in a dream it shows you are an open-hearted and sociable person.

PERSECUTING

Dreaming of a man being persecuted indicates that you have encountered an unexpected obstacle in your work which only a practical, rational approach will get you past. If your dream involves a woman being persecuted, you will be the target of malicious remarks made behind your back: if you can track down the person who is doing it, you will have the support of your superiors at work.

PERSUADING

To dream of persuading someone to give in to temptation means you have a considerable need for protection, and persuading them to commit a crime, gamble money or do something illicit means there is trouble on the horizon for you. The extent of this trouble depends on the seriousness of the action the person is persuaded to carry out. Persuading someone to buy something means you are having trouble getting others to recognize your talents and hard work.

PHARMACY

A pharmacy is a warning signal when it appears in a dream: going into one means you should pay more attention to who you choose as friends. If you go in during the day in your dream, a slight illness or injury is in prospect, but if it is an all-night chemist's, there may be more serious illness involved.

PHEASANT

A pheasant is a favourable sign in dreams, and coming back from the hunt with a brace of pheasants shows great honours in prospect.

PIANO

An upright piano in a dream indicates struggles and disagreements where love is concerned, while a grand piano shows that your pride and ambitions are both excessive. An out-of-tune piano means that you are likely to get much busier socially and at work, and a brand new one means professional successes and long-term well-being. If you dream about buying a piano, you can rely on the trust and loyalty of a friend you have made recently. If you play it yourself, successes in the sporting

or gambling areas are likely, and if someone else is playing it, it means new and interesting business ventures will develop for you.

PIE

Making a pie in a dream means you have a strong personality. A pie in the oven is a sign of hope; a hot one means financial gains in prospect, and a burnt one reflects a lack of balance in your character. Eating a pie in a dream means you suspect an enemy in your close circle who needs to be exposed for what they really are.

PIER

If you dream about being on a pier and looking out to sea, you are a rather nervous, restless person, engaged in a constant and unsuccessful search for personal fulfilment, but, fortunately, someone is about to come into your life who will change this unhappy state of affairs. If you dream about fishing from a pier, you will soon receive some very happy news. If there are amusements on the pier, you are playing with someone else's affec-

PHEASANT   This beautiful gamebird in a dream is a favourable omen.

tions and doing all of the taking in a relationship but none of the giving.

PIG

A pig in a dream can symbolize both good and bad luck. It suggests that something you are involved in will go wrong, but another venture – which you did not hold very high hopes of – will be a surprising success. Be careful with members of your family, as they may cause you the some distress. If you dream about a pig just before you go off on a journey of any kind, it might be better to postpone it for a while.

PIGEON

This is usually a good sign to appear in a dream. It presages the arrival of news, perhaps in the form of a letter, and if the pigeon is flying in your dream, there will be an important change in your place of work. A walking pigeon means that there are surprises in store, but they may not necessarily be pleasant ones, so be careful!

PILE

The significance of this dream lies in what the pile you see contains: a pile of stones or rocks signifies problems created by people trying to harm you, and a pile of paper indicates that someone will try to be revenged on you. A pile of bodies shows unpleasant complications are developing in your family. A pile of hay means that there will be a sudden unexpected stroke of luck which will bring you very much closer to someone. A pile of books means you have a lively imagination and a slightly eccentric and extravagant personality. Knocking over a pile of plates shows you are unusually practical and decisive.

PILGRIMAGE

Going on a pilgrimage in a dream reflects harmony and mutual understanding in your relationship with your partner. If it is a pilgrimage to a shrine, you are feeling optimistic about the future. Going on a pilgrimage to the Holy Land signifies an improvement in your working conditions. If you go on a pilgrimage on your own, it suggests you may have to fight very hard to maintain your position at work, but if you go with other people, you can trust the person you love.

PILLS

Loose pills in dreams indicate that you will undertake a daring venture with many risks involved which will help you get away from your psychological dependence on someone or something. Pills in a bottle reflect your indecision and timidity: if only you could have a little more confidence in your abilities, the sky would be the limit. If the pills are laxatives, you will shortly reach a more equable relationship with your partner; if they are headache pills, you will experience a disappointment connected with your work.

PILOT

Piloting a plane in a dream shows new and stimulating projects at work; piloting a boat indicates that you have recently got over some

PILGRIMAGE   To go on a pilgrimage shows you have great trust in your partner.

danger, and being the pilot of a big ship indicates both immediate financial gains and longer-term monetary benefits. If you find yourself flying an airliner, you are in a nervous, irritable frame of mind and need to stem your impatience if your work is not to suffer. Piloting a fighter plane indicates that you are confident, and a bomber, the likelihood of a trip abroad.

PINCH

Pinching someone else in your dream indicates that your mood at the moment is a confused, distracted one and you are finding it hard to keep things in proportion. You should try to sit back and calm down, as you have weighty problems to face up to which can only be solved by a calm, rational approach. If someone else pinches you, the indications are that your health is going to suffer, but you can lessen the impact of the illness, or even avoid it altogether, if you look after yourself properly.

PITCHFORK

A pitchfork in a dream signifies a lengthy, burdensome task, possibly with little reward when it is completed.

PITY

Feeling pity for someone or something shows an unusual level of confidence and decisiveness which will help you over obstacles at work that normally you might not be able to deal with. If someone you know expresses pity for you in your dream, attractive opportunities are being opened up for you at work, but they could also be risky or hazardous and you should be careful not to make any false moves or be over-eager to take them up. Asking for someone's pity in a dream indicates a sizeable amount of money coming in, and success in the field of romance.

PIZZA

Dreaming of a pizza piled high with toppings indicates a strengthening of relationships, but dreaming of just an ordinary pizza, with the customary amount of cheese and tomato, shows your lack of concentration and consistency at work. A burned pizza indicates an unexpected success in relations with the opposite sex. If you dream about making a pizza, you are entering a period which is favourable from every point of view, and if you buy one, you will easily get round any obstacles which are being placed in your path at work. Eating a pizza shows that you are throwing yourself wholeheartedly into a new activity or interest.

PLANET

Being an astronomer in a dream and looking at a planet through your telescope shows that projects you are involved in will develop slowly but successfully. If the planet is golden in colour, there will be a reconciliation with your partner after a difficult period caused by your obstinacy. If the planet is black, it shows you have made some ill-advised changes at work or elsewhere, but if it is any other colour it indicates your present feelings of peace and relaxation.

PLANE TREE

A tall plane tree in a dream is a sign of strong friendships unaffected by distance; if it is in leaf, it reflects a long, patient wait for a project at work to come to fruition. A fallen plane tree shows a painful ending to an emotional relationship. If you dream about resting in the shade of this tree, you will enjoy lasting physical health, and if you see one in the distance your health is on the mend after a difficult time. Seeing a large number of plane trees shows common sense and practicality.

PLANT

A flowering plant in a dream indicates unexpected happenings in the near future: if it is in a pot, there will be general changes for the better, but if it is growing in a garden or a field, you can expect interesting developments in relations with the opposite sex. A dried plant means you need to sort out an unpleasant misunderstanding, and a very small one means you have an aggressive, authoritarian personality which insists on its rights in whatever the circumstances.

PLATINUM

Despite the extreme preciousness of this metal, it does not bring good fortune if you dream about it: it shows you are entering a very difficult time of gloom and depression, possibly due to a series of mistakes or lack of success at work. You should not let this get you down, though, as you will soon have the chance to

PLANT   Plants in pots predict day-to-day improvements.

demonstrate your worth to your superiors and you will come to realize that they are still batting for you. A piece of jewellery made wholly or partly of platinum means you are unusually tense, and if you steal something made of platinum the effort you are putting into something at work will turn out to be in vain.

PLEDGE

A pledge of love in a dream actually indicates that you are not keeping your promises and a pledge of friendship shows mistakes needing to be put right as soon as possible if you are not to pay the consequences. If you dream about pledging or pawning a valuable object you will receive help from an unexpected quarter which will get you out of a very tricky situation; if you get it back, problems are piling up.

POPPY   A flower which is associated with short-term happiness.

PLOT

A plot of any kind in a dream is a warning sign: keep yourself to yourself, and keep a close eye on friend and foe alike, because someone is scheming behind your back.

PLOUGHING

The plough is a symbol of good fortune in a dream. If you are female, and you dream about a man ploughing in a field, it shows that your husband, or future husband, is likely to be an honest and hardworking man. If a man dreams about ploughing, it means that his willingness to take on new situations and his adaptability will help him to create an enviable position in society.

PODIUM

An empty podium in a dream shows unforeseen obstacles in your path which your partner will help you to surmount. If there is an orchestral

POKER   Playing poker in a dream suggests your luck is out.

conductor on the podium, you will find yourself heavily involved in a very complicated, delicate situation which it will be hard to extricate yourself from. If you are standing on a podium, you will get overenthusiastic about a success which will turn out not to be a real success at all, and if you are conducting an orchestra from it, you are prone to self-congratulation and are verging on the conceited. Falling off a podium means that the outlook at work is a very bright one.

POEM

Reading a poem in a dream shows that you will soon face a possible business involvement which you should look at very carefully before you commit yourself to anything. Writing one indicates that a solution to your financial problems is on the way. If it is a deeply serious poem, you are an emotional and passionate person, but if it is a funny one, you are in a real mess which you can only get out of by pulling yourself

together and relying on your own good sense. A satirical poem indicates a complex personality, and an epic one, good fortune in financial matters.

POKER

Playing poker in a dream reveals that your luck is not holding up well at the moment and this will mean that you will miss out on more than one golden opportunity. Winning a game of poker means you are worried and downcast by a mistake made in your work, but losing reveals your happiness at an unexpected financial gain. If you are playing for very high stakes in the dream, you are too emotional and impressionable in your personal relationships. Playing poker with strangers indicates embarrassment.

POLICE

In a dream as in real life, the sight of a policeman is usually a reassuring sight which inspires confidence. Although you are going through a difficult time where work is concerned, dreaming of a policeman indicates that you will be helped by the person you love, and their affection will help you regain your self-confidence which is waning fast at the moment. If you get into trouble with the police in a dream, there is no cause for alarm as the dream actually indicates lasting happiness and well-being. Being a policeman yourself in a dream shows that you have a (probably unconscious) desire to meddle in things which do not concern you.

POLICE STATION

Being summoned yourself to a police station in a dream to give a statement suggests that you should try to get over your anger towards a friend you feel has let you down. Going into a police station shows your involvement in a difficult venture or project; coming out of one indicates that you will form a new friendship with someone of the opposite sex which could be misinterpreted by your partner.

POPE

The Pope is usually a favourable sign to dream about. If you dream that you see him sitting on a throne, it shows that you should follow up your new ideas since these will be profitable to you; if he is surrounded by his cardinals, it means you or someone else are very much going against established precedent in your present undertakings, and if he is in procession, you have an unfortunate need to conform which is slowing down your progress in your career. If you dream that you are the Pope, the future will be peaceful and happy. But if you speak to the Pope in your dream there are some small problems to be cleared up with your partner. If the Pope is ill in your dream, it indicates you are worried about something, and if he dies, it indicates that some kind of misfortune is looming.

POPPY

Like many other flowers in dreams, the poppy indicates happiness, though this happiness often does not last very long. Picking poppies in a dream foretells a short romance.

POSTAGE STAMP To dream of collecting stamps reveals obstinacy.

PORCUPINE

Although the porcupine is a pleasant animal by nature, it can inflict a lot of pain as well, and so to dream of it shows you are a likeable person but you often hurt others without realizing it.

PORTER

Seeing a porter carrying someone's luggage in a dream shows that there is a certain amount of hostility going on behind your back, though if the porter is using a trolley, a piece of work you are involved in will turn out very much to your advantage. Being a porter yourself shows fatigue and exhaustion caused by overwork.

POSTAGE STAMP

Collecting postage stamps in a dream shows an obstinacy which sometimes works in your favour and sometimes against you. Buying stamps shows your horizons are somewhat limited and you need to make an effort and start looking for new friends and new interests if you are not going to stagnate completely. Licking stamps and putting them on letters shows a great number of inner conflicts which are proving difficult to sort out.

POSTCARD

Receiving a postcard in a dream indicates the arrival of a surprising piece of news, or the beginning of a favourable new development. Writing a postcard in a dream shows your sense of perspective on matters, but also your worries concerning a friend; collecting postcards indicates that you have made a decision you cannot go back on, though you wish that it was possible for you to do so.

POSTING

Posting a letter in a dream signifies a personal mission to be carried out, and a postcard, minor problems to be resolved. Posting a newspaper or magazine indicates that there are many pleasant distractions in your life at the moment.

POTATOES

Dreaming of potatoes in a field reflects a long period of peace and happiness, and if they are in a bag, unexpected improvements on the financial scene. Picking potatoes means there is a pleasant visit happening soon, and buying them suggests you are making a better job of expressing yourself than you used to. Peeling potatoes means you will overcome various difficulties in your work environment. Boiled or mashed potatoes show that you have satisfied a relative of yours over some matter, but fried ones reveal your lack of understanding in certain situations. If the potatoes are especially large, you will get back some money you had written off, and if they are small, a brief moment of embarrassment can be expected.

POTION

Making a magic potion in a dream suggests that you should look out for cheating and deception going on around you, and drinking one indicates the arrival of interesting news from a long way away. If the potion is made from herbs, you will gain a great deal of money; if it is sweet, you need to be less selfish and make

"The pistol spun, went off by accident, and the bullet hit me ..."

We have already seen how dreams about death can leave us with a feeling of real fear when we wake up from them, but they actually indicate a positive frame of mind. A dream about death in fact can free us from a conflict or problem that has been troubling us.

Of course, there is no single, absolute interpretation of any one dream which applies to everyone. In most cases, situations and symbols can be interpreted along broad lines, and then their meaning is enriched by the purely personal associations they have for the dreamer so that they can be "used" as a way of dealing with reality.

Many dreams about death reveal aggressive tendencies, just as we have seen that dreams about violence do. There are also dreams about death which are closely linked with sex, in particular the idea of sex without love.

"I was standing in a garden. Not far from me there was a man with his back turned towards me. I felt sexually attracted to him. All of a sudden, he turned round and smiled at me. In between us there was a table with a gun on it: it looked like a pistol, but bigger than a usual one. He came over towards me. As he passed by the table, he bumped into it. The gun spun on the table. When it stopped spinning, it went off. I felt myself being hit by the bullet and I fell to the ground."

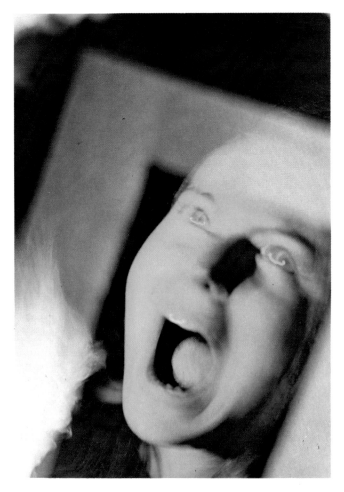

If the dream was analyzed through the personality of the dreamer and her psychological situation, it would give a clear picture of part of her life she had no other way of expressing.

132

PREGNANCY   Dreaming you are pregnant means that life is difficult.

sacrifices if your relationship with your partner is to go the way you want it to; if it is bitter, you are making your presence felt in your work. A medicinal potion means you have a decisive and resolute personality. Making someone else drink a potion shows that you have made a recent error of judgment.

POWDERKEG

A powderkeg blowing up in a dream shows a radical change is being made in some aspect of your job which will leave you disconcerted and perplexed, but if you try not to let it worry you too much you will eventually realize that it is a change for the better. If you dream about having to guard a powderkeg, you are very excited about a new friendship, but it will not work out as well as you had hoped.

PRAWN

Prawns are not a particularly good sign in dreams: if they are alive, they suggest problems connected in some way with the law, and if they are dead, or cooked, they indicate that emotional disappointments are likely in the near future.

PREGNANCY

Dreaming that you are pregnant suggests that you are going through a hard time. If a girl dreams about being pregnant, she will have no trouble surmounting her various problems because of help from other people, but if an older woman dreams she is pregnant she needs to be very patient before she can achieve her aims and ambitions. Strangely enough, it is not at all unusual for a man to dream he is pregnant: it also suggests he needs to fight long and hard to achieve the success he is hoping for.

PRIDE

This is one of the few dreams which reflects exactly what is going on in reality: it means that you are being selfish and ambitious, and creating yourself enemies in the process. Unless you mend your ways, you will very soon pay the consequences. If a woman dreams of being excessively proud it symbolizes the arrival of sad or worrying news, while if the dreamer is a man it shows that your relations with other people are rather superficial. If the pride is justified in the circumstances, on the other hand, perhaps being pride in a special achievement, it suggests you are having an agonizing wait for something or someone in real life.

PRIEST

Dreaming of a priest in a church shows that others are looking after your interests: some of whom you know about, and some of whom you do not. A priest sitting in a confessional indicates that you are harbouring unfounded suspicions. If he is celebrating communion, you will be helped and counselled by people in authority. A priest giving a sermon means you will receive an indication of someone else's concern for you, and if he is blessing his congregation, you are being selfish, vain and materialistic.

PUB

If you see any kind of pub or bar in your dreams, you have feelings for someone who does not return them. Going into a pub in a dream means someone you trust may be deceiving you. If you go in with someone else it suggests you are wasting precious time on a worthless project. Eating in a pub means a woman will lie to you, and drinking in one means you will receive praise shortly which may not be entirely heartfelt. A pub with drunks in it indicates possible enmity arising from your current social and professional position.

PUBLISHING

To dream of having your books published shows that you are bored and depressed with your work; while being published in newspapers or magazines indicates that there is unpleasant gossip about you from people who are envious of your success. If you dream you are a reporter publishing an exclusive interview, you are likely to make great leaps forward in your work. Publishing a review means you will feel less happy than usual in the future, but for no particular reason.

PUMP

An automatic pump in a dream indicates your great happiness at a business success, but a hand pump shows a temporary dissatisfaction with life in general which is getting you down. Using a pump to water a garden suggests that everything seems to be going your way: a strengthening of ties with someone you care for, and increased freedom and independence in your work.

PUNCHING

To be punched in the face in a dream means that you have recently made a bad choice which will cost you dearly. A punch on the other parts of the head means that you are experiencing joys of short duration, and a punch in the stomach signifies your present difficulty in emotional relationships. If you punch someone who has done something to hurt or harm you in the dream, many of your hopes and illusions will be shattered when you receive an unpleasant surprise in real life. Clenching your fists with anger means there will be a serious argument with your partner.

PUNISHMENT

As in real life, punishment is not pleasant in dreams. In most cases, it has an unfavourable meaning: punishing children, for instance, suggests significant financial problems are looming, and, also, if they are your own children, that you are being over-emotional about something. If the punishment in your dream is justified (for example, a criminal receiving a sentence), you have a strong sense of responsibility, but if it is not, you are not managing to make your presence felt at work and to make people feel you are an important part of the team.

PUPPET

Any dream involving puppets indicates your present and future happiness. If you hold a puppet show yourself, it suggests strong organizational capabilities.

PUZZLE

Solving a puzzle in a dream means you have finally taken control of a complicated situation in real life. An easy puzzle means that there are wrongs in your life which need righting, but if the puzzle is very difficult, your worries are fruitless and will go away much sooner than you thought.

PYJAMAS

Men's pyjamas in a dream symbolize your unstable health and unhappiness, while women's mean lack of understanding or agreement with your family. Children's pyjamas incidate a long, agonizing and ultimately fruitless period of wait-

ing. If you dream about putting on pyjamas, your passion for someone else will not be reciprocated, and if you take them off in a dream, it shows you are in an insecure and fragile frame of mind and have a desperate need for affection and understanding. Washing pyjamas means that your personality is an exceptionally complicated one.

PYRAMID

Seeing a pyramid in a dream augurs very well indeed: you are about to begin a period where things go exceptionally well for you. A new relationship with someone of the opposite sex is indicated, as is success at work in the face of apparently insurmountable obstacles. Climbing a pyramid means you are self-possessed, confident and have great willpower.

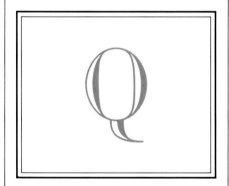

QUAIL

Dreaming of the quail signifies your general uncertainty about matters. Dreaming about a quail in flight can mean news on the way or disappointed expectations. Hunting or eating quail both stand for torment and remorse.

QUARANTINE

This long period of isolation has an unfavourable meaning in dreams. Putting someone in quarantine means an end to an activity or project which was going well up to now, and being put into isolation yourself is a sign of arguments and a possible split from your partner. If your period of quarantine passes slowly and tediously, it indicates that you get depressed easily.

QUARRY   Anticipate a journey after dreaming about quarrying stone.

QUARRY

The meaning of this dream depends on what is being quarried. A chalk quarry presages financial problems, while coal being quarried indicates your high level of energy, and stone, the possibility of a journey.

QUARTET

Dreaming of a string quartet indicates that you have a decision pending which needs to be made as soon as possible. A quartet consisting solely of violins means a long, faithful relationship with the person you love, though malicious gossip by people who are supposedly friends could harm the relationship unless you are wise enough to ignore it. Playing in any quartet yourself means you are feeling extremely confident about yourself and your abilities.

QUARTZ

Coloured quartz in a dream signifies having excessive qualms about something, while plain quartz means uncertain prospects for the future. Rough quartz means that worrying news is coming, and polished quartz, a substantial item of expenditure. If you dream about possessing large quantities of this material, or many objects made from it, you will be forced to go through some unpleasant confrontations with friends to protect the reputation of the person you love, even if you have to break long-term friendships in the process.

QUEEN

A queen sitting on her throne in a dream denotes good fortune and success in business affairs. If you see her waving from a balcony, she heralds the arrival of news from distant parts, and if she is in a carriage, it shows that you may have a lust for power and fame which makes you look ridiculous. If she is side by side with the king, this shows that your enterprises will end in success. A queen bee in your dream means you will enjoy perfect health for some time, but a queen in cards means you are over confident.

QUESTION

Asking a question in a dream indicates a threat is being made to your relationship with your partner, but answering one heralds the beginning of a long and satisfying relationship. If the question you ask in the dream is impossible to answer, you are being very rash and could easily put a foot wrong in your work. If the question has an answer, but the person you ask cannot answer it, this suggests that you are an extremely decisive person who will go to any lengths to enforce what you believe to be your rights.

RABBI

Dreaming about a rabbi in his synagogue foretells good news from a very long way away; if he is preaching, it means you will make an advantageous agreement; and if he is reading, it indicates your present difficulties are being smoothed over. If he is discussing something with others, it shows that you are in an unnecessary state of gloom and despondency over some situation, but if you can pull yourself together and try not to spend too much time pondering, you will see how unimportant these temporary problems really are. Speaking to a rabbi means you are feeling very satisfied with the way life is going at the moment.

RABBIT

Dreaming of a rabbit usually brings good luck, and in many countries its foot, whether in real life or in dreams, is regarded as a particular symbol of good fortune. A rabbit in a dream also symbolizes prosperity and fertility. Sometimes it foretokens a move to a big city, or anywhere else which is crowded. A married woman dreaming about a rabbit can expect a new child in the family. A rabbit crossing a road, on the other hand, denotes imminent danger.

RACKET

Tennis rackets in a dream show an assertive, courageous personality; a squash racket indicates something in your life needs to be cleared up, and a badminton racket, suspicious

RABBIT   A good dream-omen, signalling fertility and prosperity.

behaviour by your partner towards certain people you know. If you dream about buying a racket of any kind, many of your illusions will be dispelled by a piece of news from a long way off. Losing a racket suggests a period of dissatisfaction and unhappiness, fortunately not lasting very long; and finding it again, a large amount of money arriving from somewhere.

RADIATOR

A radiator in a dream normally indicates trouble on the horizon. Dreaming about one which is turned on indicates temporary tensions are looming, while if it is off, you are about to discover an unpleasant secret. Turning on a radiator means an embarrassing situation is coming up for you. The radiator of a car indicates you are being a little too hasty in some of your actions and decisions.

RADIO

Listening to the radio in a dream bodes a pleasant meeting with friends; while turning it off suggests that you are feeling restless in your relationship with your partner. Repairing it means a small financial loss is coming. If you buy a radio in your dream, you will be criticized by someone who dislikes you; if you sell it, you are about to go through a period of relative comfort and well-being. Giving one as a present means you are in a nervous, agitated frame of mind. An old valve radio means you will make an enjoyable business trip.

RADISH

White radishes in dreams symbolize unfounded jealousy and suspicion, while red ones show good health and a high degree of initiative. A bunch of radishes means you are being too withdrawn towards someone who could be very useful to you in your work, and if the radishes are still growing in the ground, you will go through a period in which you are tense and over-sensitive. Eating radishes in a dream means you are very hard-working.

RAG

To dream of making old pieces of material into rags means you will make a choice which will prove to have been both correct and wise, and using a rag to clean something shows that sometimes you can be a little weak when it comes to making decisions. A white rag indicates the arrival of relations from abroad, and a red rag is a symbol of anger. A dirty rag in a dream means that you need to be more disciplined and less lazy.

RAG-AND-BONE MAN

A rag-and-bone man buying something in a dream usually means a minor tiff between you and your partner, while if he is selling something, the outlook for an important project you are involved in at work is a bright one. If you are a rag-and-bone man in your dream, it means you are involved in a risky and hazardous venture which could prove to be expensive.

RAGE

Dreaming of anyone showing rage is generally not a sign of good fortune: it indicates some future unhappiness verging on desperation, caused by a disappointment you had not expected from someone you loved. If you dream of going into a rage with a friend because of what he or she has done, you are starting to worry too much about the health of a person close to you when it is already on the mend. If someone else goes into a rage at you, it is a foretaste of unpleasant news to come.

RAID

A raid by thieves or bandits in a dream shows a confused and uncertain emotional relationship: you need to sort things out in this area or you will lose the love and respect of the person you love. If you are raided by the police in your dream, you have some minor personal problems at the moment, but if you manage to avoid arrest, a piece of work you are involved in will end happily.

RAINBOW   Dreaming of a rainbow, as might be expected, brings good luck via changes for the better.
RADISH   A hard and diligent worker may dream of eating radishes.

RAILWAY

Any dream involving railways in any form indicates a healthy and busy social life, though if it is an underground railway, someone or something is getting in your way and you need to be very forceful to overcome this obstacle. A railway accident, however, suggests that one of your plans is about to go wrong.

RAINBOW

Even if you do not manage to find the traditional crock of gold at the end of it, dreaming of a rainbow is very much a sign of good luck: there is change on the horizon, all of it for the good.

RAKE

Raking tarmac in a dream is a sign both of talkativeness and unreliability, while raking a garden shows that you are now solving your financial problems. Raking a field reflects physical stamina and considerable strength of will. A metal rake shows industriousness in your work, and a wooden one that you are facing a very tricky situation. A rake which has no teeth is a very bad sign to dream of, for it means you will lose your partner's affection for ever; but one with a broken handle shows you are being too shy in relations with someone you are just getting to know.

RANCID

Rancid butter in a dream indicates loneliness and pessimism: you should be careful not to get so wrapped up in your own world to the extent that you start finding it hard to relate to other people. Any other food which has gone rancid means that your health is not all it could be and you need to discipline yourself more if it is to get better.

RARE

A rare plant in a dream symbolizes mutual affection and understanding in emotional relationships; a rare coin, your sadness and nostalgia for the past; a rare book, nervous tension and hypersensitivity; and a rare stamp, intelligence and astuteness. Eating rare meat means your actions at work are attracting praise from your superiors.

RAT

Dreaming about these animals means that a large number of relatively small problems are on the way. For someone in love who dreams of rats there is an additional, but much greater, problem: you

have an implacable rival who will stop at nothing to win your partner. If you are married, you can expect minor upsets caused by people who are supposed to be your friends.

RATION

If you dream of a very small ration of food there are major events affecting your love life on the way, but if it is a generous one, malicious gossip from people around you is indicated. If the ration consists of bread and water, there are very good prospects at work at the moment, but if it contains meat, you will make a few small, but annoying errors of judgment. If army rations

RARE   A rare stamp suggests the dreamer is clever and astute.

are involved, you may often be childish, and tend to get worked up about minor problems.

RATIONAL

If either you or someone else is rational in a dream and you approach a problem calmly and refuse to panic, this paradoxically means that there is an absence of this quality in your everyday life, and you often make silly mistakes because of a lack of forethought.

RAYS

The rays of the sun in a dream suggest you are being protected and looked after by someone important at work. The moon's rays signify that you are too weak and easily-led: your main need is for more self-confidence to help you through a difficult time in your life. If you see a ray of light broken up into a spectrum, you are a very open, sociable kind of person.

RAZOR

An electric razor in a dream is a warning to be more careful in your actions. A new hand razor reflects inner calm and contentment; a broken one shows hidden pain, and a blunt one, confusion and unhappiness caused by someone you love. If

you dream about buying a razor, you should face up to the minor differences of opinion between you and your partner before they turn into bigger ones. Using a razor indicates fruitless rebellion against a situation you can no longer put up with.

REACTION

Dreaming of a chemical reaction reflects a simple, naïve personality, but one which has many physical and spiritual resources and adapts easily to different situations. Seeing a man reacting violently to something in a dream means you will find yourself caught up in a very delicate situation and have no idea how to get out of it; if a woman reacts violently in a dream, this indicates that you are a sensitive, slightly timid person.

REBEL

A rebellious boy in a dream is a sign that an urgent piece of business needs to be finished very soon. If it is your son or daughter being rebel-

lious, you will experience a temporary setback caused by an emotional break that was not anticipated. If you dream you are at school and rebelling against a teacher, your relationship with your partner will be characterized by happiness and contentment.

REBOILING

Anything which you boil for a second time in a dream shows that you are trying to capitalize on a situation and get the most out of it before it is too late.

REBUKE

If the rebuke you make in the dream is a justified one, it signifies that you have found a clever solution to an emotional problem, but if it is unjustified, it heralds a minor but unpleasant period of unhappiness or illness. If you rebuke your son or daughter, your prospects at work have never been better than they are at the moment.

RECEIVING

Receiving money for whatever reason in a dream signifies that a

The dreams of an astronaut

To what extent does the place where we are sleeping determine the content of our dreams? Many studies have been carried out in an attempt to answer this question. One factor which has emerged is that the room temperature can often affect what we dream about; if it is cold, the situations and places in our dreams tend to be cold too, and likewise if it is unusually warm.

In 1984, one particularly interesting experiment was carried out on a group of astronauts. They were asked to write down what they dreamed about during their sleep periods on board their spacecraft. Some of their replies were: "I was playing hockey"; "A country landscape"; "I was salmon fishing in Vermont"; "My mother".

So why didn't they dream about the vastness of space, or the great blue and white ball of the earth, outlined against the pitch-black infinity of space? And what about the fears and anxieties that one might expect to be assailing people who had been uprooted from their own planet and were living in an environment that was totally alien to humans?

None of them dreamed of anything of the kind: their visions were small-scale, domestic ones. One expert remarked: "Man is clearly the one species which adapts best to any kind of environment, but at the same time we are the most resistant to influences from the outside world. Our psychological heritage, with all its richness and complexity, is where we derive our strength from, and nowhere is this better shown than in these dreaming astronauts. Human beings retain their personalities intact

whatever the situation they are in, and their interests and preoccupations remain the same. That applies whether they are on earth, or in space."

business matter must be sorted out. Being given a present means a reconciliation with someone you love occurring in the very near future. Receiving good wishes, perhaps in a greetings card, indicates harmony in emotional relationships; being given a kiss, a betrayal in love; and receiving advice signifies protection and support from someone who wields a great deal of influence. Receiving a compliment which makes you blush suggests you are probably about to undergo a gloomy, depressive phase. Being given an order to do something means there is interesting news coming.

RECEPTION

Holding a reception in a dream foretells advantageous business ventures and financial well-being. Going to a reception indicates the beginning of new and exciting developments related to romance. If it is a noisy, informal reception, you are reserved and shy in almost everything you do; if it is a solemn, formal one, you are an original, imaginative person who loves anything that is risky or unusual. A reception held in your honour in a dream indicates that something is happening in your life that you are not accustomed to.

RECIPE

Reading or using a recipe in a dream shows that past financial setbacks have turned out to be less serious than you had thought. Writing a recipe down indicates that you have misjudged a person when in reality they have a great deal of respect for you. Giving a recipe to someone else means you are very good at making the correct decision in any difficult situation.

RECITING

Reciting poetry in a dream symbolizes a worried, anxious frame of mind, probably resulting from a break with someone close to you. Reciting a story, on the other hand, indicates great self-confidence and ambition. Reciting a speech from

memory suggests that you have to get over your timidity if you are to succeed. If you or anyone else recites a prayer, it means that one of your ambitions is about to be realized.

RECOGNITION

Doing something which gains you recognition in a dream means you are involved in a lengthy, difficult task, but it will be a success in the end. Showing recognition for someone else's achievements in a dream means your optimism is so great that it will help you achieve things others might have thought were impossible.

RECOGNIZING

Recognizing a relative in a dream means you are an open-hearted and sociable person, loyal to others and confident of your own abilities. Recognizing a friend means that a mistake needs to be put right as soon as possible. Recognizing a criminal in an identification parade indicates that business and financial success are coming. If you dream that you recognize a place you have seen before, you need to keep a very close eye on your state of health. In a dream, recognizing that you have committed a wrong means you will need a great deal of patience to see a current project through to the end.

RECONCILING

Having a reconciliation with your father in a dream indicates that you will go on a business trip abroad which will be constructive and profitable; a reconciliation with your mother indicates confidence and decisiveness in matters connected with business. A reconciliation with your children means initiatives you have taken are sensible ones, and one with your husband or wife shows that you will get heavily involved in a very difficult situation and have considerable trouble getting out of it. Burying the hatchet with an enemy in a dream means you will manage to avoid a heavy financial loss.

RECORD

Seeing or buying a record, tape or compact disc in a dream means your confidence in yourself is waning and you need someone else to reassure you that what you are doing is right. Running a race in record time means that you will derive satisfaction and happiness from the success of an important project you are/were involved in. Breaking a world record means you have a decisive, clear-thinking personality, but you also have a strong need for freedom and independence.

RECORDER

Any musical instrument of this nature in a dream brings good fortune: you are about to fall in love with someone you have only just met, and are willing to sacrifice almost anything to gain their affection, though you should be careful, because there is no guarantee you will succeed. If you hear someone else playing the recorder, you are an optimist who regards the future with quiet confidence. A broken recorder means an intense but short-lived attachment.

RECORDING

Recording anything on tape in a dream signifies a strong will. Recording an item of expense on paper suggests an unexpected piece of good news will arrive, while making a note of any other fact indicates that there are difficult obstacles you need to overcome in your working life.

RECOVERING

Recovering something you or someone else have lost in a dream means there will be unforeseen changes at work which will disrupt your daily routine for a while. Recovering stolen goods means you are full of original and imaginative ideas at the moment. Recovering your sight in a dream signifies that you have a desperate need to be loved and understood, and recovering your health after an illness or injury means, on the contrary, that illness is on the way.

RECRUIT

To dream of being recruited into the armed forces indicates that you have had difficult times at work recently which have taught you something about yourself and helped you to become more independent. Being recruited into a team to play any kind of sport means you will have a major difference of opinion with relatives. Employing workers yourself means you are over-reacting to situations and being impulsive and jumpy: you should try to calm down and face up to the problems of everyday life with a little more reflection. Recruiting soldiers in a dream means that soon you will have a very favourable opportunity.

RECTOR

The rector of a university in a dream symbolizes ill-humour and irritable behaviour, while the rector of a church or other religious institution means there will be sudden and definite progress in an important project which looked as though it might be getting bogged down. A rector teaching means you will spend time worrying unnecessarily about a relative's health; if he is praying, relations with the person you love have never been better. Talking to a rector symbolizes good news.

REDCURRANTS   An unexpected proposal could influence future career prospects.

RED

Dreaming of red clothes of any kind indicates passion and sensitivity in emotional relationships; a red thread means a desperate need for love and affection; and a red pencil or crayon an ability to support and sustain others in their time of need. A red car or other vehicle reflects a craving for novel and interesting things to happen.

REDCURRANTS

A dream which involves redcurrants is a sign that you will soon receive a suggestion or proposal which may surprise you at first, but which is well worth considering more closely because your future career could depend on your reply.

REDUCING

Reducing the price of something by bargaining in a dream means you tend not to see the wood for the trees, and tend to rush headlong

REGATTA   Watching a boat race may mean news from afar.

into things without considering the possible repercussions. Reducing your weight in a dream means you are having trouble getting people to take you seriously in your work, and reducing a workforce indicates new, interesting friendships on the horizon.

REFERENCE

Showing someone your references in a dream means a financial venture you are involved in will be very successful; asking someone to provide them means you are far too egocentric and this is making you very difficult to live with. If the references are good ones, you are feeling very attached to someone you have met recently, but if they are bad, surprisingly enough, you will make undreamed-of progress in your career.

REFLECTOR

A reflector on a bicycle or other vehicle indicates unreliability and, more importantly, a lack of staying power in relationships with others, a characteristic which may mean that you will fail to get to know someone really well who would have been ideally suited to you.

REFRESHMENTS

Making refreshments, such as sandwiches or drinks, in a dream means you are steadily climbing up the career ladder which will eventually allow you to reach the lifestyle you were aiming for. Buying them means your feelings toward your partner, and theirs toward you, are serious and sincere. Taking any kind of refreshment means you are likely to enjoy perfect health.

REFUGE

Taking refuge from someone or something in a dream generally suggests a certain amount of insecurity is troubling you at the moment. If you take refuge from the elements in a shelter of some kind, it means you are afraid of starting family arguments by speaking your mind, while if you shelter from someone who is chasing or otherwise harrassing you, you are constantly worried by what other people are saying about you behind your back.

REFURNISHING

Refurnishing a house or other building in a dream indicates a period in which you are re-examining many of your values and making some major changes in your lifestyle.

REGATTA

Watching a regatta, or any kind of boat race, is very common in dreams. It means there is news on its way, possibly from a great distance, which will give you hope and confidence in your future career. If you dream about actually taking part in a regatta, you need to make a temporary change of plans; if you win the race, there are difficult family arguments in the offing.

REGIMENT

A regiment of soldiers in a dream shows that someone you know is being obstinate; a victorious regiment reflects an impulsive, flighty nature, but if it loses in battle, there are significant changes afoot at work. A cavalry regiment indicates honesty with your partner; an infantry regiment suggests that you will attain an enviable financial position.

REGIMENT Soldiers in a regiment show awkwardness from an acquaintance.

REINS

Holding reins in your hand in a dream suggests a worrying lack of confidence, and a certain amount of confusion as well: you should accept the attempts of others to bolster your self-confidence if you are to regain your former composure and balance. Putting reins on a horse means you are worrying needlessly about the health of a relative, and the act of reining in a horse means that you are being very generous and unselfish towards your partner, and that he or she appreciates it.

REINS These reveal worry about a relative's health.

RELATIVE

Dreaming of a rich relative means you are feeling excessively vain about yourself, but dreaming of a poor one indicates unexpected financial benefits or income. Seeing a relative in a dream means you are not always faithful in your relationships with the opposite sex. Inviting a relative to your home means you are feeling decisive and self-confident; if they come for a meal, it means that you still have a lot to learn about getting on with other people, and should not be so

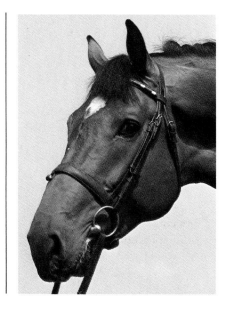

What do red and blue mean in our dreams?

Two of the colours which appear in dreams and are most often remembered are red and blue. Both have a very precise meaning, both in popular tradition and also in the light of what modern psychology has told us about the human mind.

Red is a symbol of aggression. This is not necessarily a negative characteristic: in fact it can have a very positive meaning, suggesting that we have a need to make our mark on the world rather than letting others take the lead and instead of being lazy and afraid of facing up to problems. So dreaming in red often means vitality, a desire to act, be positive and get things done. Statistically, it has been shown that women dream in red more often than men do.

Blue reflects a feeling of contentment and a need for peace and tranquillity. A person who often dreams in blue, or about blue things, is likely to be generous, understanding of others, and someone who will help his fellow humans without expecting a reward for it. The colour blue also indicates a forceful but balanced personality.

Paradoxically, then, red and blue are colours which complement each other in dreams, one appearing as the other disappears, for most of us have the characteristics represented by both colours.

The pictures on this page reflect the interesting fact that Princess Diana – as she herself has admitted – favours the two colours most often dreamed about, red and blue, in her choice of clothing. The young princess is an active and go-ahead person, who daily has to face situations needing an enterprising mind which can make decisions quickly; but she is also a shy person. So she needs to assert herself and make constant use of that side of her personality which helps her to avoid some of the stresses of contact with the public. This is the reason why she so often wears red. Likewise, her predilection for blue is very easily explained.

They reflect a personality which is generous, and always willing to share with others the privileges she enjoys. There are countless examples of this feature of her character. For example, her used clothes are given to a charitable foundation which helps needy

children, and sold by the foundation for enormous sums to rich women all over the world. But none of her altruism is in any way ostentatious or publicity-seeking, and much of it is expressed through small actions which, if nothing else, have attracted public attention to the problems of people who are less fortunate than most.

We choose the colours of our clothes – and our dreams. Our subconscious uses colour to re-establish psychological equilibrium; our conscious mind uses colour to reinforce identity.

argumentative. Discussing something with a relative in a dream means you are unhappy and pessimistic, but having an argument with them suggests you are a tactful, diplomatic person.

RELEASING

Releasing someone from prison or confinement of some kind in a dream means you are not carrying out a promise, while if someone else releases you, this indicates that someone will declare their love for you in the near future, and it could lead to marriage.

RELIC

A historical relic or ruin of some kind in a dream suggests that you feel very guilty about something you did in the past. A religious relic, such as the Turin Shroud, means you are extremely practical and down-to-earth, and others appreciate your lack of pretensions.

REMARRYING

Remarrying someone who is younger than you in a dream indicates that you are facing a delicate situation which needs to be handled carefully, but getting remarried to someone older means you often feel tired and overstressed. Getting married to a widow or widower is a danger signal if it happens in a dream: you are taking on too many burdens and responsibilities at work, and there is a serious risk of your overdoing things unless you sit back and take things a little easier.

REMEDY

A remedy which works in a dream indicates confidence and decisiveness in everything you do, but if it does not work, this dream indicates that your hopes and aspirations are rather too ambitious. If a doctor prescribes you a remedy in your dream, there is reassuring news on the way concerning the health of a relative.

REMEMBERING

Remembering a promise in a dream means you are being too obstinate; while remembering a birthday demonstrates that in your real life you are showing over-sensitive behaviour caused by an unanticipated disappointment connected with someone of the opposite sex. If you remember somebody's name in a dream, you are feeling very lively and very much in control of the way your life is going; remembering a debt owed to you means a short period of dissatisfaction and unhappiness. Remembering money that you owe someone else means there are contacts to be taken up again after a long absence.

REMOVING

Removing an obstacle in a dream means you have serious personal problems which need sorting out as soon as possible; removing stones or rocks means you are very strong-minded. Removing furniture indicates major changes which you have initiated, while removing the body of someone you have killed means you are worrying unnecessarily about an elderly relative.

RENEWING

Renewing a contract in a dream heralds a new venture at work which is virtually a guaranteed success; renewing a vow or promise shows an outstandingly strong personality. Renewing a library book in a dream means you are being astute and wise in matters at work.

RENOUNCING

Renouncing a religion in a dream suggests that an important project at work will be brought to a speedy and successful conclusion. Renouncing a right shows that you are very scrupulous in your professional life and have a considerable attention to detail.

REPAIRING

Repairing a car in a dream indicates that you are careful with your money, though you are far from mean; and a bicycle, that you are feeling nervy and sensitive. Repairing shoes, or having someone else repair them, presages a tranquil, peaceful life. Repairing damage that you have caused through carelessness in a dream means that you are not always the most tactful of people.

REPEATING

If you dream of yourself or someone else having to repeat what you have said, it suggests you have a tendency to take instructions without questioning or thinking about them. Repeating a mistake in a dream means you are worried that you are less industrious than you used to be. Repeating an experiment to see if it gives the same results means you are very rational and analytical.

REPRESSING

Repressing tears in a dream means that you owe someone an explanation concerning a very important matter in connection with your work. Repressing a passion for someone in a dream shows that you are about to make a potentially deceitful and double-edged proposal which needs a very careful re-think. Repressing a plot before it can be carried out means you have your suspicions about a colleague at work, but they are totally unjustified. Suppressing a rebellion suggests you will have to make an unexpected trip abroad.

REPRIMANDING

Reprimanding your children for something they have done in a dream indicates professional difficulties, and giving your husband or wife a ticking-off means that you need to keep an eye on how much money you are spending. Reprimanding any other relative means you are behaving in a confused and uncertain way at the moment. Reproving a man in a dream means you should be able to profit from a very favourable opportunity which is going to be given to you.

REPRISAL

Carrying out a reprisal for any reason in a dream suggests you are impulsive by nature. You are also being particularly jumpy at the moment, and this could lead to serious errors of judgment in your work environment. If the reprisal is for a good reason, you have great hopes and ambitions for the future, but if it is unjust, you will incur an unexpected expense. If the reprisal involves bloodshed, you are at risk and financial difficulties.

REPRODUCING

Reproducing a picture in a dream, either by copying it by hand or by photocopying it, means you are entering a phase in your life where nearly everything is going against you. Reproducing a text, or someone else's handwriting, means that there is a problematic situation at work which should be cleared up at the earliest available opportunity.

REPULSIVE

Dreaming of a man who is repulsive signifies a financial venture going decidedly wrong, and a repulsive woman suggests that things are reaching a crisis point in your life. A repulsive old man means slow but constant progress in your career. If you find the food you are eating in your dream repulsive, it is because you are about to get involved in painful arguments with your partner; if something you smell is disgusting, it means you will be the object of criticism and slander.

REPUTATION

Losing your reputation is not a pleasant thing to happen, either in reality or in a dream. In dreams it denotes jealousy and suspicion involving you and your partner. But even if you dream about having a good reputation for something, you could have a major conflict of opinion with someone you work with. If the reputation you dream of having is anything less than good, you are likely to be feeling ill at ease about something.

REQUEST

A request for a favour in a dream means that you need to review your priorities in your approach to life, and one for any kind of material goods means that your emotional relationships are on a shaky footing. If it is you issuing the request, you are an ambitious person who worries little about what the future can throw at you, but if the request comes to you from someone else, a period of peace and contentment is on the way.

RE-READING

Re-reading a newspaper in a dream suggests you are making slow but sure progress in your job and eventually this will lead to a healthy financial position and more independence than you have now. If your dream involves reading a book you have already read, things are about to start going your way in love and romance.

RESIGNATION

Resigning from a job in your dream suggests that a period of major change is on the way. Resigning yourself to having lost something means you are emotionally very sensitive, and resigning yourself to a defeat indicates that your first impressions of someone you have just met are wrong. If you resign yourself in the dream to the task you are doing cheerfully and gracefully, it suggests you are an open, sociable person who reacts spontaneously to people around you, and even if you resign yourself to the task reluctantly, you have a surprisingly intuitive and reflective personality.

RESIN

This is a fairly rare subject for a dream; it usually has to do with relations with the opposite sex, and is a symbol of an almost obsessive attachment to the person you love. Extracting resin, perhaps from a tree, shows minor satisfactions in store for you, and buying it reveals a rational person good at making quick decisions. Rubbing resin onto something, such as the strings of a violin bow, suggests that you are going through a phase where everything in your life, both public and private, is confused and uncertain.

RESISTANCE

Meeting resistance to something you are doing in a dream suggests you have an innate desire for freedom and independence. But if you resist doing something yourself, there are problems and hostilities at work and it would be a good idea to accept the help and advice of someone older and more experienced than you are if these small problems are not to turn into big ones. Resisting pain indicates emotional stability and a good relationship with your partner, but resisting fatigue means you need to review some of your priorities. Resisting temptation in a dream means you will be plagued with doubt and uncertainty, and resisting attack means an unexpected stroke of good luck.

RESPONSIBILITY

If your dream involves your taking on a major responsibility, it is not a good sign: you are being tetchy and irritable with your loved one and are putting a long-lasting relationship at risk as a result. If you dream of refusing to take on a responsibility

RESTING   A difficult situation is looming if you dream about resting.

because you regard it as too great a burden, it means you are being unnecessarily unfriendly to someone you have recently met.

RESTARTING

Starting a lesson again in a dream after it has been interrupted indicates that a matter needs clearing up on your part; recommencing work means you have an exceptionally strong personality and a spirit of enterprise. Starting an argument again suggests that unpleasant news from a very long way away will arrive. If you dream that you have to start a speech again that has been interrupted by a heckler or unforeseen event, you will enjoy a pleasant but short-lived personal success. Taking up a relationship where you left off in a dream suggests you are excessively preoccupied with the past.

RESTAURANT

Dreaming of a restaurant in a town symbolizes the fact that someone you know is keeping a secret, while one in the country means that problems are on the way for you. A crowded restaurant indicates difficulties with your partner caused by

your timidity, and an empty one, a worrying emotional problem caused by your partner's unpredictable behaviour. If you have a meal in a restaurant in a dream, it shows that you will receive an attractive proposition, perhaps connected with your work.

RESTING

In dreams as in real life, working for long periods without having a rest inevitably leads to physical and mental stress: you should try to find new interests to stimulate your mind and lead you away from this overzealous preoccupation, or there is a chance you may lose your job by wearing yourself down. Resting in an armchair in a dream shows that a difficult situation is just around the corner, while taking a quick nap on a bed means that you feel confident in yourself and have a sense of responsibility.

RESTORING

Restoring a picture in a dream symbolizes aspirations not being fulfilled, and a statue, the fact that you will receive help and advice at work which will help you to stand on your own two feet. Restoring an old

building such as a palace means you have a vivid imagination, and restoring a monument foretells a particularly comfortable time from the financial point of view.

RESULT

Dreaming of receiving the result of a sports match shows that you are being particularly calm and rational in your actions. Finding the result of a piece of research or an investigation indicates you are being encouraged in your work and it is more satisfying as a result. Getting the result of a calculation indicates that someone you have known for a long time needs your help and advice.

RETOUCHING

Retouching a photograph in a dream is a very good sign: it shows that your initiative and determination are helping you achieve results you would not have thought possible. Retouching any other kind of picture means that you are astute.

RETREATING

If you retreat from some kind of danger in your dream, it reveals wisdom on your part in real life. A

RESTORING   Restoring pictures mean aspirations are not being met.

military retreat from the enemy indicates a difficult period ahead from many points of view. A retreat because you are frightened indicates that a project in which you are involved is coming to a close, but if you show unwarranted cowardice, it paradoxically indicates that you are exceptionally decisive and will not keep people waiting for an answer.

RETURNING

Returning home in your dream suggests you have considerable personal qualities which have still to be put to good use in your career; returning to your native country means there is jealousy and bitterness between you and your partner which probably has some grounds for justification. Returning home from a war means you are self-confident and verging on vanity. Coming home from prison means you have considerable gifts of patience and perseverance. Returning something borrowed signifies that you have received a favour but you have not acknowledged it.

REUNITING

Reuniting people in a dream is a sign that fortune is smiling on you and business matters are taking a turn for the better. Reuniting children suggests you have great talents which are still not being put to good use in your career, and a reunion of soldiers indicates heated and possibly hostile discussions with your partner. Reuniting school friends indicates the arrival of a major piece of good news, and reuniting relatives who have not seen each other for a long time means you are soon to embark on an emotional relationship which is perhaps unlikely to last.

REVENGE

If you dream about seeking revenge, or obtaining it, you are likely to receive a bitter disappointment in love. If someone else exacts revenge on you, you can expect problems at work.

REVIEW

The appearance of a theatre review in a dream denotes a visit from someone a long way away, while dreaming of a film review suggests an ambiguous situation with your partner which needs to be cleared up as soon as possible if it is not to harm your relationship seriously. A military review shows that you are full of creative ideas in your work, and a naval review means a pleasant piece of news is about to arrive. Reviewing troops yourself means you are being far too ambitious.

REVIVE

Reviving someone who is unconscious in a dream means you have been placed in a very responsible position at work; if they were near death before you tried to revive them, it shows you are being careful and considerate in your actions; and if they were drowning, you are lively and full of initiative. Resuscitating a child means you are sensible and intelligent. If it is a man who is being revived, you need to put right an error made in your work, and if it is a woman, you will be involved in an argument about money.

REVOLUTION

Dreaming of a revolution by the people means that your business affairs need a close eye kept on them, while if the army takes part as well, troubles and setbacks are indicated in your private life. If there is bloodshed involved, you are being too rash and hasty in your actions.

REVOLVER

Firing a revolver in a dream shows you are physically very fit and full of mental energy: this would be a very good time to start on a project at work you have wanted to be involved in for a long time. If you hear a revolver being fired in your dream, you are full of brilliant ideas at the moment; if it is daytime in the dream when you hear it, you have financial problems which need sorting out before they start to snowball, but if it is at night, you are in a

nervous and restless frame of mind. If someone is killed in the dream, it means you have put an unpleasant phase of your life behind you for good.

RHUBARB

A rhubarb plant in dreams symbolizes unforeseen satisfactions and pleasures, but stewed rhubarb is a much less auspicious sign: many of your hopes for the future will founder because of a financial loss. Serving rhubarb to your guests means you are likely to miss out on a perfect opportunity.

RIBBON

Any dream involving ribbon shows you are an open-minded person who makes friends easily, as well as having a well-ordered mind which

REVOLVER   Firing a gun in a dream suggests surplus energy.

helps you relate to people at work and outside it. A pink ribbon means that a project you started on some time ago will come to a successful conclusion, and a silver ribbon means you are a little excessive in your enthusiasms.

RICHES

Gaining riches in a dream actually signifies the reverse in real life: you will experience a worrying financial loss of some kind. Conversely, losing one's wealth in fact means you can look forward to a very comfortable financial position. Giving away your riches means you are very worried about something, and gambling them away suggests you are being over-emotional in your relationships with others. If you dream about being careless with your savings, there are improvements about to happen in your work environment, but if you covet someone else's, you can expect a period when nothing goes your way.

RING

If you dream you have lost a ring you should be very careful what you do, as your marriage is hanging in the balance at the moment. But if you take off a ring in a dream because it is hurting you, your marital problems will only be short-lived. If someone else gives you a ring, this symbolizes a night of passion. If they actually put the ring on your finger, you will be going to a wedding soon.

RINGING

Bells ringing in a church reveal hidden anxieties, while ringing them yourself indicates that you have made, or are about to make, lasting friendships. Someone else ringing a doorbell symbolizes women gossiping, and ringing one yourself means you have a strong need for love and understanding.

RISK

Running a risk of any kind in a dream indicates that you will have to make a very tiring business trip, though dreaming of a needless risk,

which you run just for the sake of it, means you are being too enterprising and independent, and this will lead to mistakes in your work.

RIVER

Dreaming of a river flowing along slowly and gently, or with clean water in it, signifies good fortune of some kind, but if it is rushing along, or if it is polluted or muddy, it indicates the opposite. Falling into a river in a dream means there is some kind of danger lying in wait for you; bathing in one indicates financial or material gains on the way; and swimming across a river foretells hopes coming to fruition.

ROAD

This is a symbol which can have several different meanings. A road sloping downhill indicates your differences of opinion with relatives, and an uphill one denotes the painful problems which you have to face in real life. A wide road means

your relationships are untroubled at present and a narrow one foretells a strange meeting or encounter. Walking along a road in your dream means that your honest intentions will receive their own reward.

ROAR

Hearing a person or an animal roaring in a dream is not a good sign: there is an unpleasant surprise in store which will upset you more than you might expect it to. If the wind roars in your dream, you will lose or waste a substantial amount of money, but if the roar is made by water, you will have an unpleasant experience connected with the opposite sex.

ROAST

If you dream about a joint of roast meat, it indicates that you will receive affectionate greetings of some kind from a friend.

ROOF   A tiled roof is a good sign, foreseeing long-term happiness.

RIVER   A dream of rushing, broken or white water is an ominous one.

ROBBERY

If your dream involves your organizing a robbery, it suggests an inner conflict or dilemma which could have a permanent and injurious effect on you if you do not solve it as soon as possible. Committing a robbery yourself in a dream shows your lack of self-control in real life, and being robbed means you will have an illness or injury which, fortunately, will soon be cured. Watching a robbery and not doing anything to prevent it suggests that you are insecure and full of self doubts.

ROBIN

This bird has long been regarded as a sign of good luck in real life: it is also one of the few birds in dreams whose significance is a wholly fortunate one.

ROCK

Seeing a rock in a dream means that you have new opportunities for advancement at work, while moving one indicates your present gloom and dissatisfaction. Breaking a rock in a dream means that your emotions are empty and lifeless. Climbing up a rockface foretells your desires being fulfilled, and getting off one indicates that you will

launch a new venture with an uncertain future. If you fall off a rock in a dream, you will have to face up to the loss of a friend.

ROLLING

Rolling downstairs or down a hill in a dream shows that you are going through a short period during which you feel off-colour, but should avoid the temptation to take it out on other people. Rolling in the mud suggests that people around you are unfairly having to shoulder your problems and to make personal sacrifices for you. Rolling on grass means you feel deeply and genuinely towards your partner. Rolling something along, such as a barrel, means you are having an uphill struggle dealing with relatives.

ROOF

The roof of a house in a dream symbolizes new ideas which need to be put into practice, and the roof of a church stands for the help and support you have received from someone important at work. A tiled roof foretells a long period of happiness ahead, but a thatched roof is a sign of a disappointment in love.

ROOM

A waiting room in a dream reflects your uncertainty about a work project which looks promising but which could go wrong. A ballroom indicates that emotional problems are looming, and a games room shows that suggestions being put forward may not be all that they seem. A dining room signifies your annoyingly obstinate behaviour, and a living room foretells unexpected guests.

ROOT

The appearance of the roots of a tree in a dream indicates that you will overcome difficulties, and those of any other plant show that you will make an acquisition which will prove to be of very good value. The roots of a tooth represent family quarrels. If you uproot a tree or plant in your dream, you are good at making rapid, effective decisions; if

ROOT   Tree roots in a dream denote an ability to overcome problems.

you cut its roots, you are unlikely to be a person who acts in haste but are thoughtful and perceptive. Burning roots shows that you are upset and disappointed about a love affair. Eating roots of any kind means you have extremely good health.

ROSARY

In dreams the rosary is a symbol of the protection and support you are receiving from someone influential. If it is made of ivory, it stands for your apathy and lack of initiative, and if it is wooden, it shows sentimentality and timidity. If you buy a rosary in a dream, it suggests that you have high hopes of a project you have just embarked upon.

ROSE

Buying roses in a dream indicates that you have a likeable personality; growing them shows that emotional relationships are going smoothly; and picking them symbolizes a new

ROSE   Buying or giving roses is always a favourable image.

involvement, either in romance or business. Watering roses signifies support received from friends; giving them to someone, a great deal of personal prestige following on from a success; and being given them, receiving as well as giving love.

ROWING

Rowing a boat strongly and effortlessly in a dream means you are too impulsive, and need to curb this side of your behaviour at any cost; rowing with tiredness shows your success in business matters; and rowing upstream shows your confusion of ideas and arguments with a superior at work. Rowing on the sea means you will receive support and protection from others at work, while rowing on a river suggests you are very much aware of your considerable abilities and are prepared to exploit them to the full. Rowing on a lake indicates that you are feeling highly-strung and irritable.

ROYAL

Dreaming about a royal family heralds your financial success in the future, while dreaming of a prince foretells a pleasant and interesting discovery. A royal palace in a dream shows that you have had an unexpected stroke of good fortune. If you dream about putting on a royal gown, unfaithfulness in a relationship is indicated, and if you carry a royal sceptre, you will be criticized behind your back by people who are envious of you.

RUBY

Seeing a ruby in a dream suggests that you are too impulsive and hasty in your actions, and buying one means your finances are shaky at present; being given one indicates that your illusions are short-lived. If you steal a ruby in your dream, you will be helped out in a difficult situation at work.

RUDDER

Dreaming of the rudder of a ship shows inner confidence and decisiveness in everything you do. If you are at the helm yourself, the dream implies that you will attain a goal you have been striving very hard to reach.

SAINT If a saint appears in a dream, you should accept any proposals made to you, unhesitatingly.

SABRE

A sabre out of its sheath in a dream symbolizes short-lived hopes; if you see it being used to cut someone or something, it suggests you are gradually wearing yourself out with overwork. If the sabre is a very old one, it shows that you may be an obstinate and vindictive personality, which could make you impossible to live with as far as your partner is concerned.

SACK

A sack of coal in a dream indicates interesting and stimulating prospects are awaiting you, while a sack of potatoes denotes possible sexual indiscretions which you must avoid making at all costs, otherwise you will receive a severe setback. A sack containing anything else suggests you are putting financial gains before something which is more important, and an empty sack indicates a great deal of business acumen and astuteness on your part.

SACREDNESS

Listening to any kind of sacred music in a dream means you are becoming over-emotional and over-sensitive in an uncharacteristic way: if you try to go back to being the calm and reasonable person you are by nature, you will be able to avoid the unpleasant consequences of this touchiness. Dreaming about any sacred object, such as a crucifix, means you are exceptionally strong-willed.

SACRIFICE

Sacrificing an animal in a dream suggests a minor disagreement with someone you work with; sacrificing a son or daughter foretells a serious difference of opinion with the person you love which could signal the end of your relationship if the matter is not resolved amicably.

SAIL

A square sail in a dream shows that you have problems to be faced up to; a triangular one signifies that you

150

have to make an embarrassing choice. If it is white, your business or financial affairs need to be properly organized, but if it is any other colour there is very happy news on the way. If you hoist a sail in your dream, you have emotional problems which need sorting out at the earliest opportunity.

SAILING

Sailing across the sea in a boat in a dream suggests that you are an open, sociable person who also has considerable initiative, and this might be the time to put those qualities to good use by starting on a project you have been planning for some time. Sailing in a yacht which uses sail power shows you have confidence in the future and in your own talents, but if your boat uses a motor, you have a strong mind and an awareness of your responsibilities, and there is also a letter on the way which may induce you to make a trip abroad to a particularly fascinating place.

SAILING   Dreams of crossing the sea in a yacht reflect self-confidence.

SAILOR

If you dream about being a sailor yourself, it indicates that two of your main traits are a passion for travelling and a great spirit of adventure, and you need a change of scene to recover some of the freshness and vitality which have been missing from your life for so long. Seeing one or more sailors in a dream is a prelude to success and good fortune in your working life.

SAINT

Seeing a picture of a saint in your dream means a potentially very profitable suggestion is forthcoming which should be taken up straight away. Seeing an actual saint in a dream heralds a long-awaited reconciliation with someone you love. Seeing an effigy of a saint on an altar indicates that you have high hopes for a very ambitious financial venture.

SALAD

A salad is a healthy sign to dream about; it means that you will make your mark at work through your abilities and talents. If you dream about mixing a salad, it suggests harmonious family relationships.

SALESMAN

Dreams involving salesmen are generally positive ones, indicating your financial successes. Dreaming about being a salesman yourself means you are a sympathetic person who is always willing to help those in trouble. Dreaming about selling arms or drugs, or anything else undesirable, means there are dangerous temptations in your path.

SALMON

If you dream of seeing a salmon in a river, fate is smiling on you at the moment. A cooked salmon which is about to be eaten means that financial gains are coming to you, but smoked salmon represents future difficulties in business matters.

SALT

The appearance of sea salt in a dream denotes determination and physical strength, while ordinary salt reflects your good state of bodily health. If the salt is coarse, an upturn in financial matters is on the way, and if it is fine, you have strong powers of imagination and a need for freedom and independence. If you dream about buying salt, you are about to throw yourself wholeheartedly into a major work project. Putting salt in water means more than one perfect opportunity is being handed to you on a plate, and putting salt on food suggests you are downcast at a series of errors.

SAND

If your dream involves walking along an expanse of sand, it suggests you are jealous and suspicious by nature. Lying down on a sandy beach means that you have to defend someone's interests, and sprinkling sand on the ground denotes money slipping through your fingers.

SATIN   You are very thoughtful if you dream of wearing satin.

SANDAL

Seeing white sandals in a dream shows that you have a great deal of unrecognized talent; those of any other colour show you thrive on the unknown, rather than being afraid of it, and you also have a lot of initiative. Men's sandals in a dream indicate that a brief but pleasant emotional relationship is on the way; women's ones suggest a bond or connection is in danger of being broken, and children's show that favourable suggestions will be put to you.

SARDINE

Seeing a shoal of sardines swimming in the water, buying them, or eating them, are all favourable omens in a dream: they indicate health, happy family relationships, and pleasant news. Sardines in a tin indicate that the time has arrived for you to make a decision.

SATIN

White satin in a dream symbolizes your recuperation from illness or from being under strength, and black satin, your considerable intuitive abilities. Red satin is a warning of violent events or disputes. Wearing any clothes made of satin means you are a reflective, careful person who nevertheless has a great confidence in yourself and everything you do. If you see a tent made of satin in your dream, you will receive the praise and recognition you deserve, having brought an important project to a successful conclusion.

SAUCE

The appearance of tomato sauce in a dream shows that a letter is on the way, and mayonnaise means you have a minor but irritating disagreement with a work colleague. Chilli sauce means deception and cheating going on behind your back, and curry sauce indicates that you should not give full rein to an emotional attachment which you are feeling at present. Apple sauce means you are being too proud and conceited.

SAUSAGE

The appearance of a whole sausage in a dream indicates a combative mood, and one which has been cut up shows a new direction in your career. An uncooked one stands for important family discussions, and a cooked one suggests a minor difference of opinion with your partner.

SAVING

The meaning of this dream depends very much on what is being saved. If it is money, the dream means that there are financial worries coming which will make life a great deal more difficult; if it is time being saved, you are astute and sensible in everything you do. Saving someone's life in a dream in fact indicates, paradoxically, that you are a selfish person who will not put yourself out for others. Saving a goal in any sport means the sudden and unexpected arrival of a friend.

SCABIES

This unpleasant disease also has an unpleasant significance in dreams. If you or someone else suffers from it, you will soon be at the centre of a

confused situation without much idea of how to get out of it.

SCAFFOLD

Seeing a gallows or scaffold in a dream means you can expect major gains following the success of a financial venture, but if you yourself are condemned to death on one, you will be persecuted by people who are envious of your success. If you also see a hangman in your dream, you are running a great risk in your emotional life. Climbing onto the platform of a scaffold means you have a reputation for being serious in your work, and if you are accompanied by a priest, it indicates that you will be plagued with feelings of fear and anxiety, but they, fortunately, they will not last for long.

SCANDAL

A woman creating a scandal in a dream indicates that you have made an unwise decision, and a man signifies that you are in a compromising situation. If it is an old person who creates the scandal, it shows your indifference to people around you. If it is you that are the centre of the scandal, you tend to underrate yourself and have very little ambition or pride in your achievements.

SCAR

Despite what one might think, a scar is a positive sign if it appears in a dream. If you dream you have one yourself, it means you have the capability to avoid threats and difficulties lying in your path: in fact, the larger the scar, the more evident your ability is in this. A scar on your hand indicates you have made a loss of money, and one on your face signifies there are minor obstacles to your progress. A scar on your leg reflects your lack of enthusiasm for something, and one on any other part of the body, some short-lived bitterness.

SCHOOL

A primary school in a dream means there are aspects of your behaviour that need to be changed; a secon-

---

The idyllic dreams of criminals

Psychologists are more or less united in the belief that all of us, to a greater or lesser extent, have latent criminal tendencies. This may come as something of a shock, but it should be noted that by criminal tendencies we normally mean an instinct for self-preservation, which in certain circumstances can drive even the most harmless people, or animals, to defend themselves using violence.

But what we are particularly interested in here is people who have an in-built need to express themselves through acts of violence. Despite what we might think, most people of this nature tend to have non-violent dreams, while the majority of us who do not have criminal leanings often dream about violent situations. All of us have, at one time or another, unleashed our violent tendencies through the medium of dreaming.

What is the reason for this apparent contradiction? Why do violent people have non-violent dreams, and vice versa? William Steckel, an authority on dreaming, has stated that once criminals are able to give free rein to their violent instincts in real life, they no longer need to do so in dreams, and the exact opposite happens in people who would never dream of displaying these particular types of instincts in real life.

Steckel's theories have been reinforced by experiments carried out by another expert on dreams, Sancte de Sanctis, who showed that

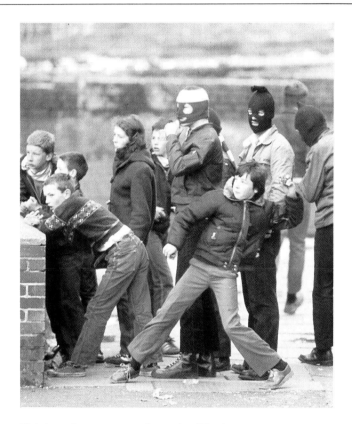

If violence becomes part of everyday life, the subconscious may compensate with dreams of pastoral serenity.

criminals tend not to dream very often, and when they do their dreams are serene. As Steckel remarked: "Feel free to murder someone you can't stand when you're dreaming, but don't do it while you're awake!"

dary school, that you have a choice to make from a great number of options. A boarding school represents the support you are getting from friends at the moment, and a private school means you need to take precautions against potential risks. If you dream about going back to school, you will see some of your financial ventures finally being successful. If you are given a school report, it means you need to take a look at the reasons for your partner's unpredictable behaviour, and if you are given someone else's, you will suffer a loss of money.

SCISSORS

Like many sharp instruments in dreams, scissors are not a particularly positive sign. They are a warning to watch out for false friends and not to confide in anyone for the time being. A tailor using a

SCHOOL   Dreams about returning to school often bring financial reward.

pair of scissors means you are full of original ideas; a surgeon using them means that your present rebellious feelings are not going to achieve anything, and nail scissors indicate a travel-loving personality that is always on the move.

SCRAPING

Scraping anything made of metal in a dream suggests an annoying setback at work; scraping wood, that you have a strong need for freedom; scraping a wall foretells the long-awaited return of someone you love; and scraping a bone means you are perplexed by what to do about an unexpected piece of news. If you use a knife to scrape anything, it means a major disappointment in love, and if you use sandpaper your projects for the future are decidedly rash and over-ambitious.

SCRAPS

Scraps of paper appearing in a dream suggest that you should look

twice because appearances can be deceptive; scraps of cardboard show your inner dissatisfaction and disappointment with an unexpected personal failure. Scraps of parchment show that you are a person others can rely on, and scraps of food, that an emotional relationship is now well and truly over.

SCRATCHING

Scratching oneself in a dream normally indicates inner insecurity and lack of satisfaction. Scratching your face reflects a temporary setback, and scratching your hands suggests you might be being unfaithful in a relationship. Scratching your legs means you have serious doubts about something, but if the dream involves scratching your head, an unexpected boost is indicated.

SEA

To dream of swimming in a calm sea suggests that things are going exceptionally well for you: like the water, you are feeling relaxed and tranquil, and various opportunities are opening up both at work and in romance, which will be successful provided you make a positive effort to take them up. Falling into the sea from a boat, on the other hand, indicates that you have difficulty in reaching an agreement. Most dreams involving the sea also indicate that there is travel in prospect.

SEALING WAX

Sealing a letter with wax in a dream means you are extremely reserved; seeing someone else do so suggests that you have emotional problems.

SEAPLANE

A seaplane taking off in a dream suggests that an old love affair is about to be rekindled, but if the plane crashes, it shows that you are experiencing major problems in your life. A moored seaplane indicates a capricious nature, and getting into one yourself means a successful but difficult conquest.

SEARCHING

Searching for someone male in a

SEA   Visions of the sea in a dream symbolize opportunities for travel.

dream indicates that you will find an unexpected obstacle to the smooth running of your plans at work which it will take all your considerable powers of practicality and intelligence to remove. Looking for someone female in a dream means that you will be the object of criticism and dislike from someone at work, but if you defend yourself, you will be supported by your superiors. Searching for an escaped prisoner means you will have to be careful not to get embroiled in a difficult situation. Searching for an object means you are being over-imaginative and over-ambitious with regard to your plans for the future.

SEEING

To dream of seeing something but not being able to tell what it is suggests you need to clear up a complicated situation before it gets even worse. Seeing something in the distance but not being able to reach it indicates that your plans for the future may be over-ambitious.

SELLING

Selling something on credit in a dream means you are uncertain and unconfident. Selling something retail suggests you have a major burden or responsibility, and selling wholesale indicates a morbid imagination. Selling something by auction suggests your emotions need controlling. Selling things cheaply means work problems.

SENTRY BOX

This is a favourable thing to dream about whether it has anything in it or not: if there is a sentry standing inside, it signifies successful results in your work, and if there is not, you can expect pleasant news.

SERMON

A long sermon in a dream shows that you are undergoing a moral conflict between practicalities and utopian ideals, while a short one means you are decisive in your

SHEEP   A prospect of grazing sheep is generally a good dream-omen.

business dealings. If you dream about listening to a sermon in church, your position at work is not safe, but if it is given outdoors, you will be forced to postpone a project. Giving a sermon yourself shows that something exciting will happen.

SETTING OFF

Setting off on a journey in a dream means a desire to escape and a craving for new experiences. Setting off on the right road means you have serious doubts about something, but setting off on the wrong one suggests that you will be successful.

SEWER

Dreaming about a sewer heralds good news: if you put your experience to good use, your hopes can be brought to fruition.

SHAME

Being ashamed in a dream indicates a bumpy emotional life, which could be damaging in the long term. However, if someone else is ashamed of themselves in a dream, it means that you have planned great goals for the future.

SHARPENING

Sharpening a knife in a dream means you have major doubts and anxieties about a new project at work, but these are unjustified. Sharpening a razor means that your relations with your family could be improved.

SHAVING

Shaving yourself is a sign of financial loss, or uncertainty in business matters; shaving someone else indicates a forthcoming provocation, but you should not rise to the bait.

SHEEP

If you dream about sheep grazing in a field, it is a sign of good fortune. Sheep being sheared indicates that wealth and a good marriage are on the horizon. But if the sheep are running away, you feel someone is persecuting you for no reason.

SHEEPFOLD

Dreaming of a sheepfold full of sheep means there are some excellent opportunities being offered to you at the moment; an empty one shows that you feel your life lacks direction at present. Opening the gate of a sheepfold means discussions, possibly arguments, with friends; closing it, that you have a lack of trust in someone close to you: if you try to see things from their point of view the situation should get better.

SHEET

The meaning of this dream depends on the type of sheet you see. If it is white, it signifies your changing moods, while if it has a pattern on it, or is any colour other than white, it indicates that your curiosity has been satisfied about something. A dirty sheet shows your present intolerance and bitterness, and a crumpled sheet signifies that a small financial gain is coming.

SHELL

Finding seashells on a beach during a dream means that you are experiencing an embarrassing situation in real life, especially if the shells are empty. A shell which still has a creature inside it indicates a victory on the sports field. Seeing a shell which has been fired from a gun indicates that your love affairs have burnt out, but if the shell has still to be fired, there are interesting developments on the way relating to someone of the opposite sex.

SHEPHERD

Dreaming of a shepherd with his flock promises success in a project you are involved in at work, and if you also see a sheepdog, it indicates sincerity and faithfulness on the part of the person you love. A shepherd robbed of his sheep suggests you will be briefly upset by a misfortune of some kind. A shepherd lying asleep while his sheep are straying reflects your own negligence at work caused by your preoccupation with matters in your private life. A shepherd being attacked by a wolf means you are having minor upsets with your family.

SHIP

A ship can have different meanings in a dream, depending on the exact circumstances in which it appears. A cargo ship symbolizes temptations which you must overcome; a passenger ship indicates family quarrels; and a battleship signifies serious setbacks in your professional life. A ship crossing the sea indicates a difficult and introverted personality, but if it is tied up in port, it shows that you have a childish, illogical side to you. If you are on board the ship in your dream, it means you will receive both praise and riches as the result of a successful gamble.

SHIPWRECK

Like most disasters in dreams, a shipwreck – if you are involved in it – is a portent of things going badly. You can expect a number of upsets and difficulties following a break with someone close to you, all of which will cause you to become very depressed. It also suggests your health is not as good as it could be, probably because you have been working too hard. If you see a shipwreck from a safe distance, on the other hand, the prospects are much brighter both in the area of work and that of health.

SHIRT

In common with other items of clothing, the meaning of this dream depends on the type of material the shirt is made of and on what sort of

SHELL Collecting shells suggests you are in an embarrassing situation.

shirt it is. If it is made of a very expensive material it is not a sign of good luck for you; likewise if it is white. If it is made of cotton or wool, or if it is coloured, it suggests that there is about to be a dramatic upturn in your life. A dirty shirt indicates problems in your family, while a night shirt means there is agreeable news on its way.

SHOE

Men's shoes in a dream mean that a superior at work is looking after your interests, while women's shoes indicate a disagreement with a brother or sister. Children's shoes in a dream mean you are achieving promotion at work. If the shoes you dream of are new, there is money on the way, but if they are old, you can expect a period of despondency. High-heeled shoes show that you will make an unexpected move, and flat shoes reflect troubles at work.

SHOEMAKER

This is a favourable sign to dream about, showing the possibility of a profitable business deal. Dreaming of a shoemaker at work indicates that you should not pry into the concerns of others or you will get an unpleasant shock, but if you employ him to repair your own shoes, the dream shows you should follow your own hunches more often.

SHOOTING

Shooting a rifle in a dream means you have made mistakes which need patching up; firing a pistol indicates that you should keep your impulses under control, while a cannon symbolizes fleeting, meaningless relationships. If you shoot a person, you can expect a disappointment involving someone of the opposite sex, while if an animal is shot, it marks the end of a harmful relationship.

SHOP WINDOW

Seeing a shop window in a dream means you can expect significant financial gains; putting goods in it yourself reflects a romantic conquest, and decorating it suggests that appearances can be deceptive so you must examine everything thoroughly. A broken shop window indicates a time of tension, and an empty one shows that you should cultivate a business relationship.

The guide to perfect dreaming

Did you know there is a "Good Dreamer's Guide"? This describes the position you should be lying in as you fall asleep, which way the bed should point, techniques to use if you want to wake up at a particular time, and how to conquer insomnia . . .

THE IDEAL POSITION for a good sleep is lying on your right-hand side; as early as ancient Greek and Roman times, this has been the accepted wisdom. Sleeping in this position allows you to make use of the positive aspect of the magnetism you possess.

THE BED should be facing in a north-south direction so that your body can make maximum use of the lines of magnetism running from the north pole to the south pole. Many doctors recommend this position, as well as suggesting that you get rid of any surplus static electricity before going to bed by running cold water over your hands for a few moments.

WAKING UP AT A SPECIFIC TIME is accomplished by visualizing the time you want to get up. This is best done by imagining a huge alarm-clock, with very large, clear numbers, and with the hands pointing to the desired time. If you do this at least three times before you go to bed, the results are almost always successful.

CURING INSOMNIA, provided it is not caused by a medical condition, can often be

done using a simple breathing exercise which takes only two or three minutes. This consists of breathing in very deeply through your nose, and expelling the air slowly through your mouth so that your lungs are as well ventilated as possible. This calms the mind and is particularly worth trying a few times if you wake up in the middle of the night and cannot get back to sleep.

SHORE

The shores of a body of water are not generally an auspicious sign in a dream. Riverbanks represent your having impractical or dreamy ambitions, and a seashore shows inertia and laziness. The shores of a lake stand for sudden anger. If you land on an unknown shore in your dream, there is pleasant news on the way.

SHOVEL

A workman's shovel in a dream is a sign of guaranteed financial success, though if it is a gravedigger who is using one, your finances will be rather more shaky. A baker using a shovel to put bread into an oven or take it out means that you are facing a long and burdensome task which nevertheless gives you considerable personal satisfaction.

SHOWER

Having a shower in a dream indicates your hard work being to no avail. A cold shower indicates a setback in matters of the heart, and a hot shower, receiving an important explanation or clarification of an action or situation which puzzled you. A shower of rain symbolizes a problem which goes away almost as quickly as it arrived.

SHUDDER

Causing someone else to shudder in a dream means excellent prospects as far as your work is concerned, and shuddering yourself means you are indulging in a secret emotional relationship which you should give up if you do not want a more lasting relationship to be destroyed. If you shudder with revulsion at an item of food in a dream, you can expect major financial worries, and if it is a drink of some kind that makes you shudder, you need help and understanding to get used to an unfamiliar environment.

SHYNESS

Dreaming of a shy man indicates a lively discussion with someone at work; while the appearance of a shy woman reveals your uncertainty and doubt relating to someone you love.

If it is an old person being shy, you should take the advice of others into account when deciding how to get round a major obstacle at work. If it is someone else being shy in your dream, it indicates you have a low level of confidence in your own abilities, but if it is you that is being shy, there is a period of despondency on the way.

SICKNESS

Dreaming about being bedridden through any type of illness indicates that you could succumb to a temptation which may harm you in the longer term. If someone else is sick, it suggests you should keep a close eye on any potential rivals, either at work or in love, who are threatening to make life difficult for you.

SIGNING

The meaning of this dream depends on what it is that is being signed. Signing a cheque means there are difficulties in prospect, and signing a receipt indicates a recent outburst of anger on your part. Signing a letter indicates financial prosperity, and signing an agreement foretells of progress in your career.

SILVER   Silver objects mean promotion is still distant.

SILVER

Dreaming about silver coins means you could lose some money, though if you or someone else use these coins to pay for something, there will be an improvement in your business and financial affairs. If you dream that someone else has a large quantity of silverware, it suggests a step upwards in your career, though if you dream about owning objects made of silver yourself, you may be held back from this promotion for some time to come.

SINGING

Any kind of singing in a dream, whether it is by you or someone else, means that although you may be cheerful at the moment, there are problems and worries around the corner. Fortunately they are unlikely to trouble you for very long and will resolve themselves.

SINKING

If you dream you are sinking into water, mud or anything else, it suggests you have just lost some money or spent it unnecessarily, and you should not get involved in any other financial ventures for the time being, because your faulty judgment is liable to make them equally expensive.

SINNING

Committing a sexual indiscretion with a woman in a dream foretells obstacles in your work environment leading to acute anxiety; while committing a sexual indiscretion with a man indicates your fear for someone's health. If you commit a sin of omission in a dream by failing to do something, it means a favourable but potentially risky opportunity is about to be given to you, and you should consider your decision very carefully because it could affect the rest of your life. Committing a crime deliberately in a dream means you are being greedy and taking more of something than you need to.

SKATING

Dreaming about rollerskating is a sign of your anxiety and nerves, while ice skating suggests that an emotional relationship is being threatened by the malicious influence of someone who envies your success. If you dream about taking skating lessons, you will be pleasantly surprised by an opportunity which allows you to make your mark at work, but if you see other people skating, you can expect to be the object of bitterness and rancour from people who are supposedly your friends.

SKELETON

A human skeleton in a dream indicates that serious financial worries lie ahead, and an animal's skeleton suggests that you have a tendency to feel lonely and depressed, though if you accepted the help of someone who cares about you, you could shake off this state of mind. If the skeleton walks or talks, it indicates that you have a secret which you would be reluctant to tell anyone.

SKIER

A skier doing a jump in a dream symbolizes your increasing physical and psychological strength, while one speeding downhill means you should avoid fits of anger. If you dream you are skiing yourself and you fall over, your financial and business outlook is very bright.

SKIP

Skipping with a rope in a dream means you are open and giving in your relationships with people around you, and skipping along a road heralds the long-awaited solution to a monetary problem.

SKIRT

The interpretation of this dream depends on the type and colour of the skirt you see. If it is a white one, it symbolizes joy; if it is any other colour, it signifies your desires being realized. A short skirt means you are getting involved in something you should not, and a long one shows that you are considering the possibility of cheating or deception over something. A cotton skirt indicates a romantic conquest; a silk one, a good social position; and a velvet one, excessive ambition.

SKULL

A human skull suggests a sense of worry and lack of trust in someone close to you, and an animal's skull indicates that you are in some embarrassing situation. A talking skull symbolizes your well-kept secrets.

SKYLARK

A skylark in dreams is a sign of great good luck. It symbolizes future health and wealth, and if an unmar-

SLEEP   Dreaming of deep sleep promises new business associations.

ried woman dreams she hears a skylark singing, she will have a wealthy, loving husband and children with musical tendencies.

SLAP

Although it is an unpleasant experience in real life, being slapped in a dream is not entirely an unfavourable sign: although things may not be going your way at the moment the future looks much brighter, provided you keep calm and think carefully before you make any major decisions. Slapping someone else in a dream suggests you are being unfeeling towards someone in your everyday life.

SLEEP

It is quite common to dream about seeing yourself asleep or seeing someone else asleep. If it is a restless sleep, your health is less than perfect at the moment, but if it is a deep sleep, it indicates that you will make new business connections. If you dream about waking up after a long sleep, you are likely to be full of energy and vitality. Sleeping with someone else in a dream means you are both optimistic and trusting.

SLIPPER

Women's slippers in a dream are a sign that an emotional relationship may be in danger, but men's indicate that you are in a strong, lasting relationship. If the slippers are made of fabric, they show that there is a need for changes to be made in your life, and if they are leather they signify your satisfaction with a person or situation. Buying slippers in your dream means a piece of speculation will turn out in your favour, and giving them to someone else means that you are in a period of calm and contentment. Putting on slippers shows that you are certain about what to do about a proposal being put to you at work. If they are falling apart, they symbolize a step upwards in your career.

SMELL

A strong, unpleasant smell in a dream such as smoke or sweat indicates that you will make an important new friend or acquaintance soon. A more pleasant smell shows that you are receiving advice which would be best ignored, though the smell of flowers or perfume can also suggest the need for a break with someone who is not doing you any good. If you or someone else smell unpleasant in your dream, it is a warning that you should take more care of yourself because you are taking on too much responsibility and working too hard.

SMILING

Smiling with pleasure or happiness in a dream means that you will have an unwelcome encounter with someone you have not seen for a long time, but smiling slyly or maliciously indicates that you are making a compromise which could harm your career. Smiling at someone as a sign of friendship means that alarming news will be arriving from afar.

SMILING   A happy smile warns of an unwanted meeting with an old contact.

SMOKE

Smoke in a dream is a sign of disappointment or delusion; the thicker the smoke, the greater the disappointment you are feeling. If the smoke gets in your eyes, it reflects your displeasure at something. Cigarette smoke is a sign that you are about to make an important new acquaintance, and burning incense indicates present family harmony.

SMOKING

The exact interpretation of this dream depends on what is being smoked. Cigarettes mean you will have minor, insignificant financial gains, and cigars signify that your efforts are being made in vain. Smoking a pipe shows that you have received a just reward, and smoking drugs means you have a lot of important things to do. A cigarette holder reflects a delicate constitution and less than perfect health.

SMUGGLER

Being a smuggler yourself in a dream means you lack self-discipline and tend to get involved in short-lived, risky exploits that

SNAKE   A snake suggests a rival is threatening your romantic affairs.

may land you in trouble. Seeing a smuggler at work, or being chased or arrested, indicates rash, hastily-made decisions.

SNAIL

Snails are not a particularly good omen in a dream: they indicate your unreliability and sudden changes of mood, and it is possible that someone who is jealous of you is about to start putting obstacles in your path.

SNAKE

The snake is widely regarded as a symbol of ill-fortune in dreams. If you see one in a dream, it means either an enemy is trying to harm you financially, or a rival in love is trying to destroy your happiness. If you manage to kill the snake, you will be able to prevent this person from damaging you.

160

turned to ice on the ground, it shows doubts and problems relating to a loved one. Dirty slush reflects your discretion and carefulness, and a snowdrift indicates unexpected pleasures and financial gains. If snow is falling in your dream, there are many new and interesting events about to happen in your life, and if you are walking on snow, you have plenty of initiative and also considerable enthusiasm and imagination, but you should avoid getting some things which are troubling you at the moment out of proportion.

SNUFF BOX

A gold snuff box in a dream means you need to save money, and a silver one, that you are unpredictable and moody. If it is a very old snuff box, you need to sort out some long-standing problems before any more time goes by.

SOAP

Soap powder in a dream indicates that a meeting will go well, and bath soap shows the renewal of an old

SNUFF BOX   Antique boxes mean it is time to overcome an old problem.

SNOW   Icy snow shows that relations with your partner are problematic.

SNOOKER

Seeing or playing in a game of snooker, billiards or pool in a dream foreshadows possible difficulties on the horizon; if you are in love with someone, your family may be opposed to them or make life difficult for both of you.

SNORING

A man snoring in a dream shows that a superior at work has a great deal of respect for your abilities, while a woman snoring indicates your considerable problems with an overambitious financial venture.

SNOW

Snow in a dream can have a number of different meanings. If it is light, powdery snow it indicates whimsical, capricious behaviour; if it has

attachment. Shaving soap signifies that excessive demands are being made of you. If the soap is white, you can expect fairly significant improvements on the financial front, and if it is perfumed, it indicates a lack of understanding between your family and the person you love. Washing your face with soap indicates repentance, and washing your hands with soap means a goal finally being attained.

SOFTENING

Using a fabric softener to do your washing in a dream foreshadows a small stroke of good fortune. Fitting a water-softener to your central heating system shows that you are assailed by worry and self-doubt.

SOILING

Soiled laundry in a dream indicates a distracted and worried frame of mind; wearing soiled clothes indicates your discouragement over something and your consequent mood of unhappiness. Soiled paper means that you have formed an unfair assessment of someone, and dirty furniture shows a lack of decisiveness and authority. If you dream about getting dirty in a pool of mud, you need to make a change in your work routine before your health is adversely affected by overwork.

SOLDIER

Dreaming of a soldier within barracks marks the end of a worry which has been tormenting you for a long time. A soldier in the street shows that you are getting mental stimulation from work, and one on parade means someone has a greater interest in you than you may realize.

SOLDIER   Soldiers on the battlefield suggest problems with a younger person.

A soldier on the battleground means a difficult time with somebody much younger than yourself, and if you are a soldier yourself in your dream, it suggests you feel very strongly about something but have trouble persuading others to share your view.

SOLE

The appearance of a leather sole in a dream means you are worried and anxious about a relative's health, when there is no need to be. A rubber sole means timidity and lack of confidence in what you do. If you dream about losing the sole of a shoe, it would be a good idea to take up an opportunity which has been presented to you, before it is too late.

SON

To have a son in a dream (whether or not you actually have a son in real life) signifies success. An unmarried son reflects problems in your life, and a married one, worries connected with your family. If your son is in the army within the dream, your ambitions will eventually come to fruition.

SORE

A sore in a dream can be just as unpleasant as it is in real life. It means you are entering a critical period as far as your future career is concerned; unless you think carefully before making any decision, you could stand to lose out financially. If you have a sore on your hand, you will manage to sort out problems facing you at work easily, and if it is on your arm, you will be able to benefit from close cooperation between you and another person at work. A sore on your face in a dream promises success for a venture you have speculated some money on.

SOUP

Dreaming about a plate of hot soup is not necessarily the favourable sign one might expect. Vegetable soup indicates family problems, and pea soup indicates that you have had a brief argument. Potato soup means that you are feeling unwell. Clear soup shows that important decisions must be taken in your relationship with your partner. If the soup is on a table, it shows you will be helped out by someone you did not trust.

Sow

If you dream about a sow coming towards you, there is good fortune on the way; but if it is walking or running away, then the future holds out little luck for you.

Spade

Any dream involving someone using a spade for any purpose means new and promising alternatives are opening up in your career. Buying a spade indicates that you have secure, honest friendships, but if the spade you dream of is rusty, you need to approach a delicate situation with a great deal of care and tactfulness, and if the spade is broken, you are entering a period of aimlessness and indecision.

Sparrow

Dreaming of a sparrow in its nest shows your need for support and protection. If it is singing, it indicates that you have avoided a danger recently. Dreaming about a flock of sparrows foretells a period of very hard work ending in great personal success.

What do flying and falling dreams mean?

Dreams about falling and flying have been given a wide variety of explanations in the past, many of them very basic physical ones related to sexual desire, circulation problems, skin sensitivity, and even eye problems.

The interpretation most frequently given is a sexual one. Flying has been seen as a sign of sexual potency, and falling, as an indicator of limited potency. Dreams among teenagers which involve flying have been analyzed and a correlation has been established between this type of dream and an increase in sexual desire. Here, flying is a kind of boast, a display of sexual powers.

Freud stated that, for women, falling was a sign of resistance melting when they were confronted with the opposite sex. Studies have shown that it is more common to dream about falling than flying, and that young children rarely dream about flying, if ever.

People who dream about flying tend to be those who are unhappy, who are not in control of their lives and do not see their ambitions being realized. They are likely to have low self-esteem, and dreaming about flying is often a compensation for lack of sexual experience.

People who have this dream tend to feel pleasure and contentment when they wake up from it, as they have established a greater degree of equilibrium between their conscious and unconscious.

Dreams about falling are often seen by experts as expressions of a need to let oneself go and enjoy life more, and stem from a feeling of isolation. It is quite often the case that the more you succeed in life the more isolated you

feel from your fellow human beings. The need to preserve the status you have reached often obscures the need for basic human contact. Not surprisingly, this type of dream is particularly common among successful professional men and women, as though to make up for a part of their lives which is missing.

Dreams about falling can be seen as an unfulfilled desire for support and affection: this might be felt particularly by a child away from the warmth and comfort of home, or an adult living in a situation where they do not feel understood or accepted.

SPEAR

If you or someone else are carrying a spear in a dream, it is a warning of potential danger: you should be particularly careful. Being wounded by a spear, or wounding someone else, signifies your great dissatisfaction with something or someone. A broken spear indicates that you are confronting major problems.

SPECTACLES

Wearing a pair of glasses in a dream means there is a chance of your missing out on a very favourable opportunity, though if they are sunglasses, you are entering a period in which you are full of optimism and self-confidence. If the spectacles are for short-sightedness, you will gain interesting new experience in your work, and if they are for long-sightedness, you will reach an agreement with someone which will put an end to a difficult situation. Buying glasses in a dream indicates that you will have a brief period of illness which will cause nothing more than minor inconvenience, and taking them to be repaired foreshadows an unexpected payment of money to you.

SPEED

A train speeding across the countryside in a dream indicates a phase in your life where you feel calm and

STAGE   Actors performing on a stage predict an interesting discovery.

contented, and an aeroplane indicates that you will make a move which will prove to be advantageous. A fast car shows trust and faithfulness in an emotional relationship. Buying a fast motorbike suggests you have unjustified doubts about a new acquaintance you have not yet got to know properly.

SPILLING

Spilling cold water in a dream suggests childish, thoughtless behaviour on your part, while spilling hot water, shows that you have health worries. Spilling salt indicates family problems, and cooking oil, financial losses. If you spill wine in your dream, you will be deceived by someone you thought you could trust.

SPOON

The meaning of this symbol in dreams varies according to what it is made of and what it is used for. A tablespoon shows flexibility and adaptability, while a teaspoon suggests that you are being overly critical of someone. A wooden spoon signifies secret liaisons with someone of the opposite sex, and a silver one, easy conquests in love.

SPRING

A spring with dirty water in a dream is an indicator of good fortune, but one which has dried up or blocked up indicates future problems and bitterness. Drinking from a spring symbolizes affection being reciprocated. A metal spring such as a bedspring suggests that you are not a materialistic person and can manage without your home comforts if necessary. If the season within your dream is obviously spring it symbolizes that you are having new and stimulating ideas.

SQUARE

A square shape or a square object in a dream reflects a feeling of confidence and security. A town square is a sign of your increasing energy, both physical and mental. If the square is full of people, you can expect a period of depression, while an empty square indicates a brief separation from your partner. Walking through a square indicates a forthcoming favourable opportunity which should be grasped with both hands.

SPECTACLES   Wake up! Opportunities may be passing you by.

STABLE

Dreaming of a stable with cows in it foretells a major achievement or success, while one with sheep in indicates your over-sensitivity. If the stable has one or more donkeys in it, there are business problems ahead, but if it contains horses, prosperity and well-being are likely. If you dream about going to sleep in a stable, your business affairs are guaranteed to be a success.

STACKING

Stacking books, wood, or furniture in a dream all mean that you have some heavy work ahead of you. If there is a very large quantity of objects to be stacked, the dream can also symbolize future abundance and fertility.

STAGE

Dreaming of a stage in a theatre symbolizes embitterment caused by something involving the opposite sex. If the stage projects out into the audience, it reflects a missed opportunity. If it has scenery on it, it shows you are involved in a long and hard search for anything which gives pleasure. A stage with actors performing on it means you are about to make an interesting discovery, and if you are on it yourself, making a speech or acting, you are showing totally unjustified jealousy which can only lead to the end of a relationship.

STAIN

A stain always symbolizes some kind of misfortune, though exactly what this is depends on what causes the stain. If it is coffee, the failure of a project or venture is in the offing, and if it is ink, a person dear to you is likely to be ill. A grease stain indicates future arguments and malice being directed toward you, and a wine stain foretells feelings of jealousy on your part. A bloodstain suggests that you make decisions hurriedly and without closely examining the issues involved.

STABLE   Horses in a stable mean you can look forward to a prosperous future.

STAIRCASE

A stone staircase in a dream means you need to exert all your self-will and effort if you are to break your dependence on someone else in your work; a wooden staircase suggests that you are making mistakes at work which could harm you severely. A long staircase means you can expect a period of tiredness and unhappiness, and a short one, that you need to make your presence felt more at work.

STAR

To dream of a star is a sign of confidence in yourself and your abilities; the pole star symbolizes hopes which are bound up with a project at work. If the star is twinkling, you should try to be more careful and cautious in things you do.

STATION

A railway station in a dream heralds important news connected with work. If you are arriving at a station or departing from it in your dream, you are waiting patiently for the results of a major project you are involved in, but if you are meeting someone else at the station, the dream shows you will be helped in your career by someone who wields a great deal of influence. If the train you are waiting for is late, it means you should not move too quickly in a new relationship, but you ought to allow it time to develop naturally.

165

STATUE

A marble statue in a dream shows your considerable self-control and responsibility, and a bronze one, conversely, lack of willpower and the fact that you are easily influenced by others. If it is made of clay, you are becoming involved in fruitless recriminations. A very old statue means you are about to find yourself at the centre of a very tricky situation.

STAYING OVERNIGHT

Dreaming of staying overnight in a hotel indicates your financial successes; staying outdoors, or in a tent, a craving for more freedom and independence. Spending the night in a car means that you are receiving help and advice from friends; in a railway station, that you have to put right the results of a mistake made some time ago; and on a train, that you will make a decision which will have very favourable results. Spending the night on a boat reflects your love of solitude, and staying the night at a friend's or relative's house in a dream is a reminder that you are not as friendless as your sometimes think.

STEAK

Eating a steak in a dream is a sign of your present well-being, but seeing one without being able to eat it indicates unrealizable desires. A rare steak means possible financial losses.

STEAM

A steamboat indicates financial and material well-being, and a steam train suggests a romance of yours is at risk in some way. A steam engine means you are finding life with your partner difficult at the moment. If the steam is coming from a kettle or saucepan, it suggests you will be off-colour for a short time.

STEPFATHER

The appearance of a stepfather with whom you get on in your dream shows that you have a decisive personality that likes to be in control, is immune to temptation,

STATUE   An ancient statue heralds a potentially awkward moment.

and is orderly and self-disciplined. Dreaming of a bad stepfather indicates major differences of opinion within your family. Visiting a stepfather in a dream means you are likely to be laid up by illness, and there is also a greater likelihood than usual of your making mistakes at work. The appearance of a dead or dying stepfather means you have a fertile imagination and an extrovert, sociable personality.

STING

Being stung by an insect is, curiously enough, a favourable sign if it happens in a dream. It indicates that your relationship with your partner will be a long and happy one; at work, a personal success will gain you the trust and confidence of a superior and you will gain in responsibility as a result. If you get stung by a nettle in a dream, it suggests you are self-distrustful and withdrawn in relations with your partner. If you are stung by any other animal or plant, it means you will suffer from a brief illness or period of depression.

STITCH

The most important factor in a dream involving stitches or stitching is what the thread is made of. If it is cotton, you should avoid getting involved in pointless, time-consuming discussions which could annoy the person you love. A woollen thread means someone is being a hindrance at work, and stitching something with silk means there could be a possible deception by someone dear to you. Giving or receiving stitches for a wound suggests that a friend can help you get over a psychological traumatic experience. Getting a stitch when you are running in a dream means you should slow down at work.

STOCKING

Making or buying stockings in a dream is a reflection of your present success in romance. Putting them

on means you need help from someone and are likely to get it. If they are new, you have aims and ambitions which can never be realized, but if they are old or laddered they indicate indifference from or towards someone of the opposite sex. Mending holes in a stocking is a sign that your present pleasures will soon pass.

STOCKS

Being put in the stocks in a dream suggests there is enmity towards you from someone which you are not aware of. Building up stocks of something, perhaps in a shop, means an unexpected change of scene which will leave you briefly disoriented and may mean you lose out on an opportunity.

STOMACH

The appearance of a man's stomach in a dream indicates your tendency to laziness, while a woman's indicates that you are holding emotional secrets. If you see your own stomach in the dream, you need to keep a close check on your health. A bloated stomach means you are very shy, even with people you know closely, while if it is bare, you will solve a problem that has been troubling you for a long time. Dreaming you have stomach ache indicates temporary problems, and watching your stomach swell because you are pregnant indicates that you will soon be feeling satisfied at some accomplishment of yours.

STONE

A hard stone is a symbol in dreams of time-consuming preparations for an important event. Precious stones mean you are worrying about someone in your family, and a very old stone symbolizes that your generosity has been ill repaid by someone who received it. A tombstone reflects respect and recognition for something you have done in the past. Throwing stones signifies that you are about to make a profitable acquisition; loading them onto something, boredom and lethargy; and unloading them, help and support from members of your family. If you dream about walking on stones, you will experience painful lovesickness over someone.

STITCH   Stitching indicates that things are not going well at present.

STORE-ROOM

Opening a store-room in a dream indicates new experiences relating to romance, but closing one indicates your repressed fears and uneasy state of mind. If the store-room is dirty, you will find yourself involved in a delicate situation, with little idea of how to resolve it.

STORK

Despite its connotations, dreaming about a stork is not a good sign: it foretells a change, possibly a move, which will leave you worse off than before. If the stork is flying, there is the risk of your committing a crime, and if it is sitting in its nest, you are likely to have family problems.

STORM

Any type of storm in a dream, be it rain, snow, hail or wind, is a sign that dangers are awaiting you and you need to be extra-cautious.

STORY

Listening to someone else telling a story in a dream reflects a personal achievement you have made which can only be described as brilliant. Reading one to someone else, or to yourself, means that you are attracting unjustified criticism, and making one up as you go along suggests your efforts over something are to no avail. If it is an adventure story, you will be criticized and slandered by someone who is envious of you,

while if it is a story of romance, an appointment will be cancelled at the last minute. A science fiction story suggests you are orderly and precise in everything you do.

STOVE

A coal stove in a dream presages an important relationship, and a wood-burning one, the fact that you need to ask someone else for a solution to a problem. A gas stove indicates an impressive improvement in your health, and an electric one, uncertainty about what to do next. If the stove is off, you will miss out on a very favourable opportunity which is about to come your way.

STRAIGHTENING

Straightening a piece of clothing that is crooked, such as a tie, in a dream means you can expect problems on a number of fronts: at work you will have to justify some minor errors of judgment to a superior, and in love you will have to pay the consequences of an argument with your partner. Fortunately, all these problems are likely to be short-lived. Straightening a piece of furniture that is out of place means you will put a lot of time and effort into a new project at work, and your hard work will eventually be recognized and amply rewarded.

STRANGER

Any appearance by someone you do not recognize in your dream indicates long-lasting friendships and faithfulness in love.

STRAW

Dreaming of a bale of straw indicates problems and obstacles in your love life, and cut straw lying in a field means that you are beset with financial worries. If you dream about harvesting straw, you will get involved in an embarrassing situation without realizing it. Burning straw means you are caught up in a situation which is getting beyond your control. A straw hat indicates that appearances can be deceptive, so you should not take them at face value. If you or someone else drink something through a straw, it indicates that you are taking on a heavy burden of responsibility.

STRAWBERRY

Eating strawberries or giving them to someone else is a very favourable sign to dream of, indicating forthcoming pleasant surprises and events. Strawberries with cream, however, show your bias and lack of objectivity in dealing with an issue, and wild strawberries mean difficulties at work.

STREAM

Dreaming of a stream is not a particularly auspicious omen, although if it is clear enough to drink from, it is a guarantee of long-term health. If it is at all muddy, there are likely to be arguments in your family, and if it has dried up, it indicates that you have made a decision which is likely to cause you harm.

STRONG MAN/WOMAN

A strong man in a dream, perhaps lifting weights or doing something similar, indicates hopes being shattered and ambitions being set too high, while a female body-builder indicates a fortunate gamble or piece of speculation. An unusually strong child in a dream is a sign of good health and of your knowing where you want to go in life. If it is you in the dream that is very strong, there is a short period ahead in which nothing seems to go right.

STUDYING

Studying languages in a dream indicates that you are being deceitfully flattered and studying literature foretells of renewed hope in a project connected with your work. Studying maths means you have a habit of disagreeing with people for the sake of it. Studying in the evenings means you are uncertain and not sure what to do next in life.

STUMBLING

If you fall over in the street in your dream, it might be a good idea to put off making an important deci-

sion for the time being. Stumbling on a flight of stairs suggests that you have a distorted view of things, and tripping over a stone indicates obstacles are looming that need to be avoided and that you will make mistakes which it will be costly to repeat.

SUBMISSIVE

A submissive woman in a dream is a sign of your growing feeling of energy, and a submissive child means an offer is being made under false pretences. A submissive old person means bright prospects on the business front, and a relative being submissive indicates future professional success and prestige. A submissive man means that you would be justified in putting off carrying out your responsibilities – perhaps at work – for the time being. A schoolchild being excessively obedient shows that you should be asserting your rights, and an obedient son or daughter means you can expect most of your hopes to come true.

SUBSCRIPTION

If you dream about paying a subscription to something, the outlook is a very favourable one. It means either that you will soon obtain the

STRAWBERRY   Eating strawberries heralds a pleasant surprise.

STREAM   A clear sparkling stream promises lasting good health.

vital results you have been waiting for for a long time, or that a secret will be revealed, or that your inquisitiveness about something will finally be justified.

SUCKING

The interpretation of this dream depends on what it is that is being sucked. Sucking a toffee means you have made a correct assessment of someone close to you, but any other kind of sweet means people will try to get in the way of your progress in your career. Sucking a lemon reflects persistent arguments with your partner, and sucking a chocolate suggests that you might be over-indulging yourself, perhaps by eating too much.

SUIT

A man's suit in a dream reflects the fact that an old friend or acquaintance is in need of help, but a woman's suit shows a lack of organization in things you are doing. Mourning dress indicates that a serious loss of some kind is forthcoming; a new suit reflects your financial worries; and an old one, your determination.

SUITCASE

An ordinary suitcase in a dream shows you have a great deal of dynamism, but an expensive leather one means a journey is in prospect. An especially large one indicates your spirit of adventure, and a small one, arguments with relatives. An open suitcase means your prospects of success in a new venture are high.

SUMMIT

Dreaming about a mountain summit with no snow on it means a journey of yours will have to be put off till later, but one with snow on it means you have made an unfair assessment of someone or something. If there are animals on the summit, it indicates improving health, and if there are plants or trees, you will reach

STUDYING   If the subject is maths, the dreamer can be argumentative.

agreement with members of your family. If it is shrouded in mist, your feelings towards someone are about to be reciprocated.

SUMMONS

Issuing a summons in a dream means unpleasant events are looming in your love life, and receiving one indicates your excessive enthusiasm for something. Withdrawing a summons means you are in an agitated frame of mind and need to calm down if you want to avoid missing a favourable opportunity. If the summons is for a debt, it shows

you have great strength of character, and if it is for slander or libel, it means you will have trouble adjusting to your partner's unpredictable behaviour. A summons issued to a woman by a man, or vice versa, indicates problems and misunderstanding arising from your work.

SUN

If the sun is shining brightly in your dream, it indicates that you will get much pleasure and satisfaction from a relationship with someone you love, but if it is obscured by clouds or anything else, it shows there are unexpected obstacles lying in wait at work.

SUNSET

A sunset is a favourable omen in a dream. Although you may be feeling confused and bewildered at the moment, the help and understanding you will receive from your partner will help you regain your enthusiasm for life and your self-confidence so that eventually you will be achieving things you never thought possible.

SUN TAN

If you are female and you dream about getting brown in the sun, it indicates your present feelings of

SUN TAN   For a female, a sun tan indicates happiness and peace of mind.

tranquillity and contentment, but if you are a man, it shows a tendency to laziness.

SUPPER

Cooking supper in a dream suggests that a short period of belt-tightening is in order because of your financial situation. If the meal is for more than one person it indicates your mood of calm and serenity, but if it is for one it reflects presumptuous, arrogant behaviour.

SURRENDER

It is not very common to dream about an army surrendering, but it means that a financial venture you have been involved in is about to yield its benefits, and as a result there will be an improvement in your standard of living. A castle surrendering after a siege means you have strong intuitive abilities, and a single soldier laying down his arms shows you are feeling very confident.

SUSPENDERS

New suspenders in a dream indicate a temptation which you must avoid at all costs, and old ones mean assistance from someone important at work. If they are torn or broken, you have a great deal of will and determination to succeed. If your dream involves buying a suspender belt, you have ambitions which no-one else knows about, and adjusting your suspender belt in a dream shows that your practicality and foresight will help you achieve financial success.

SWALLOW

Swallowing food, or anything else, in a dream indicates the beginning of a project which could have a major effect on your career. Seeing a flock of swallows in a dream indicates the arrival of important news shortly, and swallows building a nest symbolize well-being and tranquillity. Swallows migrating to warmer climates indicate a strong desire to travel which is likely to become a reality sooner rather than later.

SWAN

Seeing a swan in a dream shows that pleasant news is on the way, while a swan swimming on a lake or pond indicates future prosperity and material well-being. Feeding a swan signifies happiness in love. A black swan, however, indicates that the future will be less pleasant.

SWEARING

Any kind of obscene language in a dream signifies your problems in relating to other people and to your environment. Swearing an oath on the bible in court indicates a happy future, but swearing undying love is a sign of insincerity on your or someone else's part. Swearing vengeance shows you are worried about something. Swearing a false oath, or lying under oath, means you should be careful.

SWEET

Paradoxically, sweets in a dream symbolize bitterness in real life: buying sweets or giving them to someone else indicate a difficulty in your relationship with your partner and the possibility of a permanent break. Eating them yourself means that you are in a period when mistakes will be very costly and you should be careful not to make any false moves or rash decisions.

SWIMMING POOL

Dreaming about a swimming pool full of water means prospects at work have never been better, and you should seize on any opportunities given to you, because they will not be there for very long. If the pool is empty, you are being unfair in you assessment of someone you have just met. If it is a very large pool, you have thought out a new project at work in considerable detail and you are hoping it will further increase your standing among the people you work with. Swimming in a pool yourself means this would be a good time to finish something you have left.

The dreams of the great climber

Jorge Amado, the famous South American writer, regards himself as a "professional dreamer". He states that the greater part of his work was conceived in dreams and he takes it as a matter of course to write down the images and visions he remembers when he wakes up, and incorporate them in his works. "All I am," says Amado, "is a hard-working recorder of dreams. If I didn't have dreams, I wouldn't know what to write about."

Likewise, Reinhold Messner, the famous mountaineer, says that much of the inspiration for his exploits comes from dreams. "More than once I have clearly seen in a dream something that later happened in real life. This has helped me overcome difficulties which I met with in a climb, because I had already solved them in my dreams."

Here we have two very different situations, but with one feature in common. Both Amado and Messner see dreaming as an extension of reality, and believe that in dreams we can actually do some of the work that otherwise we would have to do in real life.

This is far from being a novel concept. The Roman poet Virgil said that he first conceived the heroes of some of his works in dreams, and the Italian explorers Vespucci and Verrazzano both worked out in their dreams the routes they were to take through unknown territory.

Although as late as the beginning of this century people were denying that there was any connection between dream and reality, the tendency nowadays is to believe the opposite.

The dreamer strengthens his powers of concentration and experiences situations before they happen. Many experts dislike terms like 'premonition', but will accept that reality can be preconstructed on the basis of events already experienced.

SWINDLING
This has the same bad results in a dream as it is does in real life: a man being swindled indicates that you are undertaking a very risky venture, and a woman being swindled shows that your behaviour at the moment may be intemperate and foolhardy. If you dream about swindling a customer, there will be unpleasant gossip directed at you.

SWORD
A very old sword in a dream foreshadows a brief setback on the horizon, and one being drawn out of its scabbard reflects financial problems which need to be sorted out before they get any worse. A bloodstained sword shows that you are subject to fits of depression which could have a more harmful effect than you realize.

TABLE
A round table in a dream means that guests are on their way to visit you, and a square one shows that you will meet some interesting new acquaintances. A rectangular one reflects your present experience of new sensations and stimuli. An extendable table indicates misunderstandings and disagreements with someone. If it is a marble-topped table, you are about to enter into an exciting new relationship.

TABLECLOTH
A white tablecloth in a dream represents your experience of very happy events, while if it is any other colour it stands for your receiving a just reward. If it is clean it indicates unexpected gains, and if it is dirty, untrustworthiness and unfaithfulness in a relationship with a loved one. If your dream involves your buying a tablecloth, you are being tetchy and irritable.

TABLET
Dreaming about a medicinal tablet denotes ill-humour and irritability. Taking tablets for a cold or cough means you are being vague and indecisive in your relationship with your partner. A bottle of tablets indicates that you are indulging in rather self-centred worries. Sleeping tablets denote your desire for adventure and escape, but if you dream about someone taking an overdose of them, it suggests you are putting your own interests before those of someone close to you. A stone tablet, perhaps inscribed, signifies your present inflexibility and lack of adaptability.

TALKING
Talking to a man in a dream indicates that new experiences connected with romance are on the way, and talking to a woman foretells advantageous business dealings. Talking to an enemy indicates that arguments are going on in your

TARGET   Dreaming of target-shooting means self-repression.

family, and talking to an animal, that significant financial losses or expenses are on the horizon. If you are talking loudly or shouting, you have a major obstacle to overcome, but if you talk quietly, or whisper, there will be malicious gossip about you. Speaking ill of someone indicates a recent outburst of bad temper, and speaking well of them indicates that you have some bad habits. Listening to someone else talking indicates that you are impulsive by nature.

TANGLE
A tangle of undergrowth in a dream means you are much more nervous than usual. A tangled thread or similar suggests that a secret love affair is threatening to complicate your life.

TAPESTRY
Dreaming of a tapestry foretells joyful surprises ahead, and you will enjoy yourself without having to spend money in doing so.

TARGET
Shooting bullets, arrows or anything else at a target in a dream symbolizes repressed emotions and desires. If you hit the bullseye on a target, you are original and independently minded.

TART

Dreaming of a cream tart signifies the arrival of a pleasant piece of news, while a chocolate one shows present illness or fatigue. An apple pie or tart means you can expect a reward, and a cherry tart indicates you will make limited financial gains. A piping hot tart means that you will have an unforgettable experience together with your partner.

TEA

Cold tea in a dream indicates that there will be a gap or break in an emotional relationship of yours, while hot tea shows intelligence and sharp-wittedness. Tea with milk in it reflects your good sense and reason; and lemon tea, reserved, cautious behaviour. If your dream involves drinking tea, you will manage to break free from the influence of others at work.

TEETH

Teeth are normally an unfavourable sign in a dream. Having toothache signifies your displeasure at something, and if a tooth comes out in your dream, it shows you are afraid of losing someone dear to you. If you lose all your teeth it means you are full of fears about everything. A gold tooth indicates coming financial benefits. Having a filling in a dream, although it is a painful experience in real life, actually indicates there are pleasures in store.

TELEGRAM

Sending a telegram in a dream suggests balance and confidence in everything you do. This will help you past obstacles at work which others would not even think of attempting. Being sent a telegram in a dream means that you are slipping into a state of apathy and boredom which could be very hard to climb out of.

TELEPHONE

Speaking to someone on the phone in your dream indicates that an apparently small difference of opinion with your partner could have a much more serious effect on your relationship than you might expect. If someone else phones you up in a dream, you have problems which will need to be sorted out within the next few days.

TELEVISION

Buying a television set in a dream indicates a shaky financial future, and giving one to someone else means you are unhappy and have a low level of self-confidence. Repairing one indicates that you are making sensible decisions and have an ability to make carefully considered judgments. Turning on a television in a dream symbolizes your emotional sensitivity, and turning one off suggests your future involvement in a dangerous and potentially harmful relationship.

TEMPEST

A tempest at sea in a dream indicates that either your financial affairs or those of someone close to you need to be put into order, and a violent gale indicates harmful thoughts and ideas. If you dream about getting unexpectedly caught in a storm, there will be significant changes at work which will help you attain a greater degree of independence and confidence.

TENNIS

Dreaming about a tennis court indicates a considerable sense of responsibility and rationality in your actions, while if you see someone else playing tennis, rapid advancement in your career is just around the corner. Playing it yourself means you have a strong need for freedom and independence.

TENNIS   Playing tennis in a dream suggests a love of freedom and independence.

TEST

Taking or watching a test at school or college indicates that you have had a major personal success recently. If the test is written, it indicates faithfulness and a very strong rapport between you and your partner, while an oral test means you are reserved and diplomatic. If you are taking the test yourself, you are very good at intuitive guesswork; if you pass the test, you are involved in an exciting phase of a relationship; but even if you fail it means you have a lot of good ideas for the future. A test on a piece of machinery, a vehicle or something similar, means you are entertaining totally false hopes about how someone feels about you and should face up to this fact.

TESTIFYING

To dream of giving spoken evidence in court means you are confident and able to react to situations quickly, and this will help you solve some very complex problems. Testifying in writing in a dream means that you have a perfect opportunity to make money.

THEATRE

Dreaming of a large theatre means you are entertaining desires which can never be realized, and a small one indicates practicality and helpfulness. A brightly-lit theatre indicates that you will confront situations in which appearances will be deceiving. If you go to see a play in your dream, you will receive news – which could be either good or bad – from a long way away. Dreaming of an operating theatre is a sign of a weak personality.

THERMOMETER

A clinical thermometer in a dream shows a strong sense of responsibility and an ability to get things done, while the type you hang on the wall means you never make decisions without pondering them carefully. If you buy a thermometer in your dreams, there is a good chance of success in an ambitious project at work.

THIGH

The significance of this dream is usually a negative one, whether the thigh is human or animal. Long thighs mean you should watch out for malicious gossip; thin ones stand for intolerance – but fat ones show your generosity. A chicken thigh foretells a potential danger, and a turkey's reveals your behaviour as irrational.

THIMBLE

A thimble is not a sign of good luck in dreams. Using one yourself indicates that someone is critical of you

THRONE The vision of a royal throne assures you of confidence in dealing with problems.
TEETH Difficult times may lie ahead when you dream about teeth.

and your behaviour, and if you lose one it reflects an injustice that you have committed. A silver thimble suggests your excessive pride will get its come-uppance.

THROAT

A throat being cut in a dream is a danger signal of some kind. A swollen throat reflects your considerable powers of imagination, while if it is painful or inflamed, it signifies a successful venture.

THRONE

Dreaming of a throne for a king or queen indicates a calm confidence which will help you deal with a potentially embarrassing situation, while the Pope's throne signifies a correct decision.

THROWING

Any kind of dream which involves throwing something indicates your present feelings of dissatisfaction. Throwing yourself into a river or the sea reflects a deep feeling of bitterness, and throwing yourself out of the window, a recent loss on the sports field. Throwing stones symbolizes your present mood of anger, and throwing a grenade suggests a temporary loss of self-confidence caused by a mistake.

THRUSH

The appearance of this bird in dreams brings good luck. Dreaming about a thrush, especially if it is singing, signifies future joy and tranquillity. If it is building a nest it indicates good news on the way, and dreaming of a thrush's egg shows that you will have a flash of inspiration.

THUNDER

A thunderstorm indicates your thoughtlessness over something or someone, while thundering waves mean that others cannot understand your actions. A thundering waterfall signifies that you hold a prejudice of some kind.

TIE

Dreaming of a tie is usually a symbol of good fortune. Choosing a tie from a shop or a wardrobe heralds change for the better, and putting one on indicates your present financial success and good health. Tying a tie shows that your problems at the moment are temporary, but taking off a tie means there are future problems on the way.

TIGER

A sleeping tiger, or one in a cage, is harmless and, hence dreaming of one in this state is a sign of social advancement, but a tiger attacking a person or animal in a dream means there is serious danger on the horizon.

TIME

Checking the time in a dream shows an introverted and pessimistic nature with inner conflicts which are difficult to resolve. Asking someone else the time suggests a temporary upset has occurred in your love life. If it is late in the day in your dream, you should not react to provocation in real life, while if it is early, you should avoid involvement in a project, perhaps at work, which seems important but which will bring you nothing but trouble. Arriving on time means that you are in a

TOMATO   Ripe tomatoes in a dream signal that all is well at work.

relationship that appears eccentric to others. Travelling in time shows that a surprise journey will be made by you or someone close to you.

TIMETABLE

Dreaming of a railway timetable is a sign that a happy piece of news or development is on the way, while a school timetable signifies the fact that you are not getting much work done because your mind is on other things. A bus timetable means you should watch out for false alarms; an airline timetable, that a moment's indecision could prove fatal. Looking something up in a timetable indicates that you are behaving with unusual impulsiveness.

TIP

The appearance of a tip of a sword in a dream indicates a lack of discipline, and the tip of a knife, pointless rebellion over something which you cannot change. If you touch the tip of your nose it means you are worrying too much about a relative's health. If someone else gives you a tip, for example at a horse race, it means that someone has outstayed their welcome, while if you give one yourself, it indicates overbearing, arrogant behaviour.

TITLE

A titled person, such as a duke or duchess, in a dream stands for some reckless financial investments. Dreaming of someone with an academic title, such as doctor or professor, means that you need to make a very difficult decision. The appearance of a book or film title signifies change on the horizon, and winning a sporting title means you can expect problems connected with the opposite sex.

TOAD

Dreaming of a toad foretells a major challenge from a business rival. If you have a partner this dream suggests that he or she is unreliable, deceitful and needs constant praise and attention. Killing a toad, however, is a sign of future professional success.

TOMATO

An unripe tomato in a dream means an attractive, but also deceptive, proposition will be made to you. Ripe tomatoes, however, mean encouraging results on the work front. Fresh ones reflect excellent health, but dried-up tomatoes signify that you must stand up to hostility. Cooked tomatoes represent innovations and new ventures. If your dream involves eating tomatoes, you are optimistic and confident about the future; if you buy some, you are very resilient, both physically and mentally; and if you are picking them it means that something you are involved in is likely to be a great success.

TONGUE

A human tongue in a dream is a sign that you are prone to malicious gossip, while an animal's denotes dissatisfaction with your lot. Eating tongue indicates that you have major problems needing to be overcome. Sticking your tongue out in a dream shows that you do not delay in making decisions.

TONSILS

Dreaming about having your tonsils removed presages a period of disappointments which will make you very pessimistic about life generally. However, if you simply dream that they are inflamed, there are petty jealousies on the way.

TORCH

A torch has the same favourable connotations as light does in a dream, whether it is a flaming torch or an electric one. If the torch is alight in the dream, your respect for people around you will help you in your work, but if it is out, there is a period of apathy and withdrawal in prospect caused by a disappointment from someone of the opposite sex.

TORRENT

A swollen torrent in a dream is a sign of your making influential friendships, but a dried-up river bed shows a lack of practicality. A wide torrent indicates future tran-

The significance of dreaming about kings and queens

Kings and queens are a frequent subject for dreams, and usually they are remembered after the dreamer has woken up. They normally have a favourable meaning: for example, a crown shows the possibility of reaching a high status in society, and being crowned means both spiritual and financial success is within grasp.

According to tradition, a dream about a queen is always a favourable one, whether she is sitting on a throne, waving to crowds from a balcony, or doing anything else. But if she is dethroned, or dies, there are probably difficulties on the horizon.

A king wearing a crown is a symbol of success and wealth, though if he is sitting on a throne it means there is a danger of someone deceiving you, and if he abdicates or dies there could be a very difficult period ahead.

Dreaming about a prince, especially if he is heir to the throne, means that there will be complications in your life. Dreaming about his court, with all its splendours and intrigues, means you have considerable ambition to be in high places, meeting the rich and famous.

An empty throne symbolizes well-being, and being able to sit on a throne yourself indicates that you have gained a difficult victory.

In dreams about playing-cards, the king is always a favourable sign, but the queen often indicates problems of one kind or another.

quillity and prosperity, but a furiously raging one predicts the opposite: that you will face some form of adversity. If your dream involves crossing a foaming torrent, it suggests you are cautious and careful in everything you do.

TORTOISE

Dreaming about a tortoise is a very good sign, indicating both success and a long life.

TOUCHING

Touching a man in a dream signifies that you are keeping promises, while touching a woman reveals your need to be more flexible. Touching a child indicates both a sense of responsibility and a state of mental poise and tranquillity. Touching an animal suggests you are in extremely good health and can expect to stay that way for a long time to come.

TOURIST

A group of tourists in a dream is not a particularly favourable omen; it means that you are unusually nervous and it is more than likely you will make mistakes in your work. But if you accept the advice of someone close to you, things will eventually turn out the way you want them to. If you dream about being a tourist yourself, you have a great deal to learn before you can form a close relationship with someone of the opposite sex.

TOWER

A bell tower in a dream indicates particularly good relations with people at work, while a tower being knocked down indicates both fatigue and obstinacy. A leaning tower shows you have considerable inner resources. If the tower is very high, you will be involved in a potentially compromising situation.

TRAIL

Seeing the trail of a wolf in a dream means that your health is far from perfect and this is causing you worry. The trail of a fox means you will have to put up with sacrifices if

you are to save a relationship. The footprints of any other animal are a sign that you need to put your own house in order before you start criticizing other people.

TRAIN

Dreaming of a train arriving at a station means an important professional relationship is imminent, and one leaving shows your breadth of vision and a rational approach to everyday problems. If the train is stationary, there are opportunities on the way to be taken advantage of. If you dream about getting onto a train, you are optimistic and have confidence about the future, but if you get off one, you will go through a short-lived emotional crisis.

TRAM

Waiting for a tram in a dream suggests that you have received important help in your work, and getting into one suggests someone at work has no justification for the poor contributions they have made. Getting out of a tram suggests someone else's interests have to be looked after carefully.

TOWER   A tall tower signifies a compromising incident.
TRAIN   To dream about catching a train reflects hope for the future.

TRAMP

Dreaming of an old tramp is a sign of your depression and delusion. A male tramp indicates an unexpected meeting with someone, and a female one, surprising events of a romantic kind. If you are the tramp in your dream, you need to call on all your reserves of common sense and decisiveness to deal with some very difficult obstacles. If you have a partner, dreaming of being a tramp reveals that the few minor arguments you have in store will serve only to strengthen the relationship.

TRAMPLING

The interpretation of this dream depends on what is getting trampled. If it is sand, you are in a dangerous situation; if it is grass, there is good news in the offing; and if it is undergrowth in a forest, it indicates future prosperity.

TRANSLATING

Translating a book in a dream means a pleasant surprise is on the way; translating a manuscript indicates a talent for adapting to circumstances, and a short story, news on the horizon. If you translate something from Latin, you have high hopes for a new project at work.

TRAP

If you dream about falling into a trap, you need to clear up a difficult situation which you have created through your own unpredictable behaviour. If you try to make someone else fall into a trap, you will be the victim of injustice and abuse.

TRAPDOOR

If you dream about going through a trapdoor it indicates that you must make sacrifices for your family, or alternatively that you will be in dubious health. Falling through a trapdoor suggests imminent danger, and opening one means new opportunities are opening up.

TRAVELLING

Travelling for pleasure in your dreams is a sign that you are taking a well-deserved rest, and travelling on business suggests you will find a favourable solution to a problem. If your journey is a short one, it reflects the fact that you are nervy and irritable, and if it is a long one, you can expect to make a new and interesting friend.

TRAWLER

Although a trawler is not a very common subject for a dream, it generally has a favourable significance. If it is moored to a quayside it shows that you have put a worry

TREE   A tree in leaf signifies prosperity and a successful marriage.

behind you, while if it is sinking, you have differences of opinion with someone which you must resolve. If the trawler is being tossed around in a storm, you will be unexpectedly helped out of a difficult situation. If the trawler has its nets out, it is a symbol of financial gains.

TREASURE

Owning treasure in your dream means you are about to go on a long and successful business trip. If you find hidden treasure, you will not manage to complete a project at work which you had high hopes for.

TRAM   Waiting for a tram suggests someone has helped you at work.

TREE

If you dream about a tree with plenty of foliage and bearing fruit, it indicates future financial prosperity, and a happy marriage blessed with children. If you climb the tree, not only will you achieve both these goals, but an even greater blessing – contentment. However, a tree being cut down means a loss of a friend or of money, and a tree being battered by a storm symbolizes major family problems.

TREMBLING

Trembling with cold in a dream foretells an interesting discovery connected with work, while trembling with fear indicates you will be protected and supported by someone important. If you tremble with rage in a dream, you are going through a critical period of your relationship with your partner, but everything will return to normal soon. Trembling with hunger reflects a tiring but lucrative task. If you are trembling with desire in your dream, it suggests you have an extrovert, imaginative personality with a love of the forbidden and the unusual, but you should be careful not to let this side of you get out of hand, because it could make you very difficult to live with. If you palpitate with love, it means you have a determined, stubborn personality which insists on its rights whatever the circumstances.

TRENCH

If you dream about a military trench, it suggests you are gradually building up a brilliant career which will bring you fulfilment throughout your life. Digging any kind of trench suggests you are not strong on displaying initiative and are easily influenced by others.

TRIBE

Dreaming of a tribe of warriors is a sign of fortune and success as far as love is concerned, and a nomadic tribe foretells a brief but intense emotional relationship. A tribe of black people stands for your discovery of a secret. If you are part of the tribe yourself in the dream it means you are in an unconfident and irritable mood.

TROOPS

Dreaming of a troop of soldiers shows success and good fortune in business. If they are cavalry troops, you can expect a long and passionate relationship, while if the troops are fighting, your self-confidence will suffer something of a blow. If they win a battle, you can expect an argument with someone you love.

TROUSERS

Although trousers can have different interpretations in dreams depending on what type, colour and material they are, they normally indicate new opportunities, quite often involving money, and the successful completion of projects. Torn or dirty trousers, however, indicate that you have an emotional problem. The quality of the material is important in that the cheaper the material, the more likely the dream is to bring you good fortune financially: if the trousers are made of cotton or something similar, they are likely to bring success and wealth, but if they are made of an expensive material – like silk, for example – you can expect constant worries about money.

TROUT

Dreaming of a trout swimming in clear water is a sign of good luck. If you dream you are trying to catch one it indicates financial improve-

TROOPS Cavalry troops predict a long and passionate involvement.

ments, but cooking or eating one indicates looming doubts and the arrival of a somewhat alarming piece of news.

TRUMPET

Playing the trumpet yourself in a dream means you are likely to be severely let down by someone you thought was totally trustworthy. If someone else is playing it, however, your financial affairs are looking very promising.

TRUNCHEON

A large truncheon or similar weapon in a dream indicates an introverted, reflective type who likes solitude; if you try to be more outgoing and sociable the quality of your life will improve. A short truncheon, on the other hand, suggests you are overbearing and arrogant; this is making you very difficult to live with and could cause the breakdown of your relationship with your partner. Being hit by a truncheon indicates that now is the time to make plans.

TUB

Dreaming of a tub full of water, earth or anything else means you should avoid disputes with relatives, while if it is empty, you are being indecisive and uncertain in things you do. Filling a tub yourself indicates excellent prospects at work, and emptying it, that unpleasant news is about to arrive.

TULIP

Picking tulips in a dream indicates that you are involved in negotiations with an uncertain outcome, but buying them suggests a happy, satisfying emotional life. Giving tulips to someone else indicates your inner confidence. Red tulips symbolize love being reciprocated, and white ones, minor problems at work.

TUNA

Dreaming of a tuna swimming in the sea or being caught in a net is a sign of a lively mind which needs to be independent. Eating cooked or tinned tuna indicates both shyness and possible outbursts of rage.

TUNNEL

A dark tunnel in a dream indicates repentance for an action in the past, while if it is lit, you tend not to trust people around you and you are worried about the future. Going through a tunnel in a dream means that a period of happiness is in prospect, both with your family and at work.

TURBAN

A white turban in a dream is a symbol of happiness and contentment in relations with the opposite sex, and a coloured one indicates the long-awaited arrival of someone you have not seen for a long time. If you dream about putting a turban on yourself, news will arrive just when it is most wanted.

TURKEY

The turkey in dreams symbolizes dissent: it indicates arguments with friends, relatives, or colleagues at work. A dead turkey, or one that has been roasted, reflects financial problems, but if you dream you are eating turkey, it shows you have a very vivid imagination.

TURTLE DOVE

Dreaming of a turtle dove in its nest is a sign of unexpected gains and emotional happiness, especially if it is cooing. A wounded turtle dove means there are problems to be sorted out in your life; if it is dead, these problems may be major ones.

TULIP   Picking them suggests the dreamer is embroiled in negotiations.

TYING

Tying a rope to something in a dream indicates that you have an unusually high degree of physical resilience, while tying something with string signifies difficulties with your partner. Tying ribbon means difficulties and problems in your career. Tying a necktie means you are obstinate and self-willed, and tying up your hair means you are a very orderly, rational person.

TYPING

Dreaming about someone else typing slowly with two fingers is a sign of your financial worries, but if the typist is fast and accurate, things will go well on the business front. Any dream which involves you typing something shows that you have made safe investments.

UGLINESS

This is one of those dreams which indicates its opposite: if you dream you are ugly yourself, or you see someone else who is, it signifies your attractiveness.

ULCER

Seeing an ulcer on someone's leg in a dream means someone is getting in the way of your initiatives. A stomach ulcer suggests that you must fulfil a responsibility even though it is time-consuming and difficult. If you have any kind of ulcer yourself in your dream, it means you are far too impulsive.

URN   Be careful not to let your tongue lead you into difficulties.

UMBRELLA

Opening an umbrella in a dream means you are an open, practically-minded person who adapts easily to different situations, but closing one means you distrust someone close to you. Buying an umbrella indicates financial matters going very much your way. Losing an umbrella suggests that you will have a difficult time at work stemming from a failure to reach an important agreement, and giving someone an umbrella as a present means you will meet a person you have not seen for years.

UNDRESSING

Undressing a child in a dream reflects your realization that you must stand up for your rights. Undressing a man indicates unfaithfulness in a relationship, and undressing a woman shows that you may be displaying a lack of scruples in real life. Undressing a body ready for burial means a dangerous situation is looming. If you undress indoors you will make an unusual acquaintance, and if you undress in the street you need to rest after an exhausting piece of work.

UNICORN   This bad omen means that someone is troubling you.

UNHAPPINESS

Being unhappy in a dream indicates, paradoxically, that you have put your unhappiness behind you in real life. Indeed, the more unhappy you are in the dream, the more happy you can expect to be in reality.

UNICORN

A unicorn is not a favourable sign in a dream: it suggests that you are facing problems which are being caused by people who are less pleasant and trustworthy than they seem on first acquaintance.

UNIFORM

A soldier's uniform in a dream represents good relationships with other people, and any other type of uniform means a favourable oppor-

tunity will be given to you or someone close to you. A school uniform symbolizes important business dealings. If the uniform is dirty for any reason, it suggests you are about to get involved in a romantic relationship, but if it is torn, you will have to take on more than one onerous responsibility.

UNIVERSITY

Applying to get into university in your dream means you are of a very inventive turn of mind and very strong-willed, but actually going to a university in a dream suggests you are moody and given to alternating elation and depression. If your dream involves being a lecturer or professor, it means you are going through a period of happiness in every aspect of your life. Graduating from university in a dream indicates a fresh challenge in your work environment, possibly involving a new job.

URINATING

Urinating on the ground during a dream suggests that you are facing annoying problems and obstacles, and urinating in the street means belated regret for something unpleasant you did in the past. If you dream about wetting your bed, financial gains are on the way, and a child wetting itself means that you can expect a heated argument with your partner.

URN

A wooden urn in a dream is a sign of prosperity and well-being, and a china one suggests that your enjoyment of chattering sometimes leads you into embarrassing situations. An urn with ashes in it indicates that you are not very enthusiastic about something. If your dream involves an urn getting broken, you are trying to conceal your shyness.

When directing our dreams can help us control our lives

Have you ever woken up halfway through a dream and been convinced that if you wanted to you could go back to it and steer it the way you wanted it to go? This is a fairly common experience, and some experts believe that what we are doing in situations of this kind is not so much dreaming in the accepted sense of the word as fantasizing while half-awake.

Aleksander Pushkin (illustrated, right), the famous Russian 19th-century poet and short-story writer, was 'controlling' his dreams even as a boy when he attended the exclusive school in the imperial palace of what was then St. Petersburg. To do this, he used a technique he had learned from his nyanya, or nurse, to whom his parents consigned him at a very early age. He would start to read a passage from a book (usually a literary classic) just before he went to sleep and tell himself that he had to finish it while he was asleep. When he woke up, he would write down in some detail how he had completed it in his dream, and then compare the dream version with the real one. Very often, the two versions would be almost identical. It should be said, though, that even at this early age Pushkin had read an inordinately large number of books and had reached the stage where he knew authors so well through their work that he could tell what was going to happen.

The famous Spanish painter, Salvador Dali was a self-avowed specialist in the art of making dreams do what he wanted them to.

Many of his best-known pictures had their origins in his dreams.

For us lesser mortals, 'directing' our dreams is difficult, but not impossible. It is quite common to be able to dislike a dream, wake up, decide that you want the dream to be more pleasant, and then to make it so. Research in the United States has reached a stage where it is now possible to use fairly sophisticated techniques of dream control as a form of therapy, to exorcize fears and anxieties in patients.

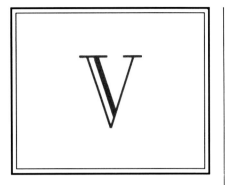

VAGABOND

A vagabond in a dream is a symbol of your excessively lofty ambitions. If the vagabonds you dream of are drunk, it means someone is misunderstanding your motives, and if they are old, you are about to reach a new agreement. If your dream involves helping a vagabond or down-and-out, you have some important decisions to make. If you dream of being a vagabond yourself, it means you have a craving for more independence.

VALLEY

Dreaming of a dark, sunless valley indicates a contented, tranquil existence. A very deep valley symbolizes a profitable venture, but if you dream of a valley with cultivated fields in it, you need to change your ways very quickly. If you dream about going into or through a valley, it means you are a lively, independently-minded person.

VAMPIRE

Dreaming about a vampire means you are full of problems and fears. Being bitten by one indicates the chance of a future unpleasant encounter, but if the vampire gets killed in the dream it means there are better times ahead.

VARNISHING

A dream which involves varnishing something indicates an excessively sensitive and impulsive nature which makes you very difficult to get on with for other people. Dark-coloured varnish indicates a misunderstanding that needs to be cleared up, but clear varnish symbolizes the possibility of an interest-

VALLEY   A deep valley often suggests a financially successful project.

ing new relationship. Varnishing a door means you have a high degree of responsibility and self-control; varnishing a window frame suggests that minor problems are slowing down your progress; and varnishing floorboards heralds unexpected pleasures to come.

VASE

Dreaming of a glass vase is a sign of doubts and indecision, while a china one means good luck is on the way. A marble vase indicates a major success in your romantic life, and a metal one, money being recovered or repaid. A vase with flowers in it means there will be a radical improvement in your financial situation.

VEGETABLE

Dreaming about vegetables is not a good sign. Dried or cooked vegetables stand for family arguments, and eating vegetables represents a loss of money. Vegetables growing in a garden or field indicate that you have more than your fair share of worry at present, and picking them suggests you are attracting some strong criticism.

VEGETABLE GARDEN

Cultivating a vegetable garden or allotment in a dream means that your business and financial affairs are about to take a dramatic turn for the better. Putting fertilizer on the garden indicates your renewed hopes on the romantic front; watering it, unexpected financial gains; and sowing seeds on it, a practical and sociable nature. Any dream which involves your working in a vegetable garden suggests you can expect some good news, though digging up a garden with a spade suggests you are getting rich at the expense of others.

VELVET

Anything which is made of velvet in a dream indicates the beginning of a complex and difficult situation. If you buy some velvet, or something made from it, you will suffer a major disappointment in love, and if you sell it, you are being lazy and unhelpful.

VENDETTA

Having a vendetta against someone in a dream means that in real life someone – though not necessarily the person dreamed about – does not feel as strongly about you as you do about them. If someone else has a vendetta against you and wants revenge, you can expect problems in your work environment.

VERANDAH

Dreaming of a verandah with flowers on it indicates that a pleasant surprise is in store, and one with green plants on it means renewed hope and ambition for a project you are involved in at work. If you dream about reading a book while sitting on a verandah, you will eventually reach a situation of complete harmony with your partner, even if things have been rather unpredictable up until now. If the dream involves sleeping on a verandah, there may be enemies waiting to pounce on you.

VERSE

Writing verse or poetry in a dream suggests you are about to make a trip overseas, and reading verse, either to yourself or other people, means you are very clear in your mind about the issues that face you. Making the poetry up completely as you recite it indicates setbacks and annoyances at work, while cutting out or substituting some of the lines which are written suggests you are tired and irritable. Reading or writing free verse means that you have a certain amount of hostility from relatives to contend with.

VET

Being a vet yourself in a dream means you will achieve financial and personal success in your job, and going to see one indicates a lasting friendship. If the vet comes to you to treat your pets, it means you have to face up to some important issues concerning your career, but if you go to the vet, you have problems that need sorting out.

VETERAN

A war veteran in a dream indicates good relations with people at work, though if he is wounded or crippled there is an unpleasant meeting in prospect with someone you have not seen for a long time. If you dream that you are a veteran who has just returned from the war, you can expect a very happy period from the romantic point of view. Dreaming of a veteran car suggests you have to overcome a number of difficulties before normal life can resume.

VICTUALS

Seeing or eating a large quantity of victuals suggests that you have ambitions which could be misinterpreted by someone who is unaware of your real motives, while if there is not much to eat, the dream indicates that your present circumstances are favourable. Asking for victuals in a hotel or inn during a dream means that you feel very close to someone you have only just met.

VASE   A vase of flowers means lucrative times ahead.

VILLA

Dreaming of a magnificent villa with a beautiful garden means that your illusions will be destroyed and you will have to set your sights lower.

VILLAGE

Seeing a village in the distance in a dream is a warning that what may seem like a golden opportunity could have damaging consequences. If you dream that you live in a village, or find yourself in one, it means you are contented.

VILLAIN

Meeting someone who is really evil in your dream actually has a favourable significance: it means that there is a letter or present on the way from someone you have a deep affection for.

VINE

The appearance of a vine with black grapes on it in a dream shows you are enterprising, and if it bears white grapes, your friendships are particularly strong. If you are growing or harvesting a vine in your dream, you have a trusting relationship with your partner, and if you are pruning it there will be an improvement in your finances.

VINEGAR

Drinking vinegar in a dream suggests that you could make yourself ill through over-indulgence. It can also symbolize bitterness in yourself or someone you know.

VIOLENCE

This is not a very favourable subject for a dream, as it indicates major difficulties are getting in the way of your progress at work. If you are violent yourself in the dream, your feelings about your partner are no longer what they used to be.

VIOLIN

Buying a violin in a dream means unexpected financial gains which will help you gain the independence which is so vital to your self-fulfilment. If you or someone else play the violin in the dream, there is a complicated and potentially compromising situation in the making and you may have considerable trouble untangling yourself from it.

VIOLINIST

A young violinist in a dream is a sign of your unjustified resentment about someone, and an older one suggests that the time is ripe for a new venture. If the violinist is applauded, it means important correspondence is on the way, but if he or she is hissed or booed, it suggests you are being much more angry and irritable than usual.

VIPER

A viper or adder in a dream suggests that enemies are poised to attack, though if the snake gets killed, they will not manage to gain the upper hand over you.

VINE Growing grapes reveals a trusting relationship with your partner.

VIRGIN

A virgin is a symbol in dreams of happiness and joy, though a dead virgin means unexpected complications at work. If your dream involves starting a relationship with someone who is a virgin, you are about to begin a period where fortune smiles on you in everything you do. If you dream about being a virgin yourself, it suggests you are being naïve at the moment and this is causing you to drop in other peoples' estimation.

VIRTUE

This is not a very common thing to dream about, but if you or someone else displays a particular virtue in a dream, it means that a project or venture will eventually turn out to be a success. If you discover a hidden virtue in yourself or someone else in your dream, this suggests that you are enthusiastic about a new acquaintance or connection.

VISION

Dreaming about having a vision, for example seeing a ghost, is not normally a favourable sign. It reflects a vain, selfish personality which is unsociable and unenthusiastic about everything: unless you can do something about this aspect of your character, it will lead to some unpleasant consequences in your social and emotional life.

VISIT

Dreaming of a lengthy visit to a person or place indicates that a difference of opinion is being ironed

VIOLINIST Older violinists suggest it is time for a new project.

out, and a short visit suggests that you should put off making a decision for the time being. If someone pays you an unexpected visit, on the other hand, it means you have an urgent problem to be sorted out. A visit to a relative means you have strong organizational skills and a great deal of energy, and one to a friend or acquaintance indicates that you need to be patient in waiting for the career advancement that you undoubtedly deserve.

Vocabulary

Learning a foreign vocabulary in a dream means you are slowly regaining your energies after a tiring period in your life. If you or someone else employ a large vocabulary in a dream, it suggests you are not paying sufficient heed to the needs of others, but the appearance of someone whose vocabulary is severely limited represents a need to turn over a new leaf and start afresh with revised plans.

The extraordinary book of dreams of Artemidorus

Freud considered Artemidorus the great master of dream interpretation. Artemidorus was born in the 2nd century AD at Ephesus, in Asia Minor, and made history with his monumental *Book of Dreams*.

The book is divided into five parts. The first two describe the writer's theories about the difficult art of 'reading' dreams, including practical instructions. The third consists of 'everything which Artemidorus had forgotten to write'; the fourth, his replies to criticisms of the work, and the fifth contained interpretations of 95 dreams he considered important.

We have reproduced here a few extracts from the book, which we will preface with Artemidorus's words: 'The same dream does not always have the same meaning in each case and for each person. It can vary depending on the time and place, and it can vary in length and content. In particular, if we wish to interpret a dream correctly, we need to take note of whether the person dreaming it is male or female, healthy or sick, a free man or a slave, rich or poor, young or old'.

BIRTH Dreaming that you are being born, according to Artemidorus, means the following things, depending on circumstances. If you are poor, it is a good sign, because as a baby you have someone to look after you and feed you. But for a rich person, the opposite meaning pertains: the fact that the baby is dependent means that you will also be dependent, because of lack of money. A married man who has this dream when his wife is not pregnant is likely to lose his wife, because the fact that he sees himself as a helpless child means he cannot have sexual relations with anyone. But if his wife is pregnant, he will have a son who is exactly like him: it will be as though he has been reborn. A slave who dreams about being

reborn is being shown that his master loves him, but is not going to set him free, just as a child is loved by its parents, but nevertheless is not its own master. If you have this dream when ill, it suggests there will be complications because children are always swaddled, as if with bandages. If you are trying to escape from someone or something, you will be unable to, because babies cannot walk. If you are on trial, your opponent is likely to win because as a baby you cannot talk properly and convince the judges of your case. If you have been found guilty, though, you will be pardoned because you have only just been born.

VOICE

A high voice in a dream indicates that you are temporarily in a bad mood, while a softly-spoken person, paradoxically, indicates that you are harbouring aggressive intentions. A loud voice heralds a period of happiness, and a nasal voice suggests that you might have ridiculous pretensions. If someone speaks with a gruff or hoarse voice, it means you are being too hurried in making a decision. If you hear your own voice in a dream it suggests that you should be careful not to make any false moves, because they could be very harmful to your career at this time. Losing your voice in a dream means you are wasting time gossiping.

VULTURE

Dreaming of a vulture can have various meanings depending on the circumstances in which it appears. If the vulture is flying, it indicates the harmful activities of enemies or rivals in love, but if it is devouring carrion, it suggests that fortune will smile on you and you will stop being plagued with worries. Killing a vulture is a good sign in a dream: it shows that you have finally overcome your misfortunes.

WAFER

A wafer biscuit in a dream suggests that you feel out of place in a new environment. A communion wafer in a dream serves as a warning that you are taking on too many different tasks and responsibilities for you to be able to make a proper job of all of them.

WAGON

A wagon being pulled by a horse in a dream indicates the arrival of news from a long way away. A railway wagon being used for freight symbolizes a malicious person who dislikes you, while a passenger carriage on a train suggests a need for domestic agreement.

VULTURE Dining vultures announce the arrival of good fortune.

WAISTCOAT

A waistcoat in a dream indicates that there has been a change in someone's ideas. If it is made of silk it indicates your gloom and yearning for a lost past; if it is white, a family agreement is in prospect, while black forbodes some unpleasant event in the future. Buying a waistcoat represents conflict and friction with envious friends, and putting one on suggests there will be an argument with someone you love, though everything will turn out all right in the end. A very brightly coloured waistcoat means you should overcome your shyness and throw yourself into a long and intense relationship.

WAITER/WAITRESS

Dreaming of a waiter or waitress in a hotel is a sign of good luck, especially if it is a waitress. But if they serve you in your own or someone else's house, it indicates family problems and disagreements. A waiter or waitress dressed in spotless black and white livery is a sign that there is danger just around the corner.

WALKING

This dream has different interpretations, depending on where you are doing the walking. Walking along a mountain road or path indicates future success and health, but walking along a narrow lane in a town or village foreshadows misfortune. Walking on sand or snow denotes a feeling of insecurity, but walking on grass or in the country signifies your calm and contentment.

WALL

If a wall blocks your path in your dream, and you cannot get round or over it, it suggests you are also encountering obstacles in real life, either financial or romantic. If your partner is on the other side of the wall, you can expect long and pointless arguments with him or her, in which you are unable to reach a satisfactory compromise. Walking along the top of a narrow, high wall means that you could

make an agreement which may potentially be very harmful, but climbing over one without hurting yourself is a promise of success in business matters. Being walled up in a dream means you need more independence from a partner or business colleague.

WALLET

A leather wallet in a dream suggests you have had second thoughts about something, but it is now too late to make any changes. If the wallet has money in it, you have serious problems to overcome, though if you adopt a sensible, rational approach you should have little trouble dealing with them. If you dream about finding a wallet, an unexpected meeting is in prospect, but losing one means you must now remedy one of your main faults, namely your uncertainty and indecisiveness. An empty wallet means there is money on the way, possibly from an inheritance or gambling win.

WALNUT

Walnuts in a dream can have a number of meanings. A walnut tree indicates shaky and unprofitable business dealings. Fresh walnuts reflect anger and resentment towards an untrustworthy person, and dried ones, good health and considerable resilience. Cracking walnuts means that you will have a spell of bad luck, and eating them means you will soon meet a person who is able to give you the affection and trust you need.

WALTZ

Dancing a waltz or hearing waltz music in a dream means that a minor misunderstanding could cause much harm to a long-standing relationship, though fortunately it will not do any permanent damage.

WANDERING

Any kind of aimless movement from one place to another in a dream suggests you are being decisive and strong-willed at the moment in real life, and are particularly keen to show how good you are at work. If

you carry on with this enthusiastic attitude at work, the results will be highly profitable.

WAREHOUSE

Any dream involving a warehouse indicates good luck and prosperity. You can expect major successes following on from your hard work and personal sacrifices, and if you are unattached there is also a strong likelihood of meeting a lifelong partner in the near future.

WASHING

Washing clothes in a dream indicates health and financial security, and washing crockery suggests family difficulties. Washing a floor indicates your experience of minor setbacks, and washing windows indicates that you have recently avoided a danger of some kind. Washing yourself indicates future joy and happiness, though washing your face foretells a short-lived sadness, and washing your hair shows there is a surprise in store.

WASP

Provided the wasp or wasps are at a safe distance from you in the dream, they indicate a forthcoming announcement. If they are buzzing around you, the dream suggests you should be looking after your interests, and if you or someone else get stung, it symbolizes bitter recriminations on your part.

WATCHING

Watching someone else without their knowing, or them watching you, in a dream means there could be an unpleasant surprise in store. Watching television in a dream means you need to reorganize your priorities, and watching any kind of entertainment or sports match suggests you are needlessly worried about your career prospects.

WATCHMAKER

A watchmaker in his shop in a dream symbolizes the arrival of an interesting piece of news or of a proposal which could change your working life for the better. A watch-

WATERFALL   A roaring waterfall symbolizes boundless energy.

maker selling something foretells a small financial loss which could grow into something worse, while if he is repairing a clock or watch it suggests you have a highly developed critical faculty and are meticulous in the things you do.

WATER

Dreaming of any large expanse of water means there are problems in store, though if you cross it successfully you will overcome all the obstacles in your path. Drinking water is a bad sign, as it indicates looming poverty on the horizon, and bathing or swimming in dirty water indicates that some kind of danger is on the way. Falling into water means that a reconciliation is forthcoming.

WATERCRESS

Dreaming of watercress is a symbol of misfortune to anyone who is in love: eating it foretells quarrels, but picking it indicates that you will have a separation from your partner which could be permanent.

WATERFALL

A waterfall is a favourable omen in dreams. If it is exceptionally large, it reflects a sensible, reflective personality, and if it is only small, you are likely to be a patient, tolerant kind of person. If the waterfall is noisy, you are likely to be very energetic. Even falling into a waterfall yourself means a win on the sporting field.

WATERMELON

Dreaming of a large, ripe watermelon signifies that your love for someone else is being returned, though if it is sliced it indicates that you have undergone a recent sacrifice or privation. Eating melon, however, suggests that your hopes are all in vain.

WATERING

Anything being watered in a dream is a sign of good fortune, happiness, and exciting events. Watering a garden or field also means that improvements are in store and unfounded fears will soon go away.

WAVES

Dreaming about the waves on the sea symbolizes recent short-lived friendships, while those on a lake suggest that you are an intolerant and uninspiring personality. If your dream involves battling against the waves, either swimming or in a boat, it means you are strong-willed and obstinate and this can either be an asset or a drawback in your relationships with other people. If you or someone else is knocked down by a wave, you need to clear up an unpleasant family misunderstanding as soon as possible.

WEALTH

More often than not, dreaming about being very wealthy means you are going through a prolonged period of gloom and self-doubt caused by your partner or by someone who loves you. If you try not to get too upset, but instead try and talk things through, the situation will eventually sort itself out.

WEATHER

Good weather in your dreams denotes decisiveness and confidence in your actions; bad weather, uncertainty and a jittery mind. If the weather in your dream unexpectedly changes for the better or for the worse, it suggests you are courageous and others feel they can rely on you. If you have to cancel something due to bad weather, it suggests you have an abundance of energy and vitality.

WEEPING

Weeping with happiness in a dream means you are worried and anxious. Weeping with rage indicates malicious gossip by people close to you. Weeping with sadness or grief, strangely enough, indicates a good financial position and success in love. Weeping in torrents in fact means that you will learn that somebody loves you, when this was quite unexpected on your part. Any dream where someone else is crying means you are letting yourself be panicked unnecessarily.

WEIGHING

Weighing gold in a dream means you have an excessively vivid imagination. Weighing silver indicates that you are being helped and supported by someone in a position of power. Weighing meat foretells an advantageous move, and weighing fruit, that you have decided to make a go of your present job despite initial misgivings. Weighing yourself suggests that you will incur unexpected expenses. Weighing any kind of grain indicates lasting prosperity.

WELL

A dried-up well in a dream suggests that you are undertaking new but risky projects, while one with water in it suggests a situation is about to turn sour. A very deep well indicates emotional, excitable behaviour. If your dream involves drawing water from a well, you and your partner are very much in love with one another, and if you fall down one, you need to make a vital decision.

WHEEL

The appearance of a car wheel in a dream foreshadows the arrival of important news relating to your job. A cartwheel signifies annoying arguments with your partner. A mill wheel indicates your worry and doubt. A Ferris wheel in a funfair means an unexpected change is imminent.

WHIPPING

This is an unfavourable sign to dream about, whoever or whatever is being whipped. Whipping a horse is a sign of anger and displeasure, and whipping a child means your emotions are running away with you. Whipping a prisoner suggests unobservant behaviour on your part.

WHISTLING

Whistling in the street or in the bath during a dream means you are feeling relaxed and content at present. Whistling to summon a dog is a sign of close friendships, and whistling approval at the theatre or elsewhere shows an adaptable, flexible personality.

WIDOW/WIDOWER

Dreaming of a widow or widower dressed in mourning suggests sadness at the loss of someone close to you, perhaps because they have moved away. If they are crying, they symbolize your present weighty responsibilities. If you are widowed yourself in the dream, it means you will be seriously worried about something, but this will not last too long.

WIFE

If you dream about your own wife, it suggests there will be arguments and jealousy between you which can only be overcome by your being patient and caring. If you are not married and you dream about having a wife, it shows you are not ready for a long-term relationship and would feel too tied down by it.

WIG

The appearance of a blonde wig in a dream denotes idealistic, but also eccentric, behaviour. A black one reflects naïveté and lack of common sense, so unless you are a bit more thoughtful you will find yourself missing out on some very favourable opportunities. If you dream about

WIG   A man wearing a wig suggests a measure of deceit and untruthfulness in yourself and others.

buying a wig, you are likely to be unfairly judged by your partner about something you do, and this could harm the relationship. Trying on a wig in a dream suggests disputes with your family or your partner.

WILL

Making a will in a dream means you are about to get involved in a delicate situation which will need a great deal of tact and diplomacy, if things are to draw to a satisfactory conclusion. Reading a will in a dream suggests you should accept the help of someone who is more experienced than yourself.

WIND

A pleasant, light breeze in a dream indicates a healthy financial position, but a violent gale signifies that you are facing an extremely tricky situation where you should be very careful before acting. If the wind is blowing against you, it indicates family problems, but if you have to shelter from the force of the wind it means there is reassuring news on the way. A bitterly cold wind means you are involved in discussions or negotiations, the outcome of which is uncertain.

WINDOW

Looking out of a window during a dream means there is travel in prospect. An open window means an improvement in business or financial matters. A lighted window in the distance represents imminent change of some kind, while a window with shutters is a sign that particularly good fortune is on the way. Closing a window in a dream symbolizes your assumption of major responsibilities, and opening it, denotes surprises in store.

WINDOWSILL

The appearance of a windowsill in a dream represents your contentment, particularly if it has flowers on it. Standing on a windowsill, however, suggests you are something of an exhibitionist and have a tendency to exaggerate things.

WINE

The appearance of red wine in a dream is a reflection of your cheerfulness and optimism, while white wine signifies sincere friendships. Sweet wine symbolizes the pleasures obtained from romance, and dry wine is a warning to avoid excess. Pouring wine in a dream suggests you will be upset by an unexpected setback, but drinking it means lasting good health and physical strength.

WINNING

Winning a bet in a dream is a sign of shyness and timidity, while winning a competition or game suggests an imminent journey. Winning an argument or debate indicates good, co-operative relationships with people at work. Winning a game of chess means you are very much aware of your responsibilities and take decisions carefully and with forethought.

WINTER

Any winter landscape in a dream is a highly favourable sign, for it symbolizes financial and material successes.

WISH

If you make a wish in a dream and it comes true, it suggests you are a sympathetic, caring person and this will stand you in particularly good stead in a new relationship which is just starting to develop. If your wish does not come true, it suggests

189

you have been taking too seriously criticism which, although well meant, is not justified.

WITCH

An old witch in a dream suggests your ideas about a new project are misguided and unlikely to be feasible, and if she is also especially ugly, it means you are indulging in an empty flirtation which will not do you or the other person any good in the long term.

WITHDRAWAL

Withdrawing money from a bank or somewhere similar in a dream stands for a minor family argument. Withdrawing into your house and becoming a recluse means many of your problems are about to be solved, and withdrawing into a monastery or convent means that you have a secret passion for someone you have just got to know. Withdrawing your support from something in a dream means you need more freedom and independence in your life.

WOLF

A wolf is a distinctly bad omen if it appears in a dream. Hunting a wolf means there is danger on the horizon, and being chased by one means you are anxious and worried. Killing a wolf, on the other hand, means a success of some kind is imminent.

WOMAN

Surprisingly enough, any woman in a dream – whether she is young or old, naked or richly dressed, beautiful or ugly – indicates insincerity, uncertainty, bitterness and resentment. A woman in the company of a man, however, is a symbol in dreams of confidence and decisiveness.

WOOD

Dreaming of a piece of furniture which is made of wood suggests that your health may be at risk for some reason. Any other wooden object suggests you are making a decision prematurely. Burning wood in a dream indicates an embarrassing situation, and collecting firewood is a symbol of lasting friendships. Chopping or sawing wood in a dream suggests a favourable solution to a problem, and buying timber suggests that someone else feels the same way about you as you do about them.

WOODCOCK

A woodcock in flight is a sign of good luck in dreams, suggesting a future success in romance. Hunting, skinning or eating woodcock shows problems of various kinds: jealousy, resentment and petty intrigues.

WORKER

Any kind of worker in a dream suggests that the effort you are putting into something important will be rewarded with success. Dreaming of a manual worker at work means that you have ambitious projects for the future. Dreaming about a clerical or managerial worker suggests that you are at a difficult stage in your career. If you employ workers of any kind in your dream, it suggests that your career prospects look very bright indeed, but if someone else employs you, it may be that someone in real life is taking advantage of your good nature and friendly disposition.

WORKSHOP

Any kind of workshop appearing in a dream is a good omen. Working in one yourself suggests you are a decisive person who does not hesitate to take the initiative, and if you use this aspect of your character to the full, the results will start to show straight away. Going to a workshop to get something done, such as a repair, suggests you are anxious and worried about something which could have a major effect on your future career, but you need have no fear, because luck will be on your side.

WORM

Worms are not a pleasant sign in a dream: they indicate diseases and illnesses caught from other people.

WOOD   Collecting wood in a forest symbolizes fidelity in friendship.

WOUND

Being wounded, or wounding someone else, means the opposite of what one might expect in dreams: if you are young, it is a symbol of love, and if you are in business, it represents profits and prosperity.

WRAPPING

Wrapping up goods in a shop in a dream means you are consolidating and strengthening your position at work, though if they are very large items, such as pieces of furniture, which are difficult to wrap up, the dream suggests that a friendship or relationship will end. Wrapping up a present means you are keeping your feelings about someone to yourself for the time being until you are sure they are reciprocated.

WRITING

Writing anything by hand in a dream reflects your satisfaction, possibly obtained by exacting revenge on someone who has hurt you. But writing something using a typewriter suggests you are wasting time and effort in disputes with people who are envious of you. Writing a newspaper or magazine article means you can expect to be depressed for no particular reason, and writing a novel means your hopes will be fulfilled beyond your wildest dreams. Writing any kind of letter indicates that you are feeling happy and contented, while writing a piece of music symbolizes happiness with your partner.

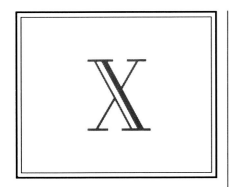

X-RAY

Being X-rayed in a dream means good news is coming from a long way away. A doctor looking at the result means you are confident about yourself and your future. An X-ray of your head suggests you are going through a period of reflection and reappraisal of your life, and one of your chest foretells the beginning of a new friendship, or perhaps some deeper involvement with a member of the opposite sex.

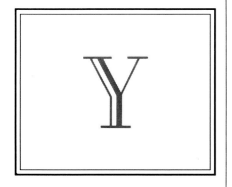

YARN

The appearance of white yarn in a dream foretells a short journey, while black means you should be giving due consideration to another person's individual way of doing something. If it is any other colour, it heralds new developments in business or at work. Tangled yarn means you should not be so obstinate with someone you have just met. A ball or yarn means you should continue to keep a relationship secret, as it could make life very difficult for you if it were revealed now.

ZEBRA   This animal heralds danger. Be on the look-out for troubles ahead.

YEAST

Putting yeast into anything during a dream means you stand to inherit a large sum of money which someone else has patiently built up over many years.

YOLK

Although egg yolks are not a common subject for dreams, if you do dream about one it suggests you should slow down a little and not set your ambitions quite so high. Beating an egg yolk means you will receive a very attractive business proposal which you should look at carefully from all sides before committing yourself.

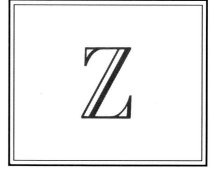

ZEBRA

A zebra in a dream is a warning sign: you should be very careful and keep your eyes open, otherwise something unpleasant could happen to you.

ACKNOWLEDGMENTS

'Sleep – The Pathway To Your Dreams' was written by Lynn Picknett

Translation of A-Z Entries: Lesley Bernstein Translation Services/Phil Goddard
Editorial team: A. Jefford, T. Rose, J. Kuhn, L. McOwan, M-C. Jerram
Art Editor: Pedro Prá-Lopez
Designer: William Mason
Picture Research: Kate Fox
Production: Peter Colley, Eleanor McCallum

The majority of the photographs in this book were reproduced by kind permission of Fabbri, with the exceptions listed below.

The following photographs were taken specially for the Octopus Picture Library:

Bryce Attwell pp. 43 right, 87 above; Jan Baldwin pp. 168 below, 183; Michael Boys pp. 44, 118 above; Martin Brigdale pp. 65, 117, 129; Michael Busselle pp. 22, 57, 64, 84 above, 102 above, 114 above, 176 above; Chris Crofton pp. 23 below, 68, 71 below, 74, 90 right, 115 above; Ian Dawson pp. 29, 52; Robert Estall pp. 49, 53 above, 79, 127, 135; John Freeman pp. 36 above, 41 above, 42 above, 91 above, 121 above, 134, 148 right, 168 above, 177 above, 187; Jerry Harpur pp. 124, 179; Chris Harvey p. 101 left; Neil Holmes p. 180 below; Kit Houghton p. 80; James Jackson p. 149 below; Barry Jell p. 94 below; Peter Johnson pp. 186, 191; Chris Knaggs p. 90 left; Bob Langrish p. 81; Sandra Lousada pp. 4, 17, 19 below, 24 above, 54, 59 below, 96, 107, 112 above, 114 below, 145, 159, 164 below, 165, 172; Steve Lyne pp. 20 above, 21, 26 above, 40, 69 above, 71 above, 72 above, 73 right, 101 right, 155 left, 164 above; Stuart MacLeod p. 175; Duncan McNicol pp. 28 right, 33 right, 34 above, 61 above, 62, 73 left, 111; Colin Maher p. 184 above; John Miller pp. 136 right, 190; Colin Molyneux pp. 13, 60 above, 91 below; James Murphy p. 86 left; Roger Phillips pp. 123, 27 right; Spike Powell pp. 63 below, 95; Peter Rauter p. 12; John Sims pp. 104, 122, 177 below; Mike St Maur Sheil p. 30; Charlie Stebbings pp. 16 below, 41 below, 88 left, 118 below; Clive Streeter pp. 60 below, 97 left, 121 below; Grant Symon p. 15; Sally Anne Thompson p. 141 below; Victor Watts p. 147; Paul Williams pp. 20 below, 26 below, 32, 48 below, 69 below, 97 right, 109, 115 below, 126 right, 136 left; George Wright pp. 43 left, 70, 93; Jon Wyand p. 51 above.

The Publishers thank the following for providing the photographs in this book:

Ace Photo Library p. 85 left; Colorsport p. 88 right; Robert Harding Picture Library p. 67 below; Michael Holford Photographs p. 87 below; Andrew Jefford p. 82; Rex Features p. 153; Science Photo Library pp. 11, 77; Tony Stone Associates p. 83; Telegraph Colour Library p. 8; Zefa Picture Library p. 157.